Read like the Devil ☀
The Essential Course in Reading Playing Cards

CAMELIA ELIAS

READ LIKE THE DEVIL

The essential course in reading

Playing Cards

EYECORNER PRESS

Read Like the Devil: The Essential Course in Reading Playing Cards
© Camelia Elias 2021. Published by EyeCorner Press. Designed and
typeset by Camelia Elias. Images: Goodall & Son Playing Cards, 1897,
in public domain (vector rendition courtesy of Adrian Kennard).

ISBN: 978-87-92633-73-6
ISBN EBOOK: 978-87-92633-74-3

March 2021, Agger, Denmark

WWW.EYECORNER.PRESS

Chance is the first step you take, luck is what comes afterward.
— AMY TAN, *The Kitchen God's Wife*

CONTENTS

THE EXCELLENT FORTUNE

WHEN DOGEN ZENJI, the founder of Soto Zen, was asked about miracles, he was not in doubt. A miracle is not a feat that sorcerous monks can pull off. Rather, a miracle is the ability to see how people feel. We think we're good at this, but how *can* we be, when most of the time what we do is *not* be present? We're always in our heads somewhere else than in our material bodies in the here and now, so we can't even see how *we* are feeling, let alone how others are feeling.

Hold this great challenge in mind, as it is with this that fortunetelling rises, surpassing often the best consecrated professions dedicated to fixing people's pain in the soul. Fortunetellers of caliber have trained themselves in the art of knowing how others feel by simply looking at how people react when they encounter playing cards in a divination setting. We call paying attention to reactions 'cold reading' because reactions betray a whole range of emotions, disclosing in the process just what cloth a person's emotional fabric is cut from. As most people have feelings, uncontrollable at that, they are very easy to read. Even the ones who are good at control can be read the cold way when we consider just what is absent from their gestures and gazes.

Something happens when bodies out of balance step into a fortuneteller's parlor that is quite different from the situation when the bodies out of balance try the office of a shrink. This something 'other' that happens is related to expectation. What people expect from a fortuneteller is that the fortuneteller reads their fortunes. At the psychologist's or psychoanalyst's the expectation is that the consecrated professional imparts advice that touches the cognitive or the affective mind. The fortuneteller touches these too, but because she operates with chance first and choice later, she is at an advantage that the other professionals are not. This advantage is called the ability to calculate risks against the background of randomness inherent in the visual language of the cards. While it may be by choice that people step into the fortuneteller's 'shady business den,' the attraction to knowing one's fortune is related to how every individual already perceives at the intuitive level a basic fact: what we call choice is not subject to our will, but rather subject to chance events. In Zen parlance this perception has to do with the perfect clarity we all possess when we find ourselves in a moment beyond linguistic and cultural constraints, that is to say, the moment when we realize that we can live life excellently.

As someone who practices fortunetelling for a living and also wrote academic books on Lacanian psychoanalysis for a living, I'm interested in what we make of living life excellently, especially if we advance in our understanding that if there's pain in the soul, it's because of desire. The fortuneteller learns to weave desire into the fixed patterns of the cards only so that these patterns can be shown to emerge as fragile, vulnerable, and weak. Even before it's built on desire, the house of cards falls for the fortuneteller, leaving her with an uncanny ability to point to just what is ridiculous in any one set of beliefs, the belief that desire makes the world go round being chief among them.

While it is correct that desire makes the world go round, culturally speaking, when it comes to the soul, or a person's 'true nature,' as the Buddhists would call the state beyond pre-conditioning, it is not desire that makes us tick. Rather, it's positioning. How do we position ourselves vis-à-vis the world? If desire is in play, is it appropriate or transgressive? According to whose rules? The psychoanalyst shakes her head every time she gets to the realization that the person she listens to is never positioned in the now, in the current circumstances, but rather wandering in the wasteland of imaginary futures or memories of the past.

As any sage, clever monk, or sorcerer martial artist can testify, living life excellently is directly proportional with living life beyond desire. You get beyond desire when you realize just what constitutive force language has. If you're *you* or some *other* desired identity, you're *it* because of this constitutive power of language. Just think of this phrase: 'nothing succeeds like success.' What we find here is a narrative of desire flung to the emotional core. We all want success, we tell ourselves, or we let others tell us that we do. Yet, as anyone who promises success is basically unable to deliver, simply because success is not something that others can deliver unto us, we are left with the clarity of what is actually the case, if we care to look closely. There is no success, only stories of success. Hearing stories of success makes us feel good. If there's something wrong with the story of success, then we experience mental imbalance. Why we can't hold on to our education, job, lover, or dwelling, becomes a mystery to us. We go to see a shrink, or a fortuneteller. We want the excellent living. Who can blame us? Desire leads the way, that is to say, desire leads the way of what we imagine is a story of success.

The Greeks were obsessed with excellence. For good reason, for what's the alternative? In his *Nicomachean Ethics* Aristotle makes a case for the tripartite relation between excellence, resilience, and execution, highlighting the idea of knowledge, choice, and a strong resolve as the premise for mastery and a skillful approach to any undertaking. Thus he says the following:

[W]hat pertains in the arts is not at all similar to what pertains in the virtues. For the excellence in whatever comes into being through the arts resides in the artifacts themselves. It is enough, then, for these artifacts to be in a certain state. But whatever deeds arise in accord with the virtues are not done justly or moderately if they are merely in a certain state, but only if he who does those deeds is in a certain state as well: first, if he acts knowingly; second, if he acts by choosing and by choosing the actions in question for their own sake; and, third, if he acts while being in a steady and unwavering state. (Aristotle, 2011: 31)

Aristotle's example is based on the observation that a writer can be a master of his craft by chance or on the instruction of another, thus suggesting that chance contributes to the 'fixation' of one's destiny or path. You get inspired and start working. Applying intelligent execution to the inspiring factor leads to mastery and self-affirmation. You discover that you don't speak the language of imitation anymore. Rather, you use your own voice and authority. Apply this to reading cards. The more you practice decoding the visual cues in the cards, the more skillful you get at detecting the precise state of a situation and then acting accordingly. Although the cards fall at random on the table, telling a story by chance, you can choose to prescribe rules for a particular behavioral conduct. You work with what is close to your heart, or the heart of the ones you read the cards for. What you see in the cards is this closeness. That's why there's a question to begin with. Without a question, no clues, only uninspiring generalities.

Now, as already hinted at, if anybody should be familiar with the tension between choice and chance, then it's the fortuneteller. People come to us to hear just by what chance they might choose, so that success in any matter of concern is assured; so that destiny runs its course 'under control.' As a Zen deconstructivist I'm keenly aware of how we use language and to what end. The cards that fall at random to answer a tight question may seem a contradiction in terms, and as far as Aristotle is concerned, that won't do. Either we're with the random, or we're with the formal. But think of it this way: if a reading of randomness is executed intelligently according to sincere, high intentions, would that not lead to excellence? It would.

Also, when we consider the fact that choice almost always falls in the category of the random by virtue of the fact that we're always subject to conditions that exceed our control – if that wasn't the case, we'd need to make no choices whatsoever – then we begin to understand why chance has such an appeal, why some think that taking a chance on life is a good idea. Especially if a fortuneteller is involved. In fact I can say that this is exactly why I have returning clients who swear that because of my consultancy their taking a chance on life has gone up a notch where excellence is concerned. That is to say, the excellence that goes into living life to the fullest. Either you live excellently, or you don't. The condition for it is simple. It's called seeing things as they are. It's not about having an edge, authenticity, a cool integrated shadow.

The whole point about reading fortunes with the cards, where 'fortune' stands precisely for the ability to see things clearly, is that is allows us to find a way to position people's desires, resolved and unresolved, beyond fears. If you never tried reading a pack of playing cards for other people, I invite you to think about just how a person reacts when the spades are on the table. Many of them. Only one red card. Like in this mini tableau here.

14

You can talk about leveling the ground, and about how all is well when it ends well, but I can assure you that the fully capable body, now crushed, that you read the cards for will have a hard time listening. What do you do? Reading cards for me is always about the miracle of having perfect clarity about how the other is feeling. I don't even let my own Zen inclinations – and the fact that I laugh at feelings all the time – inform my seeing other people's feelings. As not all of them are Zen, there's work to do. You start with the cold reading, classic style, and move into an even colder territory. You're the excellent fortuneteller who lives her professional life excellently because the focus is on the obvious, not on some story that renders the obvious hot, fraught with emotion, stories of desire and success that not even the poorest fortune would want to be caught dead near.

It is this excellence that is the 'other' thing that people seek from you, when life fails them, and when mainstream society and culture fall short of offering something that is useful. You can tell a troubled soul that all they need is more money, not their mother's love – or vice versa – in order for their story of success to get somewhere, but when it comes to putting on display some essential questions that the troubled soul would benefit more from if they answered for themselves, you realize that the visual language of the cards is there to make a sharp point where precision is concerned and when the blind spots need piercing. How do you get beyond conjecture when you advance an argument towards a solution or make a prediction? This is the question that interests me in fortunetelling with the playing cards along with how I develop a method of reading the cards in such a way that my voice and authority get through in unambiguous ways. Before I interpret the cards I work with the notions of seeing first and understanding later. I work with awareness of what we perform, and how we scale the truth. Clarity is not subject to scaling. Truth on the other hand is, as we talk about constructed convictions and beliefs contingent entirely on specific places and geographies.

In this course book I want students to find a similar voice of authority that's firmly anchored in their own excellence. Only when such a premise is established will they be able to enjoy what divination is all about both as an interpretative art and as an art that's finely attuned to the dance of chance, randomness, probability, risk calculation, and the poetry inherent in the robust, visual stylization of the playing cards.

I started teaching method as an answer to the essential questions in divination, and along the way developed techniques of using cartomancy to enhance the experience of what it means to be both skillful and precise in the interpretative arts. The book you're reading now is the second in a trilogy based on a series of foundation courses in cartomancy that I began to offer just before I retired in early 2017 from my professorship in Literature and American Studies at Roskilde University. To date, over a thousand people have joined me in my martial arts approach to cartomancy, an approach based on making sharp cuts through the visual language of the cards, engaging a penetrating and keen eye on context, the question, clarity, and composure. You're here to learn more about this.

Also part of the trilogy are two books dealing with reading the Marseille Tarot and the Lenormand Oracle respectively. My cartomantic blogs, *Taroflexions* and *The Cartomancer* with Patheos, have been a wealth of resources for over a decade, where I first introduced the readers to rigorous deconstructive critiques of cartomancy on the one hand, and fresh approaches to more traditional modes of fortunetelling, on the other hand. As this work has been very rewarding to me, proving as well to be extremely valuable to my students, I decided that it was high time to share more widely the steps towards the art of reading cards beyond introductory levels, something I've explored already in my other cartomantic books.

The *Read like the Devil* trilogy gathers the main course materials for reading cards at both foundation and advanced levels. As was the case with the first volume in the trilogy, the Marseille Tarot course book, I begin here as well with establishing a solid foundational tone for deconstruction in divination. This means that I look at the cards from the perspective of their significance in terms of function rather than arbitrary symbolism. I then move from the principles of reading the playing cards to exploring and fine-tuning the mastery of precision as it combines with an elevated and sophisticated sense for coherence in language.

The three books in the trilogy are identical in this premise, moving towards a shared goal as far as the student's cartomantic competence is concerned.

WHAT YOU LEARN

As was the case in the first volume, the learning program is the same here. You learn to develop snappy skills in identifying the essential in the cards and how to practice reading cards with an eye for the immediate. You learn to differentiate between receiving 'intuitive' messages from the cards and logically putting two and two together. You also learn different tactics of developing penetrating vision by giving equal attention to the use of courts and pips in a reading situation.

An important learning component here is also the learning from the mistakes of other students. As I'm not the type of teacher who thinks that every interpretation, opinion, or take on the cards is awesome, I have many objections. This whole book is full of objections and pointing to errors. But it is also an anchoring of these objections in solid demonstrations of why an idea doesn't work. My encouragement is implicit, rather than based on hyperbolic speech devoid of substance. I point to what's wrong, and then offer a concrete solution that nails the student's work, making it stronger and better.

What I also do in this course book is go beyond the scope of what is technically beneficial to know, and stress having command over language and the ability to not get personally entangled in a reading. All examples of readings discussed are derived from live encounters as well as student work. Every chapter starts with a selection of direct feedback to the work that students have provided throughout a series of course runs with the playing cards. We discuss both small and large sets of cards and layouts, always focusing on what makes a reading strong and sharp.

In addition to method and philosophy, the book also features a practical dimension. Each chapter concludes with a number of assignments — all original in design and conceptual thinking — and essays for further application and comprehension.

In terms of other applications, the usefulness of this course book can be judged especially if you're a reader or a student of the Marseille Tarot and the Lenormand Oracle or a variant of fortunetelling cards that all feature playing card insets. If you want to simply have a better grasp on how to read the pip cards and court cards in the Marseille Tarot, or draw on the playing card insets that accompany the symbols on the Lenormand cards, then this book draws your attention to how you can do precisely that. As the backbone of reading with the playing cards is found in the ability to combine the cards across their suits, numerical progression, and color, often disclosing marvelous ambiguities, developing the ability to entertain two or more contradictory ideas can be particularly enlightening.

What I aim for is a top level cartomancy. I work towards bringing the students to the top-level competence in cartomancy. What I mean by 'top-level' is the idea that the students reach the stage where they are beyond comparison, in a league of their own. This means the following: you don't just learn to read the cards and the mechanics behind the method, but you also learn about the value of divination and why we can rely on it to instruct and inspire. I don't tell you what to do and what symbolic meanings to memorize. I show you how to *think* in practical terms, rather than in terms of theory and history of the cards. Who is the Queen of Spades when she meets the Jack of Hearts? How do you discover the force of your truth, when you look at three cards whose number is 7? Do you get excited and see this as an ominous sign, or do you read form, lines, and color on point? In this book I teach effective strategies of owning your readings beyond the cliché – this includes dealing with the cliché called 'owning your readings.'

My method of reading cards operates with a simple elastic. I don't do 'schools': French this, German that, 'Gypsy' this, and Psycho that. I read the cards according to the basic principles that allow us to see the logic behind the system that places the court cards in analogy to societal functions and the pips in analogy to nature, seasonal cycles, cardinality, and culture.

While I draw on classical methods, I don't let these methods rule over my common sense, or take the high seat of my divination practice that I see anchored in noticing the obvious. I take the idea of reading the cards like the Devil seriously, in the sense that I make no compromise regarding what I teach you to see. By following my pointing out instruction, you'll master the essential in what it means exactly to read like the Devil. Chief among the characteristics of reading like the Devil is the notion of reading your cards for clarity, rhythm, coherence, and precision.

The idea here is precisely to consolidate the logic behind the function of the four stylized suits and the court cards, as this logic follows form and content. How are the cards laid out — from the simple 3-card spread to the larger sets — and what content do we assign the individual positions in a spread, if what we're looking at are predetermined conceptual markers? While I answer these questions, I also stress that a reading like the Devil is a reading that dares to invent its own agenda, suggesting counter-intuitive solutions to the tried and tested fortunetelling formulas. While I introduce the students to the most common or classical card-layouts, I also come up with some of my own, allowing the brain to twist the conventional and the habitual in seeing.

For instance, from seeing the pip cards with spontaneity we go to reading the court cards beyond the ambiguity of identifying 'who is who.' We also look at how we can punctuate with the pip cards. We can see the spades as full stops in a sentence, the clubs as a comma, and the hearts as an ellipsis. We employ conceptual, spatial, and temporal metaphors when we use the cards. How about your clubs signifying a pause, or breathing? We look at how the cards can represent speed and flow, timing, rulership, and connectivity.

Generally, when we look at what else we can say about the cards that's not a cliché already, we expand our topical interests. In addition to the classic subjects in method at the visual level, what

I'm also interested in is observing the relation of function, embodiment, voice, gesture, tone, rhyme, and rhythm in the cards to the prescriptive, the *do and don't* in a reading session with the playing cards. In this sense I could say that I'm interested in the magic of form: pips & courts, and the idea of trumping confusion in accordance.

Topics such as agency, rulership and timing also play an important part in any card reading, no matter what the approach, while card-linking opens the realm towards full-fledged storytelling with the cards. Love, health, work, and money are subjects that we can put *sous rature*, that is to say, directly under the signature *Read like the Devil*, when we need to erase completely the traditional, when 'the traditional' equals utter nonsense. We can then point to what *does* make sense and to what works. Bringing out the relation between hot & cold cards to predictions about investments is a valuable way of demonstrating how we can see that the playing cards as a whole set itself is a process, not just a tool that merely participates in a process of decoding a divinatory setting of ominous proportions.

'What of history?' some ask me, and I usually say that it doesn't concern me. Not in my practice of reading the cards. As this is a book about that, and about enhancing divinatory skills, I don't see why I should fuss about history. This is not a course in how to navigate or manage the pretense in vogue, populating many a cartomantic group, full of pomp and circumstance on the internet. In my personal observations, many who talk about the history of cartomancy don't actually read the cards. Or else when they do, their readings are not always as sharp as they could be. The trilogy books ask the same question: can we have more focus, please?

In this course book I make references to cartomancy history and scholarship when relevant, but mainly only for the sake of reflection and analysis, rather than description of different divination practices in different ages. However fascinating the history of cartomancy is, I'm more interested in the actual practice of reading cards via storytelling and cunning-folk arguments. Since I have my eyes on what we actually *do* with the cards, rather than lineage, I prefer looking at the philosophy of divination in context as it ties in strongly with the human imagination and the way we end up formulating strong and interesting questions.

I hope you enjoy this course book, as it springs out of years of thinking about the cards, a type of thinking that positions itself at the exact opposite pole from shallow thinking. Now, I don't want to call my thinking deep, and deplore the superficial, as I prefer to not operate with dualistic language in spite of its instrumentality. But I do want to stress that the work put into this course took its time. Call it a martial arts approach to the craft. I try to observe a phenomenon, understand it, and then make my cuts in accordance. I don't engage in a mimetic relation to what I observe. I'm not interested in copying the universe or its blueprints, and then speak from the position of one who holds secrets, to go esoteric here. Rather, I'm interested in my own god-given common sense, the propensity for calling out nonsense, and the beauty that ensues when an interpretation stands in all its glorious clarity. In cartomancy it's best to be consistently suspicious, than robustly all-knowing.

My favorite approach is the meta-approach, one in which I test myself against my own desire and expectation. As soon as I want to say something, I test myself with the inverse of the situation. 'Really?' I ask myself, and then deconstruct the habitual with a simple, 'I don't think so.'

A final word here about seducing endorsements: as EyeCorner Press is not interested in validations of any sorts, I'll refrain from quoting among the hundreds of glorious testimonials pertaining to the efficacy of this course, but I will refer to one line about this course that I like. It comes from artist Moira Thompson: 'it was the perfect course which brought together the three sides of reading, the triumvirate, the Father, the Son and the Holy Ghost of reading like the Devil.'

SIMPLICITY OF NUMBERS

literalness
stretch
the name of all things
sense of a symbol
temperament
leading questions
aces of singularity
permutations & representations
risk analysis
practice
comprehension

THERE ARE MANY WAYS OF READING CARDS, each more elaborate than the other. Also, in this world there's competition for it. Who can invent the most intense spread? The Americans like to do that. Who can count in chunks of fives or nines? The French like to do that. I prefer the simple way, which is looking at the cards and understanding the essence of what I see. I look at 9 Clubs, 3 Spades, and 8 Clubs.

I go like this: something 9 pieces of clover or wood have an encounter with 3 shovels. Something 8 pieces of clover or wood are still on the ground. I conclude: the shovels are not very efficient.

While you may think that this reading is a literal reading of the cards, in reality, what I read is signs related to what I'm able to recognize at the level of linguistic and cultural competence. When I look at these images, words form in my head that designate what I'm looking at it. While I'd like to think that I respond spontaneously to the cards, just this little fact that my recognition here is already informed by language is enough to make me cry. Where is my authentic originality here? Help... It works though. I'm not sure what mark I hit here, but I do hit a mark that's difficult to argue with. Clubs are a stylization of trees, and spades are a stylization of shovels. When we want to clear some ground of dead trees, we use a shovel or a similar tool that gathers the branches. It's good if this tool is sharp, because if we have to give the trees an extra hack, we can use the cutting edge. This is all context. There's no mystery to what we can make of this plausible scene.

If I added another context here in the form of a question, I'd note that my initial basic observation only changes in form, not in the essential idea. If the question was one of stress at work and how to resolve it, the answer would be that while cutting the work load is a good approach, the outcome of such an act is less cheerful if looked at predictively. If the progression is from 9 to 8 Clubs, then we can infer that it's no good. The stress is still high. Who to blame? The lame Spades. They are not efficient. We would thus advise in accordance: sharpen the blades or get more of them.

Another example: 5 Diamonds, 7 Diamonds, and 8 Spades.

I go like this: something 5 Diamonds meets a greater fortune. Now there's 7 of them. 8 shovels are at work. Man, someone is busy getting all them Diamonds under the ground.

I now look at the Jack of Clubs, King of Hearts, and the Jack of Hearts above. I go like this: someone, man of woods, is in a relation with a father and his son, men of hearts. They are in the same picture. What's cooking? Only the context can tell me what this encounter or relationship is about. I could invent things and call it 'tradition,' but do I want to die from boredom? Fat chance.

Now you're welcome to ask: why do I prefer this method to all the other sophistications, meanings galore, and symbolisms stretched all the way to the moon? The answer is simple: I have no interest in dying of boredom while performing any reading of the cards. Hearing myself on repeat and auto-pilot delivering the same, regardless of what context is put on my table is a sure way to hell or a place much worse. What would I say here? 'A young man of passion meets two more men of passion?' Or, if I went 'French,' would I say, 'a most fortunate man comes to dinner?' While I may say the very thing, I'd prefer to find some evidence in the card-combinations for these notions, rather than merely resort to a list of set phrases. If the context is not about dinner, then I refrain from delivering the idea, even though there's a long tradition for sounding oracular when out of context.

If there's a strong cultural stereotype representing the fortune-teller as a mean, cynical gypsy out to con you of your money, I can assure you that it's because of said fortuneteller's immense loathing of her job, as she has to deliver the same line at least 10 times a day. If I had to do that job, I'd also con people out of their money, not to mention the fact that I'd be close to suicidal. How would I live with myself delivering 'list things' 10 times a day, if I saw these cards below?

'Yes, he's cheating on you, the 7 Spades tells me, but it's better to stay with him, as he's a man of genius, the 3 Hearts also tells me. You're, after all, most fortunate, as the 10 clubs tells me.' This is the French/Romanian/Gypsy style reading.

The thing is, one can divine with any method whatsoever, but are they all equally good? They aren't. Not if nuance and fresh insight is what the fortuneteller is after. For this, you can try the simple method that will prevent you from loathing what you do, and from loathing the people who come to you, asking almost always the same type of questions. Your answers don't have to be equally uniform by the great book of *Veritable Fortunetelling*, a

French instruction manual I have in my library in the section of antique books.

Great fortunetelling is all about the willingness to kill it, which is what you do when you when you read for the essence of what's put on your table in the form of a question and its context. You take this essence and mirror it with the essence of the 4 cleverly stylized suits of the playing cards pack. You make a quick judgment that's not based on regurgitating meanings à la 'this means that...' Your judgment must be the result of what you see is happening in the cards, with the sound conclusion based on what is plausible in context.

Let's look at another example, where we have the King of Spades, the Ace of Hearts, and 5 Clubs on the table.

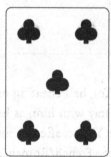

If you said: 'This someone, shovel master, is looking at a big heart. Something like 5 pieces of wood surround it,' what would you conclude? You'd conclude that the shovel master, King of Spades, is interested in working on it, the heart, one way or another, either giving it a fence or getting rid of the 5 sticks following it. But which one is it, exactly? Can you be precise here, and demonstrate why you picked one option above the other? Is the fence around the heart going up or down?

Generally speaking, we like to think of the big heart as free. If it's not, we make an effort to free it from its ties. But how likely is this action here in light of the function that the King of Spades performs? When was the last time a general in the army got rid of all fortifications? I never heard of such a thing. The King of Spades is not the Dalai Lama. So what are you going to conclude? That the King of Spades will open widely the door to his heart? Because that's what the 'ancient' French cartomancy manual tells you? If you came up with that conclusion, I'd pray for you...

So this is the work. My work. I bet that if you've read this far, you may conclude now that whatever you feel about my teaching is actually irrelevant in the face of having to admit that you didn't get bored. You'd probably like me to keep going. Which I can. I can tell the wildest stories with the cards, all tall and true. No cynicism, cross my heart. Only seeing what there's to see.

THE NAME OF ALL THINGS

'What's in a name?' Shakespeare rightly asked, because names capture the essence of existence. 'If you can name it, it exists,' the Buddhists say. They are also right. Though when they say that, what they point to is the shifting signifiers, that is to say, the shifting names of all things. Since we're after the simple truth, we want to halt and say, 'now wait a minute: if names are shifting, then what's up with the 'essential' qualities of existence? The Buddhists would say, 'what existence?' while Shakespeare would go: 'thou art a boil.'

31

Here's my first theory: what a set of playing cards consists of is a discourse on the human condition, or a way in which we are always subject to conditions, to cause and effect, to perceptions of love, hate, vitality, and pain. There's perception of reality that our minds create through names, through the conceptual value of language. So there's no primordial 'meaning' that has any substance in and of itself. This boils down to the fact that whatever we perceive is subject to our linguistic competence based on arbitrary cultural conventions.

We're here to read like the Devil. Think about the playing cards: two colors and four symbols. That's it. The whole human condition reduced to six variables. Two colors: red and black. Why?

Think: the sun rises in the East and it's red hot. The earth is black without the sun on it. We're some stardust subject to gravity, ping-pong'ing between day and night. So far so good. Four Suits: diamonds, hearts, clubs, spades. Why? Think: 'Will you marry me?' May the diamond glitter on your finger. 'Let's roll in the hay, heart to heart, buy a house, have some children, and dig the earth.' We get born, we live, and die. That's it.

The question to ask is the following: if we were to place the human condition – we get born, we live, and die – on a horizontal axis for the metaphorical idea of direction, what would we say? That love is fixed? Like hell it is. That pain is fixed? Like hell it is. That work is fixed? Like hell it is. That money is fixed? Like hell it is. There's hell in convictions, a hell we create to avoid the hell of non-fixity. We can say this: whatever our human condition subjects us to, that very thing – love, pain, work, and money – is subject to an elastic. Ergo: what we do when we play with cards is hold in our hands the secret to life, which is to stretch it.

When we craft a desired identity in an image we want to embody, what we do is stretch it. When we put on our best suit to score at a job interview, we stretch it. When we bring flowers to our beloved, so she'll swoon, we stretch it. Stretching it is the underlying structure to all transactions. The genius of the playing cards when used for divination consists of taking stock of all that we can stretch.

Note the obvious: spades: bad (they cut); clubs: bad enough (they hit); hearts: good (they pump); diamonds: good enough (they sparkle). By inference, and because the obvious is always aligned with function not symbol, if it's a heart, it's yes. If it's a spade, it's no. If it's a club, it's probably no. If it's a diamond, it's probably yes. Let's see this in action. We pose this classic question to the cards: 'will I get the promotion?'

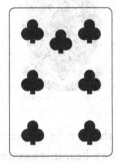  

We can say, probably yes. Why 'probably?' Well, think: The Jack of Diamonds is preceded by Clubs. Trouble. The context being work, we can quickly and logically infer that the trouble is about competition. He gets a letter. A diamond for him. He gets the job, just barely. One diamond is a lot less than ten.

What we did here is to stretch it according to the situation *and* our spontaneous response to it. What we operate with is this: context (and question); common sense (aka the heart/mind complex); color (pump it up or drop dead); number progression (1 is little, 10 is a lot).

Now think of this scenario: what would you say if the Ace of Spades finished the string? That it's in the bag? Metaphorically speaking, since bags are known to be dark inside, that could go, but given what we know of the function of the spades, how plausible would that scenario be, how possible too? Not very bloody likely. More like, no way in hell.

A certain literalness can be imposed here that can be stretched to what we normally say. We say, 'brilliant,' if we hear that a young man got a promotion. We say, 'what a shame,' if the opposite is the case. One situation has light in it, shining like a diamond, the other bites the dust, like the spade.

In cartomancy naming takes the shape of our cultural awareness of how things stand in relation to one another. Once we see this position clearly, we can start measuring the temperature of it.

In the cunning folk method of reading cards, that is to say, the method that combines common sense with the spontaneous response to seeing the obvious — a rather tall order, actually, as hardly anyone is free of cultural pre-conditioning — we associate the cards with natural elements and seasonal cycles, though this can vary greatly all according to how we equate the suits with the elements.

Each of the four suits can be thought of as having a specific temperament: fast/slow, eager/languorous, hot/cold. The way in which we have come to understand the suits comes from traditional astrology of the Renaissance time and before, when people would talk about the humor of the planets and how they influence our bodies. A sympathetic relation of correspondences was established, and with it, the idea of type, and then archetype, took off. The specifics of the four suits is related to an understanding of their function, as each of these functions can be said to mirror the four temperaments. This distillation here of the correlation between temperament and the four suits forms the basis for my own understanding and experience with reading the cards.

Let's have a concrete example based on people's motivation to seek advice with the fortuneteller. People come to us because they're motivated by the desire to know their fortune, or as the case is actually, to know where they stand in relation to others, in relation to the uncontrollable conditions of life, or powerlessness. So people are motivated by the desire for power. If you have power, it's likely you can overcome many things. People often ask: 'what does it take for me to experience smoother relations with my spouse, children, boss, parents?' Suppose the person gets these cards: 10 Diamonds, 4 Clubs, 4 Spades.

We could say the following, using both the snappy way of putting it and the unpacking of the implications of what we say for a future course of action: 'you have too much brilliance (10D). The people you have a relation with can't keep up with it. What people need are clear structures to cover their bases with, structures that are clearly (10D) working (4C), not just sparkling. Also, leave people to their own (dark) sheep (4S). Not all want sheer enlightenment. If your temperament is one of eagerness – what you know, everyone else must know because it's exciting to share – you're going to be in trouble, if your goal in life is to pursue the work of persuading others of your brilliant polish. Ergo: you could have smoother relations with others, if you simply dropped the act of convincing.'

Note here how I started with assigning the 10 Diamonds Mercurial qualities, chief among them being precisely the power to sell others an idea. But persuasion without recognizing the boundaries of the others you work with fails without exception.

Now what did I just do here, essentially speaking? I read the damn cards. I didn't read according to any set 'meaning.' I looked at the cards and read color and design. Lots of reds flanked by very square black arrangements. How conservative! Even this evaluation, 'how conservative,' is the result of not reading the cards according to meanings, but rather according to cultural competence. I happen to have learned the meaning of 'conservative' and how it manifests: not as 10 sparkly diamonds.

Your reading of the cards is in your interpretation of your place, your position in that place, and your knowledge of your place. Nail this wisdom to your head: 'know thy place,' as this is the formal premise for reading like the Devil.

TEMPERAMENT AS TYPE

Let us look at temperaments as they participate in the conceptualization of types, and see if we can further understand the four suits of the playing cards as a narrative that's framed by a list of attributes. We look at them in groups for instrumental purpose.

The sanguine type

We find our merchants here, scribes who calculate taxes and issue directives. Tricksters ruled by reason and cunning. Note: the word 'sanguine' relates to the blood, but in the context of temperament it relates to fire, to alchemical processes, to calculating and measuring, to knowledge, which alchemy is all about. In astrology, the sanguine type is not Mars, the hot-blooded, but Mercury, the cold-blooded planet. Note also that my idea of alchemy is not informed by the Golden Dawn Hermetic Order that set the agenda for much of the 19th century esoteric and occult undertakings, with many elements from the German polymath Heinrich Cornelius Agrippa's *Three Books of Occult Philosophy* (1533) being rehashed to fit the Orientalism in vogue. Rather, I think in simple terms: if you polish a stone it will shine. Throughout the ages people have been attracted to shiny objects, the rich at some point paying with castles in exchange for a glass bead. Usually such transactions are enabled by a persuasive mind, quick wit, and boldness. So my associations here are informed by a deductive chain of reasoning that's anchored in following a cultural praxis. Let's look at what associative story emerges here, if we have this approach in mind.

Diamonds: sparkling like the Sun rising in the East; morning, spring and fire; a fresh idea is a hot idea. Diamonds are chiseled and cut for exchange and culture. We hold diamonds in our hands. They denote working with the head. Diamonds are faster than the Hearts, and slower than the Clubs and Spades. Diamonds represent the nervous system.

The phlegmatic type

We're here with the type that favors the family, relatives, friends, servants, and healers. The phlegmatic is ruled by desire and marked by sentimentality and craving. We find naivety here, daydreaming, a softness in the head, or knees, that the sanguine type knows nothing about. Note: types are neither good, nor bad, neither positive, nor negative. They just *are*. If we must impose good or bad attributes on them, then we must do so on account of other variables in play than the strictly typological ones.

Who is invested in desiring the most? Culturally speaking, that would be the heart. After the freshness of the morning, noon comes to us with languor. When Eros releases his arrow, we feel a certain heat. We melt. It's summer again. We want water, or red wine. If we got an idea in the morning, now we want to share it with someone before we get to implement it, make it tangible. Sharing makes us feel good. We feel the flow when others get what we're about. Hearts are inside the body and enable the blood to circulate. The blood connects us to the world of both our anatomy and that of others. With the heart we live and love. But hearts are slow. Very slow. It can take ages for the heart to decide on what it wants. And then even longer to admit to it. Hearts represent the circulatory system.

The melancholic type

We're here with builders and forest rangers. If they compete it's because they have high (read that as airy) aspirations. They hold unto their sticks, unto things, hence the idea of melancholic stubbornness. The melancholic is ruled by steadfastness. Marked by pessimism – the harvest season is here and with it, the twilight – there's a certain urgency to finish things, end cycles; sometimes end things to death. Hence the notion that if a club ends a string of cards, it's 'probably no' if the question is a yes/no question. When the Romantic melancholic asks: 'does he love me?' she anticipates the end not the beginning of the relationship. She says, 'probably not,' pining in dreams for what is already belated.

Clubs stand for autumn and air. Now is the time to not only harvest the idea, but also test it. Trees grow in the air. Tall trees are at arm's length. We give form to clubs and sticks according to what we want to achieve: exercise, discipline others with, or build a cottage in the woods, giving life to trees in design. Clubs represent the muscular system.

The choleric type

Here we are with warriors, policemen, magistrates, lawyers. This type issues parking tickets, they act in accordance with the law, get things done without speculating, and cut to the chase. The choleric type is not necessarily logical, as that's the domain of the sanguine type, but certainly principled. The choleric is ruled by action. Note: if you think that only some types are passionate and some not, then think again. No one can be more passionate than a stubborn melancholic, or a cunning merchant. The choleric is not ruled by passion, as some would have it, as passion requires a sinking into strong desire. If the choleric is strong, it's not in desire, but rather in indifference.

Spades stand for winter and the earth. After the spark, the heat, and testing, an idea also needs to die to make room for a new one. Spades are forged for protection and conquering. You kill someone, you bury them in the ground. Only the bones remain. Spades are slower than clubs, but faster than diamonds and hearts. In a duel, the sword stays in its scabbard until the moment to draw it is just right. Some thinking goes into it, before the sword is drawn, hence the deliberate movement compared to the spontaneous swinging of the clubs. Spades represent the skeletal and immune system.

Reason in the morning, desire in the afternoon, steadfastness in the evening, and resolve at night: 'tomorrow I will do it like this,' we say, after a day of living and labor. We then go to bed.

Sometimes I could swear that our humor sits in the eye, in the gaze we cast upon things and others. Perhaps this is what the Renaissance artisans were thinking too when they painted their masterpieces, in the process depicting yet another variation on the four suits. Hieronymus Bosch's classic example in his allegory titled *Christ Mocked* (ca. 1480) represents not only the four temperaments, but also the idea of the quintessence, perhaps a model for the cartomancy spread, *The French Cross*.

Note the sanguine type (top left) with his pen in his hat. He has a calculated, yet disinterested gaze. The choleric type (top right) with his sadomasochistic collar is ready for action. The Melancholic type (bottom left) contemplates Christ while holding on to his possessions. The phlegmatic type (bottom right) is filled with desire; the desire to feel, grab, and have visions. If you contemplate carefully this image and the types it represents, you will notice that when you engage the court cards and the pips, they will act exactly according to these principles. Let us then truncate the idea even more in a quick reference list that you can glance at:

Diamonds: fire: hot/dry; east; sanguine; reason.

Spades: earth: cold/dry; north; choleric; resolve and action.

Hearts: water: cold/wet; south; phlegmatic; desire.

Clubs: air: hot/wet; west; melancholic; contemplation.

Question: 'Will she say yes?' Answer: 'No.' For the visual impact, you can continue: 'she is a woman of method, holding a list in her hand. That is her sharp knife. Whatever brilliant idea you present her with about the value of marriage, she will find a counter reason to refute it. She will say no to all your points, her 'no' being the jewel that she wears on her finger.'

By temperament, the Queen of Spades' aim in life is to have a strong resolve. The Diamond may be sparkling in her face, but before she'll fall for it, she will ask what the purpose of it is, beyond its transactional value anchored in a constructed belief.

Let this be the premise for our working here. We stretch it — original and borrowed ideas — and we permute, all according to the variables and possibilities available to us ('borrowed' in the sense of accepting the general stylization of the suits to fit humors, seasons, cardinal points, and human types designed according to such understanding).

If we have a question that addresses a concern, we answer it with the cards by always looking at what is plausible and what is possible in relation to the given context. We never depart from the question, whatever it is. Nor do we rush to tell an irrelevant story, just because we happen to see, in a context about betting on horses, the arrival of what is culturally defined as a tall, dashing and dark stranger, ready to trouble your heart. Follow the money. This is the basic cartomantic law here: stretch it, and if the elastic breaks, permute.

As any divination session operates with establishing situated meanings, it makes no sense to use lists of fixed meanings, as the backbone of our approach to the cards is through commonsense primarily and only then through the instrumentality of a list of symbolic associations. Just as in court houses judgment is passed on evidential records, not imitations of random opinions, so in divination. First there's the question anchored in a very specific context, and then there's deliberation. In a question about love, the combination of the Queen of Spades next to the Ace of Diamonds doesn't signify the potentiality for it, just because the Ace here is a 'red' card. What it says is that she needs to see first how the other is thinking, not feeling, before she makes a move.

43

In his play *Hamlet* Shakespeare associated weakness with the woman. 'Frailty, thy name is woman,' he said, putting lamenting words in Hamlet's mouth on the hasty marriage of his mother to his uncle. The woman was no Queen of Spades, calculating odds and risks, leading Hamlet to fire himself up and instigating him to act on his own prediction that this marriage will end badly.

When we read cards we're looking for the strength of our re-solve to read to precision. This strength is anchored in naming the game. 'Divination, thy name is context,' we say, and then we move towards accounting. How does what we see in the cards, down to the formal arrangement of the elements on the cards, relate to what we know about the context of the question?

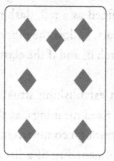

A student asked: 'what am I going to get out of The Playing Cards Course?' The answer followed the cards above, 7 Diamonds, Queen of Diamonds, Jack of Diamonds. 'All diamonds so value to be sure. Some magic and the teacher looking over the eager student who is willing to learn?' In response I asked this student: 'why the question mark at the end? Surely you already know this is so, because you've just managed to answer your question to the

44

point, first in relation to the context, and then also in relation to how the cards essentialize the function of the diamond: to be used for transaction, the premise being that a diamond stands for value (financial and mental).'

When I say that context is everything in divination, lest we want to indulge in Shakespearean lamentations, what I mean is exactly that, down to noticing not only how a question is phrased, but also what tone inflects the formulation. We pay attention to voice inasmuch as we pay attention to punctuation. We take the words at face value, and then read the lines in between what is not verbally articulated. We're with keeping a vigilant eye on our ability to cold read a situation. Reading cards is like going to war with a question, divination itself being a battlefield. If you can't read the whole landscape, you have slim chances of winning, of coming up with the right answer.

When students ask a question about the value of a teaching they invest in, what they're asking is a question about how to win at this game. It's for this very reason that I refer to my cartomancy as a martial arts form of divination. We wrestle with questions, chop off the unnecessary and irrelevant details pertaining to the 'general meanings' of the cards, and we essentialize the matter to its core concern. That's the first step in an encounter with a sitter. Then we charge. *En garde!* Draw, cut, and sheathe. That's the principle. Some sitters are generous with context. Others are not. Classical fortunetelling in fact rarely addresses context, as there used to be none in the early days of cartomancy. People wouldn't just entrust their lives and secrets to the diviner. They would consult the oracle that would shoot blanks, and then take the highly poetic and ambiguous answer as an omen inciting to action.

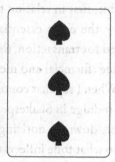

Another student asked: 'what am I going to get from this car-tomancy course?' Three cards fell on the table: 7 Spades, Queen of Spades, 3 Spades. 'A hard road or a difficult question leads to an encounter with a powerful woman who sets or shows a direct and difficult but clear path to follow after? Trouble, trouble, trouble. Maybe I asked the wrong question...' Before I said anything, asking again about the presence of the question mark at the end disclosing insecurity, two other students had this to offer: 'from trouble to growth, through the cunning magic woman. No worries!' Clearly a message of support. 'Magic, and then under the guidance of the grand witch, even more magic.' Empowerment.

But do we read to impress, support, sympathize, or encourage? I don't. I don't let any of that contaminate my clear seeing. I read with the head/heart compound, not just one of the two. Here we have all black cards. Trouble, trouble, trouble, the old books say, but is that really so? What if we considered the context again, as it's put on the table *ad verbatim*. What is the context for the question here? We're dealing with a foundation course. What do we do in a foundation course? We dig for the essentials. The basics. Even metaphorically, where do we find all this? In the basement, close to the structure of the house. What suit is associated with digging and base structures? The Spades. If you remember the context and what is plausible to expect, then you take the Spades as a good sign. So much for the established models in cartomancy that also purport to keep it simple. Keep it simple, but not that simple. Here we have a situation when the black card ending the string is actually a good omen. Context trumps the reductive method, and gives us just the right nuance for the precise answer.

You can now thus intone this mantra: 'the context leads the reading, not the predetermined meaning of the cards.' Somebody says to you, 'but it means this,' just retort back: 'No, it doesn't.' All the cards are a play of representations. They can represent people, actions, thoughts, modifiers, qualifiers, instances, forces, energies, rumors, desires, stumbling-blocks, enablers, power, and magic. The context of the question will tell you what's what. Intuition? Sure. We like it when it doesn't stand for a nebula of intangible feelings and impressions. Before you get to the type of intuition that's useful to you, you have a brain. Use it. Intuition only works when you have perfect clarity. Think about that for a moment, and intone this other mantra: 'intuition *is* perfect clarity.'

A SENSE OF A SYMBOL

Often the lists containing symbolic associations are derived from the metaphors we live by. A metaphor is a figure of speech that has representational function. Metaphors operate with symbolic associations of abstract relations that are not true. If we say,

47

'the roof is up and the basement is down,' the words 'up' and 'down' are abstract representations of an idea that's arbitrary and relative to the plane of perception. We're not really going 'up' when we go upstairs, as the action of going upstairs actually consists of just 'going,' stepping on the stairs. We want to keep this in mind as we don't want to commit the fallacy of confusing the images on the cards with the thing itself that the images stand for. Standing in for a relation is not the same as the relation itself. We use metaphors and symbols when we are unable to tangibly grasp the idea behind an action.

By its very nature to combine word and image, cartomancy operates with metaphorical and analogous planes of perception. When we say to a sitter, 'you're so like the Queen of Spades,' what we're saying is not that the person *is* the Queen of Spades, but rather point to a relation of similitude. Some sitters get excited as they 'so relate,' but in actuality there's no such one-to-one mapping other than as an abstract idea in people's heads. When you read the cards, you must be constantly on the watch, as you don't want to dispense advice that speaks solely to the image, the metaphor, or the symbol behind what the cards represent. A figure of speech is a figure of speech, not reality. People can mirror their situations in the cards, and that can be very useful for an ensuing course of action, as in, 'ah, I can also be more *like* the Queen of Spades,' if the context lends itself to such an occasion, but what the diviner must do if she is to perform a precise job, is to push beyond the metaphor, symbol, and analogy.

Therefore in this book if I offer a list of meanings, I point to its instrumentality, not its truth value, as truth can only be established outside of method, model, or associative thinking.

What do I mean by instrumentality? Think of this binary system:

YES/NO (red card/black card)
A LITTLE / A LOT (1, 10)
BIG/SMALL (King, Jack)
UP/DOWN (10, Ace)
INSIDE/OUTSIDE (Hearts & Diamonds/Clubs & Spades)
SLOW /FAST (Hearts & Diamonds/Clubs & Spades)

What I'm doing here is point to the metaphors we live by, that is to say, symbolic representations of verbal communication, space, time, distance, and speed. Because we operate with nothing but the figurative and the symbolic, rules and conventions, there's no such thing as a cartomancy system that has answers for you through a set method that rules. Method rules nothing. You do. There's no such fixed thing as, 'if it's black, it's bad.' No, it's not. Not if you're a general in the army.

QUESTION: 'Will I win the war?' This is a warrior asking.
CARDS: Ace of Spades & 10 Spades.
ANSWER: Rejoice. You win the war.

Whatever you come up with in terms of answering a question will be entirely the result of the way you're able to recognize, namely, that meaning is situational, that there's always an emerging pattern that takes place in context, often pointing to an event or a behavioral trait. What is significant is how you address the situation, and offer a solution that's in line with what is necessary, not what is desired or what the cards dictate conventionally. Sometimes your tall, dark stranger is nothing but a hesitant little prick, Jack of Spades.

In terms of design and how it relates to the binary system of the black and red cards, what is important to pay attention to is preponderance. Note the preponderance of 'black' over 'red,' or vice versa — and assess to what extent the reading is fair or not. Note the tension marked by space (empty or full). As in any design that's architectonic, negative space is crucial. Just look: the Hearts and the Diamonds take up more negative space than the Clubs and the Spades.

Blacks absorb the light, reds expand it. Hence, we say yes with the hearts; probably yes with the diamonds; no with the spades; and probably not with the clubs. That's the rule of thumb. It's not *the* rule, as there's no such thing when we're dealing with specific contexts, but a rule that's instrumentally useful, especially when in doubt. Though here, just because you're in doubt does not mean that you can dispense with your deductive thinking. Unless the context occasions a reading for an expansive 'red' situation, you won't impose the red light on it because you have a rule for it, as a 'black' turn may have a different thing to say that would be more accurate. On this, the only advisable thing to say is to suggest that you watch your habits and tendency all the time, against the background of what is the case right then and there when you perform your reading. The 'here and now' idea is not subject to what you've learned in school, as it only answers the obvious. A good diviner would be chasing the obvious at all times, rather than resort to 'old wisdoms,' however useful these may be.

Do you stretch it, or do you squeeze it? Do you notice the speed or jump from a small number to a high number? Do you consider what you know culturally to be the case, regardless of moral or idealistic considerations?

You see 2 Diamonds? Not a lot when you want 10, or at least 4 to have your corners covered. You see 4 Spades between your money cards? Bloody hell. You won't get there, from 3 Diamonds to 4 Diamonds without having to survey the field first, wasting time with ground work. If you're the Jack of Diamonds, patience will not be your strongest suit.

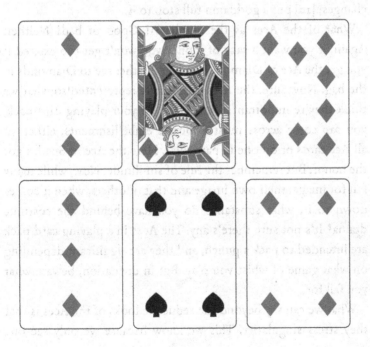

Now think of what you find in a string from 1 to 10. We go from unity to division, expansion to contraction, from one to many through the logic of numbers: [1] unity; [2] division or cooperation; [3] increment or loss; [4] stability; [5] remember your body parts; [6] paths or choices; [7] challenges; [8] wishes and fears; [9] changes; [10] put a goddamn full stop to it.

What of the Aces as the number 1? Good or bad? Neither. Again, if you want a sack of money you won't get too excited if you get the Ace of Diamonds, as you'd rather see 10 Diamonds in the bag. Now sure, the Aces are visually represented so what we think they're important. Depending on your playing card pack, you can come across most elaborate embellishments, either on all Ace cards or on one in particular. Here the Ace of Spades got the honor. But remember the rule of similitude. Now, while many fall for image, their own image and that of others, when it comes down to it, what substance do you have behind the costume drama? It's not sure there's any. The Aces in a playing card pack are intended to pack a punch, and they are significant depending on what game of whist you play. But in divination, beware what you fall for.

What we can say beyond the seductive looks of the Aces is that they stress singularity. This we know because we only see one image here, fancy or not. As such, we may think of unity in its singular expression to mark, indeed, a beginning, or more specifically, drawing also on convention: the Ace of Hearts can stand metaphorically for a house, your dwelling. The Ace of Clubs can show an opportunity. The Ace of Diamonds can signal wealthy means, and the Ace of Spades can demonstrate resolve or point to a necessity, such as making a decision or giving a situation a mortal blow. In the latter sense, the Ace of Spades can also indicate death, physical death or the death of something, such as a relation, the termination of a contract, or the death of a system of beliefs (logically speaking, a quick decision can also be seen as the death of hesitation).

But remember, reductive phrases à la 'this card is negative, this card is positive, this card is neutral, this goes to hell and this to heaven' are not very useful, as they yield close to no information. As a cartomancer, you don't want to deal with what is uninteresting. You want to prioritize process over information, and if you can choose, then you choose the nuanced type of information over the tired one. What makes you a good cartomancer is your ability to receive information from the cards and then process it with your deductive capacity and cultural competence according to context and situation so that this processed information becomes useful and relevant knowledge.

As a general rule, symbols are notoriously ambiguous. They hold multiple significations. Metaphors can also be stylistically tweaked so a certain kind of wit comes through in a conversation with the cards. The fact that this is so stresses the playful nature of the cards for divination, the idea being to constantly work with what you know of the manipulative character of language.

In divination we often operate with types of common questions: physical, metaphysical, predictive, yes/no. Most of the questions asked mirror precisely what the suits represent, whether of material, mundane, physical, metaphysical, or straight affirmative or negative nature.

We can find a number of variations across these themes: love/pain, money/work. When we talk about health, we find that health can be represented by all four suits: your body can be healthy or not, and the same applies to your finances, love, and work. Some questions revolve around metaphysical concerns or a desire to enter a spiritual relation with deities, the Devil, higher Self, or guardian angels, while others are all about predicting mundane events, or seeking a simple yes or no answer. Note the difference: 'how can I score this job? vs. 'will I score this job?' The first question is open-ended, involving you as an active agent: there's something *you* can do. The latter gives you no information beyond the yes/no, or the 'maybe' situation. *You* as a concept is subject to external conditions.

Once a question is on your table, you never judge it, nor do you judge the one asking the question. You judge the situation. Because of this, you never get overly concerned about what is ethical and what is not. It's not for you to judge what a client's motivation is for asking what they are asking. Your task is to read the damn cards, not to evaluate what you think is fair to ask or not. In various cartomantic communities you'll often hear this advice: 'if you don't feel comfortable with a question, don't read the cards for it,' but since when does reading cards is about how *you* feel?

Here's what you can practice in terms of getting skilled at asking a question or listening to one. Lay down three cards (pips and courts) and notice the 'good' (Hearts and Diamonds) and the 'bad' (Spades and Clubs). Why good and bad? Think: Hearts and Diamonds are for pleasure. Spades and Clubs are for work. Who wants to work? Not me, if I can help it. Does the 'good' end the string? Good. Does the 'bad' end the string? Bad. Note: we only use these reductions to good and bad instrumentally, not because we believe in such things. I don't. Culture enforces separations because it suits its dominant power. But I don't have to eat up what society comes up with or decides. I can think for myself.

Now consider the number progression and speed. You go from 1 to 10? That's a fast progression. You go from 1 to 3? That's slow. Generally Diamonds are faster than the Hearts, and Clubs are faster than the Spades. The court cards follow the functions of the suits (we'll look at this in the next chapter), each performing their role in the hierarchy. Numerically the King is at the top followed by the Queen and the Jack.

There's a certain rigidity to the way the suits are arranged, with the court cards mirroring this fixity. Unlike in a tarot pack, where we have many more characters in play, in the playing cards pack we only have 12 such figures representing a family unit. The hierarchy is clear and the postures and gazes can often turn one way. The playing cards I'm using here features the court cards in conversation. But in principle, the design of the body language and the gazes of the courts is meant to allude to relations that are beyond ambiguity. If the reading lends itself to considering the gazes of the characters, we pay attention to those, but otherwise, we simply focus entirely on the function that they perform.

Let's compare two readings on health and love using the same cards: King of Hearts, 4 Hearts, 8 Spades. We pose two different questions to the cards, in order to see how the context leads the answer. First question: 'how can I eliminate the stress in my life?'

  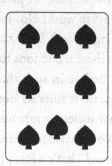

Here the answer could be the following: 'you can eliminate the stress in your life if you become aware of the detrimental effect of multitasking.'

Now let's pose the second question to the same cards: 'does he love me?' Here the answer could be the following: 'No, he used to, quite solidly, but now he hates you.'

Note: for the first question, I didn't get excited and launch into a narrative about negative thoughts and other such blah, blah of routine that springs out of the mainstream cartomantic self-help vocabulary. The question was about advice, about doing something. The question was not about describing the situation. It may well be that I have a whole legion of 'black' demonic thoughts in my head (8S), but that was not what I wanted to know. Here the helpful answer would be to say: 'take stock of what pressures you away from the things that you love.'

Now let's ask a set of questions about work and money using the same approach. This time these cards are on the table: 2 Clubs, Jack of Hearts, 8 Diamonds. First question: 'how can I improve my relationship with my boss?'

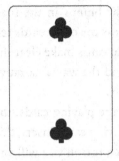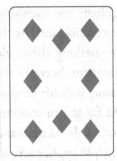

The answer could be the following: 'you can improve your relationship with your boss, if you show good will and demonstrate what value you can provide for the company.'

The second question is the following: 'will the value of my stock improve in the near future?' The answer here is simple: 'you bet.'

Note: In the first question, the context is one of rank, so I don't assign agency to the Jack of Hearts, seeing him as the boss. He's not a boss. So then, whatever I see happening around this Jack, I take it as a sign that he is the one who needs to perform whatever deed in accordance with what the surrounding cards say. Had the King appeared, I might have read the cards with the boss in mind.

The general principle to remember here is that while the court cards act, the number cards say something about the nature of this acting. The Aces and the tens are our 'margin' cards, so they acquire special status and significance because we can see them in terms of liminal circularity. What begins also ends, and the ones standing on the hedge, as it were, will always 'know' what happens on the other side. In this sense, whereas the liminal cards (1 & 10) are loaded with transitional power, bridging onto precedence and what's next, the numbers in between, from 2 to 9, highlight the transitory, the ephemeral, the bumps in the road or the quicksand. By the same token, whereas the court cards tell us something about what is at stake, the pip cards make clear the connection between the agents involved and the way a narrative or story unfolds temporally and sequentially.

As far as I'm concerned, whether I read the playing cards, the tarot, or the Lenormand oracle that uses playing cards insets, this principle applies across the board, for which reason you will encounter this same idea in the other two volumes in the trilogy. Where it gets interesting is precisely in the individual examples, as each is anchored in its own specific context.

What you also need to remember across the cartomancy board is the following: you are a brilliant diviner who reads like the Devil if, in addition to observing the obvious in the cards, you also train your capacity for self-reflection, the ability to hold in your mind contradictory perspectives, and judge with discernment.

What anchors your cards in a precise and elegant answer is not their set meanings, but rather their 'falling' into a specific context that you have a clear idea about. Again, the cards can mean many things, and they can hold many more signs than you can ever mobilize. The trick is not to run with the perspective that you like, but with the one that makes sense. Some readers can only see in the cards what they want to hear, or think the querent wants to hear. These are not good readers. They may have fun with the cards, but we cannot call what they do divination. Divination requires a cold head, not a hot one, full of opinions, likes and dislikes, superficial encouragement and niceties. The only thing that divination requires is clarity. Either you have it or you don't.

Let's see how you can train yourself towards recognizing beyond ambiguity what arises from the cards, often on multiple levels, in a set of assignments followed by a set of essays that will further your comprehension of how you can read the playing cards.

ASSIGNMENT 1: COMPARISONS

Practice the 3-card spread. Use the same set of cards to answer 2 different questions that fall within the 4 main concerns (love, money, work, health). Why do you have to do that? To develop detachment. If you can read the same set of cards as they address two different questions, then chances are that you will have learned something about going beyond the cliché readings, in which the number 3 is always increment, the 4 stability, and so on. Everything is fixed until it's not anymore.

If you can offer a commonsensical line about your cards, no matter what context they address, then you understand why answering the question: 'does he love me,' is no different than the question: 'what does it take for me to make a pact with the Devil?'

The best readings are the ones that display zero involvement on your part, whether at the cognitive, emotional, or intellectual level. When you read for another, even if that other is yourself, you're not in the picture as a reader. The other one is.

Let's give one more example here to consolidate what I'm after.

The cards above, Jack of Spades, 5 Spades, and 10 Diamonds refer to a student's question: 'will I ever just read the damn cards?' The student went like this in her answer: 'it looks like I will feel that I am in this way over my head, wondering if I will ever get to *just* read the cards, but in the end, I will get it and be able to go on. In my practice notebook I wrote of a child on a new journey, stumbling in the dark, while showing up for class, following the teacher and my fellow students, until I finally get it.'

Now, compare to this hypothetical question: 'will the teacher do her job efficiently?' Here the answer is the following: 'absolutely. She will be most efficient.' The 'over their heads' idea can easily be traced here too: 5 is for the body, together with the 10 for the top, voilà, we get the teacher's context: students who are unsure of themselves (JS, 5S). The outcome being the brilliance of 10D, however, we can pack it and say, 'it's a done deal.'

ASSIGNMENT 2: WHAT'S MY TEMPERAMENT?

Ask your cards: 'what am I prone to temperamentally that, also temperamentally, I can't see?'

What you want with this question is to get to the clash of temperament traits that you possess. The cards may disclose repetitive patterns that you're not aware of, or other sticky behavioural and character traits that you're in denial of. For example, these cards below might say the following: 'you shit in other people's pleasure. What you can't see is that your antagonizing nature leads to hard work.'

Read your cards as straightforwardly as possible, without thinking 'meaning.' Try to have direct access to what you see, and how you see it, that is to say, try to have zero preconceptions about method, model, and symbol.

ASSIGNMENT 2: THE GYPSY SPELL

Lay down a set of three cards. Take the card in the middle to be a representation of your Gypsy eye, or vision. Let the flanking cards be a representation of your divination strategy that enters the 'Gypsy current,' or lineage. Some like to think in those terms... What is the force of this lineage that your middle eye can see and use in penetrating the wisdom of divination? Let this be a spell of vision you put on yourself.

Look at these cards: Ace of Spades, 2 Diamonds, 6 Diamonds. We could go like this: 'my Gypsy eye is two sparkles. The force of this vision is the primordial cut and remote viewing.' Diamonds stand for clarity. On 'tracks' (6D), this clarity becomes a thing related to distance.

The idea with these assignments is two fold: first you practice responding to the cards spontaneously, that is to say, by taking into account what you know of the function of the suits and the cultural conventions around numerical progressions. Then discern. While we all want a sack of money, and hence may immediately respond to the 10 Diamonds positively, if the question is about focus, the 10 Diamonds is the last card you want to see, as it suggests too much of a good thing. What I'm saying is that at every step of the way, what you do when you divine with the cards is reflect on what you see. Imitation of others' ideas does not a diviner make. On my vision and my word...

For further comprehension, let us now turn to seeing the application of some of the ideas explored in this chapter to both fortunetelling in practice and reflecting on what it means to divine with the playing cards.

✦ COMPREHENSION: THREE ESSAYS

The first essay is a comparison where I look at the best and the worst in fortunetelling. The second essay addresses risk analysis with the cards, while the third talks about the fear of failure in reading the cards to precision, like the Devil.

The best and the worst in fortunetelling

'I'm concerned about my divorce.'
'There's no reason for it.'
'But it's been very hard and I don't know what's coming.'
'Listen, it's a perfectly normal divorce. Don't worry.'
'Okay, thanks.'
'Bye.'

✻

'Your New Year will bring lots of sexual vitality to you. Lots and lots of sex and lots and lots of energy.'
'I wonder about that. I'm 77.'
'It makes no difference. No difference at all.'
'Okay, thanks.'
'Bye.'

This is me, for once, in the witnessing position. A few years ago, I was staying at a cabin in the woods in Sweden. The only thing that was not slow was the German TV channel AstroTV. I stumbled into it. I made big eyes; after all, this was fast when everything else was slow. I got a drink and installed myself comfortably in the sofa. I was ready to be entertained.

The cartomancers on the TV were working very hard. It was clear that they were professional to the bone; professional in the sense of being able to handle being in the spotlight, getting questions, shuffling cards (mostly playing cards and the Lenormand oracle), and answering it all in something like five seconds flat. They called this the 'blitz' reading.

I'm accustomed to seeing this style of fortunetelling in Romania. No professional fortuneteller I've ever seen spends more than five seconds flat per question. There's something very compelling about this approach, and I use it myself. Readers who work for a psychic telephone line also know the value of speed. But here's the thing that I don't find so compelling: The lack of conversation. In the context here the cards were thrown very fast on the table, in random spreads. As far as I could follow – as the camera didn't always zoom in on the cards – the reader put as many cards on the table until they got to a specific significator, or a court card in mind. Then a few more cards fell on the table for the sake of creating context. Anything between 3 cards and 17, 21, 28, or 36 could happen, and whether there were 3 cards on the table or 36, the reader still didn't spend more than five to ten seconds per question.

No one read the cards according to any set method, school, or in any specific layout. Seemingly the reader read in line, but that was also only seemingly. I say this because if there's something I'm good at, then it's reading in line. I can do it very fast too. Sometimes extremely fast, so I recognize this type of reading immediately. This was not what they were doing here.

On occasion, when the larger sets were on the table, there was a hint of applying the method of reading cards according to distance and their position in relation to the primary significators. Mainly the focus was only on the cards around the significator. There was never any pointing to how one particular card or cluster of cards related to the question. If there was pointing then it was for positioning alone, not for context.

These readers' method followed actually the classical method for fortunetelling which is anchored in manipulating – or to be more polite, in permuting – with binary metaphors: up/down; far/near; positive/negative; inside/outside. For all its reductionism, what I actually value the most in this approach is that it's perfect for training the birds-eye view. In my own teaching I often stress the importance of rising above the cards and seeing everything on the table with hawk eyes.

The major downside was that there was never any conversation going on. I have as yet to see a professional fortuneteller in the classical style (a psychic on a phone line, or a Gypsy) who spends time on ideas, saying: 'here's an idea for you to think about,' pointing also to just the cluster of cards that suggests something to that effect. Such an approach would require a great deal of reflection and self-reflection. Self-reflection takes time. And time is money. You don't waste time on TV.

Self-reflection is also the opposite of certitude. Classical fortunetellers don't suffer from doubt, self-doubt, lack of boldness, and the pain of having to account for what logic they get it from. It's all about impression, not analysis.

What I appreciate here is not the 'I know everything' attitude, which can be very tiresome and tedious, but the Zen unwittingly present behind it, as this class of readers is not exactly trained in Zen: 'whatever I say right here and right now is the thing itself. There's no right or wrong. I'm God.' Indeed, come to think of it, not everything necessitates analysis. The grand art is, however, to know the difference.

So there are both good things and bad things to know about classical fortunetelling. Let's be more specific and create two categories here. First, the good stuff. We're here with speed, capacity for quick and clear overview, and Zen positioning. Then the bad stuff. There's zero conversation here, no reflection, yet certainty galore about just how accurate the prediction is. All shooting blanks, really, as statistically speaking, last I've checked prediction is still a 50/50 thing: now you get it, now you don't.

What I furthermore took from AstroTV that I also found entertaining was seeing how space got filled up by what emptiness: the readers got tired quickly, talking basically in a vacuum, though, since they were professionals, they didn't blatantly show it. The sitters said no more than 'okay' all the time, having nothing more to add. At best, they promised: 'okay, got it. I'll check. The lost wallet is inside the top drawer, you said.' The cards sat briefly on the table as if bewildered asking about their function, as they didn't get to speak much. The only interesting sound they made was when they were shuffled.

Now, watching how others read the cards is a good opportunity to ask yourself a few questions about what fortunetelling is for you. Here are a few such questions that you can pose for yourself before you read your next set of cards: how much do you insist on having a conversation with the cards and with the other you read for, even when you have to run a cartomantic marathon? To what extent do you think that having such a conversation is significant? If you can't afford to have a conversation, do you have a strategy that combines 'time is money' with 'self-reflection is the thing?' What is your approach when little context is provided for a big question?

SNAPPY FORTUNETELLING FOR THE PURPOSE IN LIFE

Related to how context participates in the formulation of a precise answer when you deal with the abstract stylization of the playing cards, I share here a type of reading that actually occurs with some measure of frequency. Often people ask about their purpose in life or their path. We're thus with a grand range of generality. When more concrete information is not given, you just read the damn cards, sticking closely to the essentials. Once the King of Diamonds, 5 Spades, and 8 Spades fell on the table.

 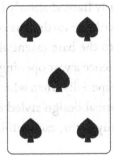 

I said the following: 'your path is to manage the pain of others.' 'Well, I'm doing that already,' the person said. 'I'm the chief psychiatrist at the loony asylum.' So there you have it. Five Spades representing an ill body, where others share the same affliction. Now to the subtle part: why did the psychiatrist ask about his path? Because he was not happy with his lot. He was looking for an alternative, but the cards here didn't give him one. So the 5 Spades for the body indicated very much *his* body, as he was the one asking the question. In divination, if we go with this system, then we always think of the 5 as it relates to the body of the querent. But in context, there's a stretching, which is what I did when I said, 'your path is to manage the pain of others' (5+8 Spades). This example demonstrates yet again how we work with a rule of thumb, but then we must remember what else the question lends itself to, and go with that.

If we have the opportunity of a face-to-face encounter, we can experience even more vividly just what it means to have a conversation with the cards when they corroborate an insight. This brings us to enjoying our position as fortunetellers beyond the aura and mystery that surrounds our oracular deliveries, when we speak in tongues and cryptic language because we can't hit the mark that ideally is clearly framed already by the sitter.

A satisfying session with the cards thus consists of recognizing the need to stay close to the bare essentials, as it's in this proximity that we can experience a vast opening towards just what we can make of the cards, especially when what we have on our hands is a few principles of formal design styled according to the types we encounter on our daily paths, each fulfilling very concrete and specific functions.

Playing cards for risk analysis

Since I like math and statistical systems, the latter mainly because in predictive settings calculation comes up as counter-intuitive, I see a ton of similarities between how scientists approach probability and how analytical fortune-tellers do the same; even the ones who are close to the state of illiteracy. I've met a few of those in my time in Romania.

In my cartomancy tool box, playing cards top the list of which cards are the most efficient when it comes to answering questions about risk. There's zero long-windedness here, what with the tight focus on the function of the 4 suits led by the court cards, long-windedness being the danger when we deal with 'picture' cards or cards that represent types in a loose way. To give an example, while no one can be in doubt as to just what bloody job the King of Spades performs, one can sit and stare at the possibility for the same when we look at the trumps of the Tarot cards.

The blade cards, Death and Justice, are obvious candidates for our King of Spades analogy. But how about the Charioteer? Isn't this one returning victoriously from the battle field, with victory representing the very premise for the bloody affair that leads to success? Just think about it. In our world, how likely is it for you to succeed unless you start chopping off the heads of the competition? You're welcome to ask me about how such acts are our daily bread and butter even in environments called 'the university,' or 'spiritual learning.' It's laughable. The higher up I climbed the academic ladder, which was pretty high at one point, the more ruthless bastards I've encountered. Ditto in the cartomantic world. Then, the Pope. 'Bloody hell,' this one says, 'unless you do what I tell you, your ass will burn.' Marvellous war stories of the twisted kind. Juicy characters to identify with, just as we like it.

Not so with the playing cards. Things are clear-cut here. Context is still king, and we deliver an answer entirely according to the wording of the question, but the nuance that the playing cards can pack is often an incisive marker of how and where exactly the answer is robust, rather than fragile.

I use playing cards when I want to go beyond mere storytelling or mechanisms of identification. The detective work with playing cards is often sharper than when we use other cards, such as the Tarot or the Lenormand Oracle. This is so simply because the style is tighter. I squint a lot when I read playing cards. The brain is at work double time, as there's no window here for reading emblematic symbols. There's even less of 'this means that' when we read the playing cards. When you stare at 3 Hearts and 5 Diamonds you don't immediately think: 'Birds. Communication. Punctum.' There's none of that sense of finality here that can easily render you in the darkest of the ditches, if your reductionism turns out to be quite wrong.

Let the King of Spades initiate the string, and you're with the idea of war communications enhanced by blades polished like diamonds. This King will have his way, which is bad news for you, if you're in it for friendship.

'But isn't it this difficult?' students who are afraid of the playing cards often ask. 'It's difficult,' I say. 'But only to the extent that you don't like to squint, kicking your habits upstairs for larger vistas and more air.' On the question of how difficult, think about why playing cards are still the most favorite among seasoned diviners. It's not because they are difficult. Rather it's because of how playing cards hit the nerve of what is risked in the game.

Think about all the questions that others come to you with. Aren't they full of risks? In this book my aim is not even modest. I want to teach you how to use a tool that addresses risky business in a most elegant, classic, and quite precise manner. But before we get to more method, let's say a word about the fear of failing at divination.

Fail, fail again, fail better. Not.

I used to be obsessed with Beckett because I was obsessed with the void. Because Beckett was obsessed with the void, I was obsessed with Beckett. Obsession works with false correlatives. But I was on to myself when I dedicated quite a chunk of pages to Samuel Beckett in my second doctorate dissertation 7 years ago.

The inspirational world is also obsessed with Beckett. Or, rather, with what the inspirational world decided Beckett's words from his absurd *Worstward Ho!* are all about. Failure. As a human thing. Hallelujah. If only we can find someone who can validate failure for good. Beckett is so delicious. You know the words, now a famous meme: "Ever tried. Ever failed. No matter. Try again. Fail again. Fail better."

I often come across Beckett's lines in magical discourses on magical practice, from divination to cursing or burying your enemies: 'Make mistakes, do it all wrong. It's delicious to fail.' Well, err. Wait a minute. As far as divination is concerned, let's try this analogy: if we forget that divination is a technology in addition to being an interpretative art, we forget that there's no difference between what a doctor does and what a magical healer does. Let me put it this way: would you go to a doctor who relishes his failures, or what's worse, can't even wait to fail better, and more, fall from all graces too because, well, it's delicious? I wouldn't. By the same token I wouldn't go to a diviner or a magician who just loves to fail. Because. Human nature. We can so relate, right? Wrong.

Magic and divination practices are about technique. The function of a technique is to be applied, not interpreted or evaluated in terms of the human condition. There's no such 'this is delicious, this is gross' parody here. If you learn a technique, you test its value by trying out its efficacy. A doctor can be very nice and full of compassion or some other vulnerable human trait that's just so endearing, but at the end of the day, what you want to know is if he can cut your gut in a competent way. Either he can do that, or he can't. There's no 'fail better' here. Imagine the surgeon who can't stop a bleeding. Beckett is so laughing.

Here's what I say. Don't fall for the endorsement of failure if you want to master a craft. There's no human nature involved in mastery. That's why it's called mastery. Learn a technique and apply it like a scientist does in an experiment. Take precautions that you won't blow yourself up in the air, which you would if your approach is slacking. A fortuneteller who applies technique to superstition is a fortuneteller who has gone beyond belief. This means that there's no one-to-one mapping of a random symbol or glyphs to an equally random idea of signification. A symbol does not equal meaning, any more than fantasy equals divine inspiration. This means that there's zero space for dicta such as, 'it can also mean this other thing' when looking at cards that hold ambiguous signals. If an answer to a question is precise, and it can be, it's because the context makes it so, as context frames a concern. If I asked the cards: 'What is mastery?' and got the Ace of Diamonds, Ace of Hearts, and 2 Hearts on the table, I could answer quite straightforwardly and without attachment that mastery is a dance with a singular idea that takes seat in the heart.

If I asked the cards: 'What is failure?' and got the King of Diamonds, 3 Hearts, and the Ace of Spades, I'd say that failure is what a king does when he looks away from the essential stacking of narratives from the heart. If you only listen to what you want to hear, then congratulations. You're in for the delicious failure.

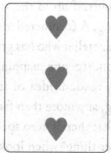

74

In my work with the cards I don't confuse mastery with narratives that make me feel good. What has feeling good about it got to do with anything? Either I cut your gut to perfection, or I don't. Not all things are intuitive. Some are counter-intuitive. The counter-intuitive falls in the category of analysis, risk calculation, and statistics.

If you want to read the cards like the Devil, then you shift into the gear that's called mastery, not failing better, as if, indeed, Beckett had the substance of our whole human nature in mind when he said that. He didn't. He was thinking of the void, devoid of substance, content, signification, meaning... In the void, he was thinking about not failing at all.

NINE: MORE THAN EIGHT AND LESS THAN TEN

The fortuneteller invested in clearing space via analytical deductions will obviously place herself at odds with most cartomancy books drawing on esoteric and occult knowledge. Since Etteilla's influential book in 1770, *Etteilla, ou manière de se récréer avec un jeu de cartes,* to Sepharial's *Manual of Occultism* in 1911, and Weldon's commissioned *How to Tell Fortunes by the Cards* for their fashion magazine 'written' by the Gypsy sounding brand Radoza around the same time, there's been no end to the entertainment called 'coming up with meanings' for the cards. Upright, reversed, across the board, hanging and dangling elaborate spreads for luck and love, special status cards, and other 'secrets' had one aim in sight: to spell out the fixity of one's fortune and fate. Without this illusion of fixity, no amazed clients. Without amazed clients, no silver to cross the fortuneteller's palm with. Indeed, enough in this spectacle alone to keep everyone entertained. Etteilla hit the mark when he put the word 'recreation' in the title of his book. Just imagine the client who has to stare at 4 Aces in a row. Magic. 'It means glory.' 3 Aces in a row 'means disaster.' Wow. But why? What's the logic here? Nobody will tell you, because there's none. It's all semantics. You can learn by heart a number of meanings based on semantics because that gives you the impression of confidence. But probing the depth of reading cards via loaded signifiers sounds to me more like a spell for disaster.

When I tell students that all they need to know about numbers is the rule of relativity, 9 is more than 8 and less than 10, 1 is whole, 2 divides, 7 is less than 8 and more than 6, they are suspicious. They want something that doesn't sound so simplistic. I refer them to the books referenced here while telling them about failure in fortunetelling. It's written all over these books. While they fascinate, they lie. Just think about why we think of the 3 Hearts as a kiss. A kiss of death, as there's no void in it that allows for your analytical brain to produce marvels against an empty canvas which is what you always start with. Although the questions may share a common concern, they're always individual. Why approach individual questions with methods that fail as far as your own imaginative cognitive capacity and field of vision goes? Although we can't wrap our heads around the magic of numbers, as they are pure abstractions, we've learnt what they mean in relation. There's no such thing as 'Three of Spades – Loss.' There's only this idea that makes sense: 3 is more than 2 and less than 4.

For the sake of accounting for my objection to lists of meanings that are merely fanciful, as they rest on mimicry and spectacle rather than logic and reason, I'll let a 'list of meanings' slip here for you to reflect on. Here's how Radoza, Weldon's Fashion Magazine's famed fortuneteller put it, when it comes to assigning special status to some number cards. I quote from the section called 'Method VII,' which I also urge you to reflect on, as in, 'what method,' when all I get is a list featuring arbitrary meanings? But have a look and be entertained. It's a fascinating concoction. On occasion I catch myself going with these fantasies, for why not? Fiction is what fiction does. It makes us think of better fortunes.

If two red tens are by you, it signifies matrimony.
Ace of Diamonds – A ring.
Ace of Hearts – Stands for your house.
Ace of Clubs – A letter.
Ace of Spades – Death, spite or quarrelling. This is the worst card in the pack.
Ten of Diamonds – A journey.
Three of Hearts – A kiss.
Three of Spades – Tears.
Ten of Spades – Sickness.
Nine of Spades – Disappointment.
Nine of Clubs – A merrymaking.
Nine of hearts – Feasting.
Ten of Clubs – Going by water.
Ten of Hearts – Some place of amusement.
Five of Hearts – A present.
Five of Clubs – A message.
Six of Spades – A child.
Seven of Spades – A removal.
Three of Clubs – Fighting.
Eight of Spades – A sweetheart.
Four of Clubs – A strange bed.
Nine of Diamonds – Business.

Five of Diamonds — A settlement.
Five of Spades — A surprise.
Two red eights — New clothes.
Three of Diamonds — Speaking with a new friend.
Four of Spades — A sick bed.
Seven of Clubs — A prison.
Two of Spades — A false friend.
Four of Hearts — Marriage bed.
Several diamonds together mean money; several hearts, love;
several clubs, drink; several spades, vexation.
(Radoza, 1910: 49)

All semantics. The point is that you can easily learn such systems of divination, and if, after years of practicing you notice that your accuracy score is high every time you have to send someone to buy new clothes because of the presence of two eights, you can declare yourself satisfied. But how are you going to know if the opposite is the case, or if something else is the case when you see the 'special meaning' cards on the table? You're not going to know, and it's exactly in this not knowing that you will have failed. The French word for Clubs is *Trèfle*, clover, so, luck. But we say Batons; no such luck here. We say Diamonds, wealth. The French say *Carreau*. 'You're dead' — *rester au carreau*. Systems follow language. The idea is not to be frequently wrong but never in doubt. The idea is to know nothing, to proceed from the void, and see where your god-given common sense takes you. Divination equals discovery, and discovery equals inspiration. It's easy to amaze people with oracular and ambiguous language, but it's infinitely more rewarding to go new places with them every time, simply because their singular and individual predicament begs it.

COURTS IN CONVERSATION

BEFORE WE LOOK AT THE COURT CARDS from the perspective of set attributes and function, let us start with a reflection on how culture works and a few examples of how students have tackled the assignments in the previous chapter. Culture works with set conventions. Conventions are established through precedence. Nowhere is this more clear than in the court houses. If there's a precedence for a case, the road for winning an argument is paved. We call this conservatism.

But precedence also works with establishing prejudice. Let me give an example of what happens in the social media. Often I get friend requests from people I don't know. As a general rule I accept them all on good faith. If good faith is trumped by insincere motives, I take the necessary steps. I swing a sword or two over the heads of the unwise, and then carry on with my regular program. But here's what happens when I get a request from men named Jack Black. I always think, 'another one of those,' winking in the direction of the Jack of Spades, famed for his status as 'the tall, dark stranger.' In other words, I'm prejudiced. I'm prejudiced because of precedence. In my case, not once did I happen to meet someone whose real name was Jack Black. Not once did I experience the fake Jack Black being interested in my professional life. They all wanted to seduce me with an aura of mysterious occultism that they'd perform to various degrees. Why they'd think I'd be interested is anyone's guess. As I don't sit and speculate on people's motives, I don't waste my time on investigating into what Devils possess them. So I let it pass, until inappropriate action is passed at me.

Once Jack Black popped into my chatroom: 'are you a real woman or a Lilith clone? This is a sincere question.' Right. I took

that at face value, though, and thought about it because it was entertaining. To make it ever more entertaining I asked the cards: 'I
got 6 Spades, Jack of Hearts, and 2 Clubs.' I answered to myself:
'I'm not a Lilith clone, but that's exactly whom horny young men
would like to encounter.'

So the 6 Spades here is a marker of the benevolent Jack of
Hearts walking the wrong path. This tete-à-tete à la 2 Clubs, is
not likely to happen. I'm not even in the picture here as the Queen
of Spades, as that would be a likely candidate for a Lilith clone.

Now, the cartomantic lesson here is to demonstrate how the
court cards work in action. Although each performs their function according to the nature of the suit they're in, this function
acquires a quality according to the surrounding cards. This means
that while we're 'blessed' with symbolic clichés galore – here
comes the seducer, Jack of Hearts, how exciting – when it comes
down to passing a correct and just sentence on what's happening
beyond how we feel about it, we find that because the surrounding cards can completely overrule the 'meaning' of a court card,
we land with a verdict that's counter-intuitive. I say 'counter-in-

tuitive' not because it is actually so, but because symbolic language often traps us into belief – à la 'I feel that the Jack of Hearts is a good person because he represents the heart.'

Here's what I say: if you want to be a good diviner, the first thing you must do is ditch all belief. All of it without exception. You don't believe in the meaning of cards, intuition as impression, or tradition any more than you believe in the sincere love of the tall, dark stranger called Jack Black.

A HUMBLE APPROACH

Here's another example of how the court cards change course when in the presence of cards belonging to different suits. This time a student asked a common question: 'what do I have to do in order to get this Job?' He got 2 Spades, the King of Hearts and the Ace of Clubs.

He went like this: 'I see the King connected to his goal, the Ace of Clubs representing an opportunity, but he needs to cut or separate something (my eyes keep seeing the King's sword). What is he cutting? I'm Not sure.' Another student offered this idea: 'the King needs to show confidence.' I intervened here with the following idea: 'the King needs to start over, as it were, as he's up against a new suit. The Ace is the beginning. Normally a King would act with the confidence of his rank. But if the question is about what he must do to score, I'd say that he needs to approach the new situation with some caution and in humbleness. He needs to see first what he's getting into.'

As the first card down, 2 Spades, announces a conflict, it would be pointless to advise this King to move with confidence towards his goal. What confidence would that be, the confidence of his heart? That would be just fine if we saw 10 Hearts here instead of the Ace of Clubs. 10 Clubs would also be preferable to the Ace of Clubs, as it would be an indication of some force. As it is, and as per the general rule, 1 is little and 10 is a lot. We're not with the idea of going forth with a lot of confidence. Quite the contrary.

So the surrounding cards tell a different story than the one in which the King is merely sovereign. Sometimes even a King needs to bow his head; especially the King of Hearts, as charging ahead, martial style in order to conquer a new territory is something that goes against the nature of his suit. We leave conquering with confidence to the King of Spades, as that one is more prone to boldly exploring new territories, or the King of Clubs, who, although lacking the winning tactics and strategies of the belligerent King of Spades, can, at least, bluff better through boasting than the King of Hearts.

The correct approach to the cards is to look first at the nature of the suits and who represents them according to what rank, and then assess the quality of action given by the surrounding cards.

83

One way in which you can be sure to stay on track when you read the playing cards is to start with practicing a few precepts: Keep it simple. Pay attention to the cards, your language, and the way you describe what you see. Go back to your question and answer it by relating to it precisely. You don't want to read the cards and get lost in details that are irrelevant to the question. Always know what you're saying and why. Differentiate between the descriptive, reflective, analytical, and evaluative dimensions of your divination.

You want to remember these precepts especially when you're dealing with a client who asks a specific question, and also wants an answer to what was *not* asked, or a client who asks vague questions and then expects utmost precision from you.

Let's have an example of the first situation. The sitter asks: 'will the mantra that was designed for my health by a shaman work?' The cards that fell on the table were 8 Diamonds, the Jack of Clubs, and 3 Diamonds.

  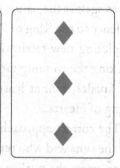

I said the following starting with noticing what was missing from the spread given the question: 'in health related questions, I'd prefer to see some hearts in the picture, not the money cards. The shaman has good intentions, but his work lacks the healing power. His mantra has focus, and it can go somewhere, but I wouldn't hold my breath. Focus is not equal to healing. The shaman must bring something else to it than personal, mental brilliance. The diamonds are good for clarity, not for making the blood flow the proper way, so they're not as good for vitality.'

There was a follow-up question from this client: 'does the presence of diamonds indicate the mantra is better suited for money making purposes?' 'No,' I said, 'the mantra was intended for health, not money. Don't mix the narratives.'

As you can see from this example, even when clients ask specific questions and they get specific answers that are even explained in terms of demonstrating why you think what you think, pointing to what's missing or to what shouldn't even be there as it doesn't fit the narrative of the question and the motivation for it, some clients get carried away when they see what else the cards can say.

But you're not here to serve the 'what else is there,' as there's already a world of other possibilities you can point to. What you're here to do when you read the cards is stay cogently within one world, not ten alternative others. Always stay on track with the initial question. Follow up questions have a good function, for instance, to clarify a point, but if they lead you astray, don't go there.

Let's have a closer look at what happens when the rule of staying on track is not consistently observed. Here's a string of student examples.

The first one asked: 'how can I support my 13-year old daughter to feel loved and nurtured with me?' For this question she got these cards: 3 Spades, 5 Hearts, King of Hearts.

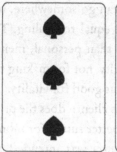  

The student's own answer went like this: 'dig through the areas that need tending, give her lots of physical affection, and lead with strong actionable love (do activities together!)' I offered this suggestion: 'you can support her over her pain in the body by siding with her father. Does she have body issues?'

Another student chipped in: 'I think I understand everything you saw in this, Camelia, except for the 3 of Spades. Is it pain, and if so, might you elaborate on that?' To this other question I offered this answer: 'Spades always inflict pain. In the absence of more concrete information at the level of context, you go with the simple *pain in the body* using *nurture* as a cue. As the mother wants to know how she can help, the answer is still to address the pain in the body. And then that thing about the father being in the picture.'

After this initial conversation about this situation, there was an avalanche of ideas pouring in. The second student who wanted my input about the Spades said the following: 'I can wrap my head around the *always pain* aspect by seeing Spades as daggers – protective, war-like, decisive in cutting a thread or choice out of the picture. The body aspect eludes me. Is it reflective of the Spades' link to the earth or the skeletal system? Or a parallel between iron Spades and the body being rich in minerals?' I offered this: 'I'm reading 3+5, the 5 being the body as cued in by context. Don't read the cards individually, but in tandem.'

Now let's see, as several things are going on here about agency and the court card in the picture, the King of Hearts. When we further unpacked this story, the mother provided ample context about the father, a policeman, who had custody and therefore a lot to say in it – 'not a nice man, with anger issues,' as she put it. And 'yes, the girl has frequent stomach pain,' we were all told. This made us consider my initial statement calling for the necessity to 'side with the father.'

If the policeman (whom we might expect to come up as the King of Spades) has anger issues, yet has custody of the girl (King of Hearts indicates blood relations), we can find support for our statement in this way, especially since generally the King of Hearts is seen as benevolent. The explanatory answer therefore is the following: 'you side with him by treating him like a father, not like the professional he is, or like someone with whom *you* have a problem. The opposite of siding with the father because of resentment backfires and hurts the girl.'

Also, consider this: when we associate the 5 with the body (5 limbs at the center of the world), what do you do when this card pops up in questions about what the querent can do about her relationship with another? Whose body are we referring to? The mother's or the daughter's? Here I went with the daughter's body as the querent's question was about a third party. Thus the straightforward reading is still to say this: 'there's trouble (3S) that affects the one that's related (5H) to the King of Hearts (it's the father that's in the picture, not the mother).

So then, this body, this 5 Hearts card, cannot represent the mother. Hence it cannot be about how *she* can nourish the relationship with love, which is already a vague and intangible thing. We're thus back to the more subtle idea, but obvious, that the way forward here is to consider the King of Hearts: 'if you must do something for your daughter, then you must consider her connection to her blood father.'

Let's have a more lighthearted example pertaining to seeing clearly. Also a student asked in class: 'Was Joan of Arc just crazy?' She got 8 Hearts, 10 Hearts and 8 Clubs for it.

The student said this: 'Joan of Arc was emotional in her wishes for her people to be victorious, but she had thought through her plans (that is, no, she was rational).' My suggestion was this: 'Joan of Arc was a mystic – excessive hearts – with a working agenda

88

– clubs. No rational intellect here. We'd need the diamonds for mental affliction next to the trouble cards.' Now think for yourself: what we call 'the rational' is very much a matter of what we cultivate at the level of the logical. We polish our thoughts in order to become rational, to have our minds shine like diamonds. As there's no diamond in the picture here, whatever motivation Joan of Arc had was of an order other than the rational. So we can exclude calculated planning. The 8 Clubs card as a representative of work is in the picture, and we go with the idea of working hard, but we won't stretch the significance of this card to a situation that requires planning when an excessive number of hearts precedes the work. We could thus say that if Joan of Arc was anything, then she was a zealot. Zealots work hard from the heart. They are not necessarily crazy, but they are not rational either.

On answering the goddamn question, let's look at these cards: 2 Diamonds, 9 Hearts and 2 Hearts.

'What is my Gypsy eye?' a student asked, and then answered: 'Gypsy vision is finding the heart's desire (does this mean that I will only answer the question that is not posed but only hinted at in the querent's heart of hearts?) I see it with a perfect balance between my mind and my heart. Juggling time!' I offered an objection here: 'what is this thing about finding things? Good you put that awareness in parenthesis. Indeed, you ask, *what is my Gypsy eye?* Surely you must answer in the descriptive, not in the wishful thinking for something you have no idea what is. So, let's hear it again, *my gypsy eye is... 9 hearts, whose force is a double deuce.* This makes sense because we see it.'

What you see for yourself can turn into a mantra, or a repetition of an essential observation of something that suddenly appears significant. That's the beauty of the obvious, when you keep it simple. Since a student got this particular message, he tried his hand at it. Here's an example of how he applied his mantra, 'This is not the Golden Dawn's Tarot' to his practice of reading the same set of cards for two different questions, introduced in the previous chapter. He went like this upon seeing the Jack of Diamonds, 9 Spades, and Jack of Hearts on the table:

'Two questions: [1] How do I grow my business? [2] How do I find new love? Answer [1]: The key to changing your business is by changing how you are going about making it happen. Look beyond that change toward new ideas about what you desire and how you will manifest healing through your work.' Answer [2]: 'The key to finding new love is changing your approach to old love; a good start would be finding someone who is more in line with your ideas but who is a bit of trickster besides.'

Looking myself at these cards I noticed a symmetry, so I said the following: 'pay attention to the courts. What do they do? They press on the 9 Spades from the margins inside. If I were the 9 Spades, I'd feel that pressure. So, what's the obvious question to ask here? Do we still read linearly, from left to right, and then go the pedestrian way: 'if it's red that ends it, then it's good?' No, we don't do that. We go with what's obvious. Two young men are dealing with the escalating trouble (high number). We can infer that they want to change that.'

Another student entered this conversation and suggested this: 'Q1: I would also add that you need to ditch (9S) the young and immature, no matter how well-meaning or promising they look (the Jacks).' Q2: 'I would also add that you (JD) need to dig deeper (9S) for new love (JH). Perhaps it's already around. Just that you aren't aware of it yet.'

My comment was to point out that this is all fine, to an extent, up until the moment when we have to ask: where does the notion of ditching and digging come from? Method over seeing is a bad idea. We may have learned that we can associate the Spades with digging, but in context, it's not sure that 'digging' applies. Other notions may be more apt. Always think: color, numbers, courts. What makes sense? In this example here, consider the number here, 9. It's high. Close to completion. 1 is excited, 9 is exhausted.

If you have to give advice, would it be about action, 'dig deeper,' or reflection, 'how has my digging been so far'? I'd go with reflection and change. Also, since we do have some method, think: Which of the numbers is more likely to spell out ditching? The sixes are for paths, ways of doing things, and transport. With the spades, we think of evacuation, discarding, getting rid of something, so 6 is a better candidate than 9, thematically speaking.

The obvious is the answer. The straightforward answer – and beyond the implicit knowledge (the student brings in the idea of healing that means nothing to us who are not in the know) – is simply to state that 2 young men must collaborate on what to do about the current troublesome state of the situation that requires change but not for the better. I would say this to my client: 'Beware of this difficult challenge.' Since two red courts flank the problem symmetrically, it's here that we must go to for our solution, to the human touch exercised in a mutual effort. We don't go to advising: 'dig,' nor offer an evaluative conclusion that entices to action: 'ditch.'

Imagine this exchange between the two Jacks pressing on the 9 Spades. Jack of Diamonds: 'Do you realize that this shit needs changing?' – the thinker realizes things. Jack of Hearts: 'Yeah, man, I can so feel it, but I've no idea how we can go about it' – the feeler feels. Jack of Diamonds: 'I do' – of course he does.

Another student added this historical insight, going back to the cartomancy of 1760: 'if we also consider Etteilla's suggestion about the meaning of two Jacks, we find that the combination points to insecurity about decisions about basic practical things. Score one for Etteilla.' My final remark on this was to offer focusing on a couple of things here if we must consider lists of meanings, why we want to use them, and why we want to ditch them or at least be careful. Yes, you can have indecision if you see 2 (immature) Jacks in the picture. The question is, however, what do you do with that information? How do you apply it to serve you in a precise way?

If the list of meanings (symbolic and other) is predicated on some specificity and not just generality, then think: where is the idea of 'basic practical things' reflected here? We can say 'basic,' since we're with the spades. But how do we know what the 'practical' is? If we go with the simple common sense behind the suits, then we have to rule out the idea that the Jacks must make up their minds in their decision about finding a practical solution. The Spades are about disputes. While it can be practical to settle a dispute, that's not an idea that's obvious here: one Jack has notions, the other emotions. So if the painful dispute in the 9 must be settled, then it's through the functions that the two Jacks perform.

Pay attention to language, text and image. At the first order level of signification, what we have here is 'Spade,' a rigid thing of culture that maintains laws, lacking both the naturalness of the clubs made of wood, and the flowing easy-going of the hearts. 'Practical things' alludes to the idea of 'many' in the 9. 'Many things' when not quarrels can be working agendas (Clubs), a family gathering (Hearts), or a bank account (Diamonds). The point to be made here is that if you score in cartomancy, you do so because you're able to account absolutely precisely for the way in which you apply the system you work with to the context of your concern. That is to say, you're absolutely conscious of the language you use to connect your words with the ideas behind the stylizations of the human relations that we find in the 4 suits. Cartomancy without language awareness amounts to a nostalgic list that's worth nothing but a dime.

THE COURTS — A LIST OF TRAITS

Speaking of lists, let's see what we can make of the court cards, if we go with creating a list of their attributes. For this I will employ a cultural narrative of the courts, similar to the one I offered in the first volume of the trilogy, where I talk about the court cards in the tarot deck. Insofar as I use the same principles regarding defining both the function of the pip cards and the courts across the board, I paraphrase my ideas in the following way:

In the playing cards pack we only have 3 representatives of the court for each suit. We find here the Kings, Queens, and the Jacks. No knight to do the King's bidding as is the case in the tarot. In modern parlance, this is a family unit: man, woman, and child. Each fulfills their functions according to their suits. Each can be in relation to the others, whether of familial or adversarial nature.

The 4 Kings can be regarded as symbols of power, each going after their interest as dictated by their suit, so we have the following representations: King of Hearts: the father, or a man of love; King of Diamonds: a man of money; King of Clubs: a man of action; King of Spades: a man of war. Depending on the context of your question, the Kings can tell you something about power relations. They can inform on dominance: weak or strong? The answer to this depends on the surrounding cards.

The 4 Queens can be regarded as emblems of truth. They mirror exactly the functions of the Kings in their control of the

94

affairs of their suits. Queen of Hearts: the mother or a woman of love; Queen of Diamonds: a woman of money; Queen of Clubs: a woman of action; Queen of Spades: a woman of war.

In structuralist terms when we deal with binary opposites, antithetical powers, and collaborative or adversarial positions, we can say that whereas symbols represent, emblems consolidate, so we gain something by thinking of the court cards as they embody these essential functions. The Kings have commanding power. The Queens have executive power, and the Jacks have mediating power, as Jacks are often considered messengers or servants.

If we go with the Greek tripartite relation: thesis, antithesis, and synthesis, we can throw into our mix of functions the idea that, in addition to composition as family members (the King represents the thesis), the court cards can also be seen as acting in opposition (the Queen represents the antithesis), or in fusion (the Jack represents the synthesis). Now, why is this model useful? Because it highlights tension in clear and unambiguous ways. In questions about clarity, what we want to know first is who is with us, who is against us, and who is willing to compromise.

Now, while you'd think that all the court cards know their place and perform their function in accordance with the law of universal equality, traditionally, or rather, conventionally speaking, things are not all equal, even though the stylized suits are designed with that in mind. Here's a rendition of the King of Spades: noble man, strategist, cuts right through it, a cold head. Compare these qualities with the way the Queen of Spades is described in cartomancy since Etteilla's days: sorrowful widow, spreads calumnious gossip, resentful, calculated, a hot head. The suit of Spades stands for law and order. While you'd think that the top heads share the same agenda, the woman here is given a character and nature that's not exactly flattering. So we can rightly wonder: the King of Spades can be a general in the army, a police chief, or a magistrate, but his consort cannot? Why? We don't find the same cultural discrepancy where the other pairs are concerned. What's going on? What about the Jack of Spades, who is considered a troublesome child until he is identified as the Devil himself making especially women fall for the promises of the tall, dark stranger? Thus in terms of 'negative' or ambiguous character, it's more helpful to think of what other cards flank the court cards, before we impose a particular meaning on them out of the blue and without motivation, the sole justification for it being that 'it's tradition.' If tradition equals 'stupid,' I suggest we ditch it.

In a reading about the intentions of a person, if we find the King of Hearts, who is supposedly the most benevolent and generous person you can imagine, next to the Jack of Hearts and 9 Spades, you can expect a description of his character in synthesis to fit almost exactly the image of the Queen of Spades, when this card is referred to 'traditionally.' We'll note that our reading will no longer be informed by the list of attributes that define the King of Hearts individually, since we'd have to consider how his 'nature' (the Hearts suit) and intention (Jack of Hearts) will acquire the less than desired qualities, the result being a description that will make the King of Hearts unrecognizable. We'd be here with someone who lies and disappoints. This example tells us that it's best to use a description instrumentally, as it makes sense, not as it's set in stone.

About the Jacks we can say the following: the Jacks are symbols of initiation, with initiation not signifying any esoteric or occult rite of passage, but rather, openness towards starting things in a spontaneous and curious way. The Jacks are the children of the higher courts, 'starting' the family unit. They have little agency or power to act. They can act as recalcitrant troublemakers — including the Jack of Hearts who wouldn't shy away from impregnating another teenager — or they can be messengers. Sometimes they can represent the thoughts of the King and the Queen when

97

they're in the same suit. In a reading about timing, such as when to perform a task, if the Jack is in the picture, it tells you that you might as well begin right now, or that things are already set in motion. On occasion, all the Jacks can also represent risks. Jacks can be daredevils, immature gamblers, or loitering *flâneurs*, initiating acts of seduction that can compromise the other.

All court cards can represent the querent, a spouse, a friend, a boss, or siblings. The court cards in the same suit can also signify or indicate a familial relation (of matters domestic, work, business, and law). For more descriptions of attributes and functions consult the essay, 'Courting the Self' at the end of this chapter.

THE COURT CARDS IN PERFORMATIVE ACTION

If we relate the court cards to the idea of functions discussed in the previous chapter, we can say that there's only one essential question that we need to ask, namely the question of what everybody does. What does a King do? Sit on it, sit on his achievements. A King is above having to prove himself, to consolidate stuff, to make transactions. He delegates. He has others do these things for him. Therefore he embodies a symbol of power in its static manifestation – again, if Hearts, man of love; if Clubs, man of work; if Diamonds, man of money; if Spades, man of war.

Sometimes the Jack in his more mature representation, such as the daredevil, can be an emblem of consolidating the King's business in an active way. He can be into developing. The difference between a symbol of power and an emblem of development is one of rank. The Jack acts on behalf of, whereas the King is at the top, commanding and controlling power.

The Queens as the creators of the world fulfil their function of being guardians of sacred knowledge, and hence of truth. They embody a different kind of power that's aligned with how we see with the logical eyes and how we see with the so-called illogical eyes – this latter idea, especially as seen from the perspective of culture.

The Jacks in their youthful and childish manifestation are agents at the mercy of others. They are sons and daughters, messengers, or apprentices. Their presence in a string of cards, especially if the string consists of the highest ranking court cards, can indicate the thoughts or emotions of these higher powers. The Jack of Hearts can be an emotional extension of what the Queen of Hearts is thinking about, or what she intends to act towards. They can also be seen as stages towards the manifestation of the mighty power that a King possesses.

If the King of Spades doubts as to whether he must engage and go to war or not, the presence of the Jack of Spades in the sequence of cards will most likely confirm this ambivalence, the Jack of Spades being a nasty little thing, always intent on splitting relations, rather than finishing them off the honorable way in a duel, or by actually going to war.

The Jack of Diamonds aspires to make money, but he lacks the cunningness of the King of Diamonds. At the other pole, the Jack of Hearts is always sweet and floundering, encouraging his single mother to find a husband for herself. Oh, the sympathy that can turn nasty, if the Queen is too impressionable herself, and unable to discern what the truth is.

I see the idea that the Queen equals truth as related to the way we make a distinction between the public and the private spheres. At least that's my conclusion after reflecting on the cunning folk cartomancy, often referenced by others in various books and online resources, yet without full explanations as to why we equate a court card with a certain idea (see, for instance, Dawn Jackson's compilation of folk cartomancy for the so-called *hedgewytch method* that, although logically wonderful and sound, often falls short of examining the root of the logical thread behind why we say what we say). This is fair enough, as the best way to go about it is to think for yourself.

Let us assume, then, that since a Queen is not considered 'a man of action,' she may sit on the domain of thought, thus approving of our attitude of thinking for ourselves. Consequently, after I was done with my own share of thinking about it (this is the second time I'm writing about this), here is what I have arrived at: no matter how civilized we think we are now in terms of gender equality, traditionally men have occupied the public sphere, and they still do, and women the private sphere, even when they appear not to. So where will we more likely find the truth? Obviously not in the public sphere where politicians set the agenda. The truth is the closest to us, our private place, our soul. Who has access to all this? Women. That's my reasoning. I haven't seen others talk about it in cartomantic settings, though it is likely that you will stumble over similar, albeit much more abstract notions.

In books about esoteric fortunetelling people refer to the court cards as having to do with an expression of the 'within and without' dichotomy, or indeed as following the hermetic axiom: 'as above, so below' (see for ex. Sepharial's *Manual of Occultism*, 1911). When not used for predictions or concrete advice on mundane matters, we can give the playing cards a psychological bent, when the court cards can represent an archetype, or be seen in terms of their helping or non-supportive attitude (from counsellors to abusers, critics, victims, champions, and so on). Suffice it here to say that if you stay close to identifying what each suit performs, then you'll also be able to read the intensity of the power of action that each of the court characters possesses by virtue of their rank, gender, and age.

KEEP IT CLOSE TO FORM

In principle, sticking close to the function of the court cards, number progression, and color division, gives you access to precision. Precision is the art of making bold statements, of risking being wrong. The only condition for precision is paying attention. When you pay very careful attention to your cards you realize that you have no time to fear anything. That's the pay off. Paying attention practically liberates you from your fears.

The court cards together with the number cards function as a unit. This means that before there's any set meaning or symbolic association imposed on a card, there's your seeing, your spontaneous reaction to the cards. If you glance at all the cards on your table at once, before you start interpreting what you see, you'll note that you're able to get a sense of what tone the reading tilts towards and what 'color.' Is it quiet or loud? I can assure you that the sound of 10 blades is loud. Is it red or black, as in heavy or light? Although you may think that your reading is all about content, the reality is that a good fortunetelling session is all about form. Granted, you deliver a message, a very useful one at that, but before you get there it's all about form. You hear the question and then you think about what's appropriate to cast: 3, 9, 13, 40 or all the cards on the table? Your interpretative job starts with making all sorts of preliminary observations.

Keeping it close to form also means that you never read just one card, or sink into your 'daily.' Your day is not static and singular, but developing and changing according to factors and conditions that are external to what you make of it. The same applies to cards in layout. Reading each card individually in a string of 3 or 10 is not only trite and boring as hell, but it will make no sense whatsoever in the context of emerging narratives, of putting two and two together based on the variations between the functions that the cards embody. What you want is to develop the ability to create a synthesis, that is to say, form an educated overall impression that leads you towards the formulation of your final sentence. Start with a 3-card. Look for function, and get going with the story.

The pip cards connect the dots and string your equations. The only principle that applies when engaging the pips relates to how each suit embodies a function numerically. Find out what that is first. Remember your math: plus, minus, and the state in between plus/minus, as the 'maybe,' or 'it's likely' or 'it's not so likely.' Which meaning applies is determined by the surrounding cards and the context of the question. Hearts and Diamonds are 'plus' as their quality is expansive and 'light' – these are your 'red' cards. Spades and Clubs are 'minus' as their quality is contracting and 'dark' – these are your 'black' cards. 1 is little; 10 is a lot. It's all about contraction and expansion, equivalence and exception, far and near, above and below. There is no other mystery to it, secret esoteric correspondence, printing error vs. intentional design, or 'this sounds good' idea. In divination what you want is to *see*, not just know things in theory.

Staying close to form is a way of accounting too for what is necessary. For instance, for all the tradition of reading the playing cards according to their upright or reversed position, I myself never think this is necessary. So I don't. Reading 'reversals' according to a new set of terms and definitions is not necessary when reading the cards is about identifying function over symbol.

Reversals fulfil no function when you read the cards dynamically, in pairs and in strings, rather than individually and in predetermined positions. Just think: what does a spade do? Cut. Is that good? Cuts are always painful, so unless you like pain, whatever the spade does is generally not good. Place the King of Hearts next to the Jack of Spades and the 9 Spades, as in the previous example, and you'll begin to understand the King of Hearts 'reversed.' He will not act according to the highest potential of his suit. In the presence of the Jack of Spades, he will feel the urge to manipulate, or more concretely, intoxicate, let a river of lies and rumours flow towards hurting and disappointing. This is not a sign of sitting in true power, but rather of awkwardness and inadequacy. So you don't need to see the King of Hearts reversed in order to get to a list of lesser qualities. By the same token, and as exemplified before, think: you are a general in the army and getting ready to go to war. You ask the cards about it. You see a lot of spades on the table. 'How excellent, a good sign,' you will say ever so joyfully. You will not worry that your drive feels 'in reverse,' as many spades on the table are your collaborators.

Thus when you divine, form is closer to your 'Gypsy' eye than content, as divination starts with the fundamental question of framing. How is the question framed? How do you frame what you see in the cards, so the message goes somewhere? A good structural form gives your reading robustness. The content can follow after you've set up the building blocks for your interpretation. Interpretation doesn't come before noticing what there is to notice. Pay attention to the obvious, and the rest follows.

9 CARDS... I FEAR THEM NOT

Let's look at some examples of reading the classic 9-card *carré*. But first here's the basic mechanics for reading: lay down 9 cards in sets of threes beginning with the top row.

If you choose a significator to put down, let it be at the center of the square. I myself hardly ever use this method, as I prefer to see if the significator pops up in my spread or not; if not, then all the cards on the table will relate indirectly to the querent. When you choose a significator, go with these physical attributes for hair and skin complexion: King, Queen, and Jack of Hearts: white/blond; King, Queen and Jack of Spades; black/dark; King, Queen, and Jack of Diamonds: red/silver; King, Queen, and Jack of Clubs: brown/chestnut.

The reading normally occurs by always considering what three cards do together. The first card down is the theme. For practice, you can try the pedestrian way: first read the rows in trios, then the columns. Activate your temporal and spatial metaphors: left column: past; middle column: present; right column: future; top row: what you think; middle row: what stares you in the face; bottom row: what you control. Finish off with a reading of the corner cards in a diagonal line, crossing the square with an X.

What determines the way you go about it that may exceed the standard or normal way is a set of preliminaries. First scan the tableau. Immediately pay attention to whether the significator is in the square or not. If yes, then pay attention to where it landed. Then think in terms of preponderance: how many black cards, red cards, or court cards? How many 'repeats' (ex. 3 Aces)? What is blatantly missing in relation to the topic asked about (ex. if the question is about love and all you get is spades and clubs, you begin to see just what tone the love question has). Lastly, pay attention to 'the last word.' Usually the last card in a 9-card spread has much to say, as it ends both the vertical and horizontal lines.

After this round of preliminary observations, here's a note about the sophisticated mechanics of reading the 9-card spread. I love rules and conventions. They form my foundation. But the way in which I move up through the layers of signification, or build on top of this signification exceeds 'rules and conventions,' as it's a matter of courage to be able to step on it and dance freely with the cards.

A glance at the way in which the trios dance, first horizontally, then vertically, and then X'ing the spot, can quickly settle the outcome. What you want to aim for is presenting your sitter with essential information formulated in what I call the master sentence, an elegant one-liner that captures the essence of what's going on.

If you arrive quickly at this line, fling it to your sitter right then and there. You can then use the booked time to unpack the implications of what you're saying. If you don't quite have the essence of the cards to begin with, proceed from assessing the function of the cards first, not their symbolic associations, as this will reveal the obvious to you. Let's now look at the 9-card classic.

Significator: King of Spades (popped randomly in the spread).

Context: Work related. The Significator, King of Spades is employed with a company and wants to know if his project proposal will be accepted, hoping also that a promotion will be in the bag if the project succeeds.

Note: You always choose significators according to physical characteristics, not function. We read the court cards primarily according to their function, but when we choose them to stand for a person, we go with the physical traits.

We start with a swift reading: the King of Clubs (boss) is assessing the King of Spades' project (10 Clubs over King of Spades), but he decides against it (9 Spades). In principle we could stop right there, as the matter is settled. But if we unpack, we note this: the project is lovingly crafted (3 Hearts below 10 Clubs), and definitely put forward (3 Diamonds), albeit in a convoluted way (3 Diamonds + 9 Clubs). Etteilla, in his influential book from 1770, *Etteilla, or a Way to Entertain Yourself With a Deck of Cards* would say that the presence of 2 threes indicates calm. Right. I'm so amused now... I don't see any calm here. I would rather say that there's some urgency towards making a decision. Threes can be eager; look at that straight line in the 3 Diamonds; with the 9 Clubs, very eager.

The King of Spades is familiar (2 Hearts) with the King of Club's intentions to create value (3 Diamonds) for the company, and hence emotionally appreciates the effort (2 Hearts). They meet in the card of 2 Hearts (when we cross or intersect their lines).

107

Let us now see how the X marks the spot. We cross the tableau with an X, to get more information. We note the following: the King of Clubs has no qualms about axing the depressed King of Spades (9 Spades to King of Spades), who has compressed it as much as he could (10 Clubs to 5 Clubs). The project (10 Clubs) is disappointing (9 Spades) and flops (10 Clubs to 5 Clubs). As a consequence, the King of Spades will not get promoted. He will feel the embarrassment (9 Spades) in meeting the great changes at work (9 Clubs), not having scored weighing down on him (5 Clubs), but he can comfort himself with knowing that less will be expected from him (10 Clubs to 5 Clubs).

Sometimes I turn over a surprise card. I turn up the cut deck and look at the bottom card. No surprises here. The card of 7 Spades enforces the sad outcome for this man. Cry baby cry, and move on. The meta surprise: although I could have gone the pedestrian way and formulate 6 sentences based on the reading of trios in the rows and columns, and then issue a final sentence, I elected to keep that option at the back of my head instead, rather than let it inform what I saw that was actually more interesting to do, which was to zoom in and out of perspective and let the cards have a say in it according to the context.

In this example my preliminary observations gave me my 'master sentence' on first, that is to say, immediately after the first glance at the cards. The ensuing unpacking of the cards merely supported this first impulse, providing evidence from the cards that testified towards the validity of my verdict.

Let us now turn to another example where the question was one about a large donation.

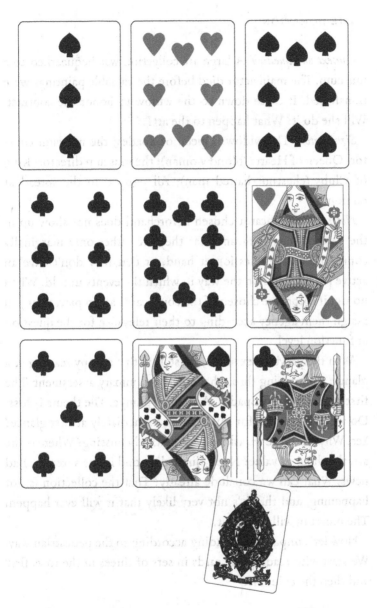

Context and question: A large art collection was bequeathed to a museum. The main actor died before the valuable paintings were transferred. It came down to the widow to honor the contract. Will she do it? What happen to the art?

Significators: The widow: Queen of Spades; the museum curator: Queen of Hearts (blond woman); the museum director: King of Clubs (chestnut-haired man); All popped in the spread at random.

Note: if a significator chosen beforehand does not show up in the spread, then it means that they are either only marginally connected to the question at hand, or that they don't have an active participation in the way in which the events unfold. When no significators are chosen, if the court cards are in play, then you assign them agency according to their relevance for the question at function level.

As in the previous example, we start with a snappy reading at a glance, while going through a quick preliminary assessment. The first card down is 3 Spades. A straight plunge. The theme is loss. Do we find support for this reading immediately at first glance? Yes. Why? Because we ask: what is blatantly missing? Where is the art, the thing of value? Not a single diamond in the spread... Bad news. What can we conclude already? That the collection is not happening, and that it's not very likely that it will ever happen. The museum will not get it.

Now let's unpack this reading according to the pedestrian way. We start with reading the cards in sets of threes in the rows first and then the columns.

We note this: it's not happening. A straight stab at the museum enlarging their collections. A community invested in beauty gets only a shadow of it (3S, 8H, 8S). The collection's road to the curator is blocked (6C, 10C, QH). This work is her body. What prevents the museum director from getting the artworks, what stands between him and the works, is the widow (5C, QS, KC).

The columns say the following: the transfer of the works is not honored (3S, 6C, 5C). The intention is good, but there's too much to deal with, and the widow is overwhelmed (8H, 10C, QS). The museum people rightly fear a negative outcome (8S, QH, KC).

This whole reading is also supported by the card looking on, the surprise Ace of Spades. No go. What you hope for (8H) happens not. We find further evidence for this prediction if we look at how the X marks the spot. We get this information from the diagonal lines over the tableau: 8S, 10C, 5C. The painful attitude towards diminishing the overwhelming pressure does not a diamond make; 3S, 10C, KC: the museum director is looking at what he stands to lose, namely, the widow's promise to act on the initial plan, even for her own sake (5C).

The final sentence was formulated thus: the collection is not happening, and it's not very likely that it will happen. The museum will not get it. Target on point. Is this the exact same sentence we started out with? Yes. This prediction turned out to be correct. Five years down the road after this reading, I hear that the collection is still not in its intended place.

At the fundamental level we can derive from these two examples this principle of reading the playing cards: keep it simple, and keep your eyes on the ball. Always think: What makes sense? Does it make sense to think of diamonds as being forged in fire, and therefore associated with the hot/dry dyad? If it does, then use that association when it's necessary. Does it make sense to think that the court cards are other people whom you engage with, rather than aspects of yourself? Search your brain: do you know a blond person, or one who has red hair with whom you might have an encounter of sorts? If yes, jolly good. If not, think: might there be a possibility to encounter a tall, dark stranger next time you set up a meeting with your bank?

Fill in the blanks: if something doesn't make sense, revise your hypothesis and move on. Getting stuck in lists, schemata, models and maps will only disclose how lost you are, not how good you're at putting two and two together. Divination is about putting two and two together according to information, processing of information, and awareness of language. Ask yourself: 'do I actually know what I'm talking about?' Use lists and systems of correspondences instrumentally, not to lead your reading.

When you divine you enter an essential dance with the cards. Bring your language awareness in alignment with what evidence from the cards you get for *everything* you say. If you don't think you can do that, then say nothing. Just sit there and stare at the cards. That would do it. Eventually something emerges that will be of infinitely more value than what you'd otherwise put on the table out of obligation or fear that if you don't say anything you'll be regarded as incompetent.

Deconstruct, but don't split hairs. Deconstruct clichés, what is conventionally perceived as 'normal,' inquire into the nature of the very thing you say, but don't be a contrarian. Language doesn't operate with realities, but with representations. Know that, essentially, everything you say, or the system of divination you use rests entirely on fiction, not truth. The truth is in your ability to combine information, context, and visual input from the cards. A strong message arises from your own justice. That's where your genius is.

ASSIGNMENT 1: SNAPPY AND PEDESTRIAN

In a similar fashion to what I've done here, produce 9-card readings in two steps based on any question you have: a snappy reading and a pedestrian reading. Let your master sentences, the final one-liners that capture the essence of what's going on, be in alignment with the cards. If they're not in alignment, account for why not. Produce an argument that demonstrates where you think you went wrong.

ASSIGNMENT 2: THE DULL AND THE MAGICAL

Lay down 9 cards. Let the card at the center be a representation of the most fascinating, interesting, and magical aspect in your life. Read the touching cards, the cards that form a diamond shape at the center, as dullness that surrounds your magical core. To be clear, the diamond shape is formed by all the cards in the middle of your rows and columns. Read the corner cards as pillars that you can rest on, or 'enlist' in your work of rescuing the interesting from the dullness that surrounds it.

Let me give an example that demonstrates what I'm after. Note that this reading is a reading for description, not prescription or prediction. We just want a snapshot of the magic and the dull.

Here, the magic is the relationship with an intimate other (2H). The dull is the swinging emotion from hot to cold (10H to QS), through having to invest the self (5D) in others (9D). The rescue is in seeing (7D) what makes you sick (5S), and settling with less.

ASSIGNMENT 3: THE GYPSY SPELL

Lay down 3 cards to address this context: 'you're powerful beyond measure.' You heard this before, and you want to believe it. Heck, on a good day, you *are* believing it because belief is all it takes, right? Wrong. If you want to know Hell, start believing in something. All beliefs lead to Hell and they stay there.

Now think: Power is power. Power is not subject to what you happen to believe in. Ask yourself: how do I know power beyond belief?

Let your formulation be the spell of power you cast on yourself. Make it poetic. Get a sense of how your words affect you at the level of resonance and tonality. A spell, after all, is a magical breath.

COMPREHENSION: THREE ESSAYS

In the following I present you first with a 'short story' about the court cards, highlighting the idea of fashioning the self according to four categories of acting in the world. The second essay deals with the logic of significators, and the third looks at how the odd card interprets the double.

One of the questions that I often get in teaching cartomancy pertains to how we distinguish between the court cards. Who is who on the table, when the court cards show up? I read the cards according to the function that I see each card embodies, whether I look at the tarot trumps, pip cards, extended court cards, playing cards, or Lenormand cards. As emphasized earlier, the narrative or 'short story' about numbers and courts is the same across the board, so let's see what we can make of the basic principles that go into conceptualizing the four suits when we talk specifically about playing cards. The suits are stylized ideas of our natural laws, as these interact with our way of coping with them.

'The wind is too strong? Well, build a house.'

'With what?'

'How about some trees?'

CLUBS

Can we think of trees in their stylized form as clubs on the cards, as having an association to the concept of building, chopping wood and all that Zen-like attitude towards routine work that would be a good idea for us all to have, lest we should succumb to too much pressure? Indeed, we *can* think of the primary meaning of clubs as 'work.'

What else do we know of trees? They tend to grow tall in the air. The wind has a funny sound through the trees and their crowns.

'Would it make sense to associate the trees with air, then?'

'I should think so.'

What else? Trees have an interesting structure in their bark. Sometimes we can think of it as heavy skin. Rough. Unpolished. The bark smells. It smells of the woods and the natural world. Sometimes animals take a pee on the trees, and then some funny looking weeds, both poisonous and not, grow by the roots. Hmm, I wonder what it all means. Very Saturnian.

If we gather the dead branches out in the woods, we can make a mighty fire with them. That is, after we build that luxury log house we dream about, the one that protects us from the strong western winds, or from the hustle and bustle of the city, its merchants and their transactions enabled by the stock value of some idea of gold and diamonds. Well, often we're not talking about real gold nowadays, as folks down history have long since given up on the necessity to have real gold passing through their hands whenever they needed to trade shit for shine.

This wise decision was, of course, mediated by the merchants of the world, the sanguine, diamonds folk, very good at rhetoric, and very good at convincing the clubs people of the benefits of working for the government. After all, when you're done with your own log house, maybe you can build ten or a hundred more just like it. All it requires is hard work. But you won't mind it, really, as what you're good at is in fact exactly that, chopping wood — whether for your own private use or for the public condo. Who cares? You get paid, and work exhilarates you.

'Is the King of Clubs a King of work, then?'

'Why, yes he is.'

What else do we know of the King of Clubs, other than the fact that he smells, he works like a maniac and demands the same? He plans a lot — all that wood needs counting — he builds connections, and he's good at figuring out which stick fits what hole. That's quite enough already. Essentially, however, all we need to do is think this: the suit of Clubs equals a whole lot of wood.

DIAMONDS

Whoever is in charge of the diamond mines, and now virtual banking transactions, belongs to the group of very smart folk. Their brains are irrigated by blood on fire in an almost mystical way. Well, so it goes with all the trickster gods. If they're good at anything, that'd be commerce and how to make others work for them. Yep. You gotta have a lot of brain power to convince the wood folk to work for you. And then, for what exactly? For losing the very thing that feeds their need for work. How many more forests must go down? Too many. The result? A cold and dry temperament. The clubs folk get depressed – 'melancholic' they used to call it – and will soon be in need of making a new transaction: more work in exchange for the lost soul.

If the diamond type of folk, the mercurial type, will not be able to provide the service, they will be sure to direct the clubs folk to a professional. They are, after all, masters of fixing ambivalence. They know everything about crossroads, whether asphalt or clay. The diamond people are *wired*.

HEARTS

The emotional people are the phlegmatics of the world. They have melted hearts. If they don't swim in emotions, they drown in

118

them. We're not with the grounding roots of the forest here, but with rivers; rivers of tears, blood shed for passion, and phlegm.

'What's that?'

'Well, that is desire with a capital D.'

Here comes Venus, the Goddess of Love and Money. We all want that, but some want that really badly. They will pray to the moon and back for it. Just think of what we do with blood in its stylized form as we find it on the cards in the form of hearts. When we wish something on our blood, spill it too for a spell, we understand that this is serious business for the heart.

With the hearts we love, have a party, make toasts, invite friends for a meal and drinks, and then watch how everybody gets their tongues untied, giving way to a whole lot of repressed emotions and desires, disclosing also just what a mighty power the power of insatiable desire is. We can find a whole range of 'human nature' in spilt emotions, for spilling is the trade of the hearts people. Just look around. The harder people feel, the more passionately they want others to take this path with them. But what is this path? These days it's called 'spilling your guts out in the most moving and heart-wrenching vulnerable stories.' It works. Some just love that sort of stuff.

If the clubs folk come to the hearts folk, the hearts folk will know how to show sympathy. On rare occasion they will show compassion, Jupiter style, but sympathy is more frequent. After all, since the hearts folk crave stuff all the time, and they are *the* masters at craving, there's only so much empathy they can display. But they will be able to hear the pulse in your veins, pumping through your heart. This pulse is close to what the hearts folk are good at identifying: circulation. Any flow of blood is their specialty.

Spilling blood. That's the domain of the choleric folk, the Mars folk, the warriors, the ones who are good with a spade in their hands. They will not hesitate to spill the blood of the hearts folk who are good at wasting emotions, theirs and others. The spades people have one mantra only, which they repeat incessantly: 'Off with their heads. Bury their bodies.' When they're done with all that chopping of heads, guess what, some digging is necessary. Where do you suppose that all those spades represented on the pips of the playing cards come from? Digging the earth. Fencing and death. Do you see the connection? The two malefics, Mars and Saturn. You don't want to go against them. Their presence in any layout spells out *trouble*. Obstacles and limitations rule.

Imagine to live in this paradox: in order to know the coldness of the earth, you need to have a very hot head, blinding your actions. *En garde*, the Solar fixated French cloak and dagger heroes used to shout all the time in those noble days of chivalric retribution, using their hottest passion and their coldest head for it, thus inverting the order of things: hot head and cold passion. But who cares, as long as somebody dies. Exhilarating.

If the choleric swordsmen play their cards right, they might even get either the clubs folk to dig the graves for the dead, or the hearts folk to officiate the burial, crying their emotions out on behalf of the community. Where do you think that all those traditions of lamentation come from? Keening, anyone? The Irish are very good at it. Not to mention the Romanians. As far as the spades people are concerned, only one question is interesting: 'Who's going to die next?'

I don't know about you, but I have participated in many funerals, including those of my parents where I've witnessed the following: the clubs folk provided the coffins and the external planning of what to do with the dead corpse, how to dress it and all that. Work. The hearts folks provided the libation and the tears. Family comforting. The diamonds folk took our money and promised to facilitate help in case of a nervous breakdown. Fast messengers. The earth folk dug the graves with their spades, and nailed the coffin. Friend or foe? We all sat at the table together, eating or stabbing each other if the drinks went to our heads. We sat together in church, and then by somebody else's grave. *Memento mori.* We comforted each other, or slandered each other. We loved each other, or then almost killed each other with some tall story.

UNIVERSAL TYPES

The point of this depiction of the four suits is to say that they represent the four universal types we all recognize from our walks of life. Some are lumpers, some are splitters. The court cards leading the numbers are all faithful representatives of their kingdoms.

Again, what does a King do? Rule, command, and protect. He rules with proven authority. He observes how competently others work for him. He displays magnanimity and ruthlessness in equal measure. Therefore he embodies a symbol of power that is both manifest and subtle. A strategist doesn't share his secrets when he plans to conquer or defend.

The Jack as the go-between the King and the Queen is an emblem of consolidating the King's affairs in both an emotional and pragmatic way. The Jack is the child that the King and

Queen love, but also one who grows up to be his own person, yet moulded in the image of the King and the Queen. The responsibility that the higher courts have for the Jack is thus not of the emotional order. When the Jacks act individually, they are into making discoveries, growing with the task in front of them. In terms of rank, they don't have much agency, but they can indicate an intention, and make a motion towards change.

The Queens have primordial power as far as creating is concerned. They wait nine months to give birth, so they are good at practicing the art of patience, noticing the subtle changes in their bodies and that of others, their children or consorts. The Queens' patience suggests capacity for reflection. She can easily be the strategist for her husband, the one keeping the books, showing how a plan can be implemented logistically. With the help of the Queen's strength, her cunningness and strategy, love, and care, the King can think of tactics to win at his war, whether we're talking about defending a territory, acquiring new land in exchange for diamonds, finding a cure for cancer, or calculating just the angle for an impossible bridge.

FUNCTIONS

As far as I'm concerned, the court cards *perform* a function all according to the suit they embody and the context of the question. Whether the King of Spades is a bad magician today and a good magistrate tomorrow will be something we can determine according to how we see the essential qualities of the suit of Spades in alignment with the context of the question. Furthermore, the distance between action and truth, the public sphere and the private sphere, and men and women is also determined by the surrounding cards. If your question is about your need to know some truth, or it has an investigative character, then the presence of the Queen will tell you what you need to focus on. If the Spades, the truth is distorted; if the Hearts the truth flows. The other suits give you a maybe. It's the question and the context that give you the answer to when the Queen acts as an emblem of truth, a symbol of power, or as a regular woman feeling the feels, doing the deeds, thinking the brilliant thoughts, or plotting to poison.

What is the question, exactly? If the question is one about how to handle the truth, then the presence of the Queen of Spades alongside with the King of Hearts suggests difficulty in admitting to suffering from blind spots. The Jack of Spades alongside with the Queen of Spades suggests intentional lying, where the Jack modifies the Queen's thoughts or intent for the worse.

Beyond cultural pre-conditioning, when we have to determine who all these court people are, populating our spreads, we can remind ourselves that we can also see with something other and more than our cognitive capacity to decode, interpret, and make aesthetic evaluations or judgments. We can see how, following the suits, we are more prone to becoming obsessed with money than with work and committing a crime of passion than passionately going to war. The reason for this is related to the closeness of the four stylized ideas in the cards of love, money, work, and war to our own concerns.

Desire for diamonds makes us sweaty and hot. The heart can beat fast and rush us into action. Work schemes won't excite us nearly as much as money schemes, and war hardly ever wins in the affairs of the heart – the head may fall, the heart, never. We keep Spades and Clubs at arm's length. We adorn our bodies with diamonds, and the blood in our veins keeps us alive. Far and near, it's all here in the four suits. We say yes to pleasure and comfort faster than to work and war. What is our most immediate need? Shelter and love. Money buys us the house and the bedroom. We only need to go to war, or compete, if the neighbor has her eyes on our property.

THE SELF AND THE OTHER

Court cards always represent other people. They hardly ever represent 'aspects' of ourselves, not even when we try to stretch our esoteric politeness. Court cards as aspects of us are pretty useless, and in mundane questions they never work. Telling someone who gets the Queen of Hearts and the Queen of Diamonds side by side that this indicates how she can sometimes be full of love and other times full of brains will hit a nerve, for sure. But how specific is that? Aren't we all like that? Aren't we sometimes loving and sometimes innovative? Generalities never move anyone. Think in specific terms beyond the cliché.

PICK A SIGNIFICATOR

The best is to go old school, and always pick a significator before laying out any larger spread of cards. The significator must be aligned first with the physical traits. Traditionally, a redhead, or a woman with white hair, is represented by the Queen of Diamonds. If she's a professor, or manages the bank, match point. In readings, however, a blond man, King of Hearts, can be a lawyer, thus functionally fulfilling the role of the King of Spades.

In matching the physical traits with professions, we say that the Queen of Hearts is a blonde mother, or a working in healthcare. The Queen of Clubs knows her business, and handles practical matters with mastery. She is an enterprising brunette. The Queen of Spades is the darkest in complexion, and works as a judge or a bad witch – the question decides which persona applies.

The King of Clubs is a manager or boss, of dark complexion, and the King of Hearts a father, a counsellor, or a priest, a blond man. The King of Spades is a magistrate, a policeman, George Clooney in *Ocean's Eleven*, or a mentalist. Usually he has the darkest skin. The King of Diamonds is a financial tycoon, freckled or reddish blond going towards silver.

The Jack has more attributes when accompanied by other courts. If the King is a general, the Jack is his soldier (Spades). If the King is a bank director, the Jack speculates on Wall Street (Diamonds). If the King is a cardiologist, the Jack is a seducer (Hearts). If the King is a developer, the Jack is a forest ranger (Clubs). The Jacks study or deliver messages (Diamonds), meddle in others' affairs without concern (Spades), work for a herbalist (Clubs), or daydream (Hearts).

What we can say here is that there's hardly any ambiguity as to who does what and for what purpose. Because of this purpose, the court cards give us a sense of direction. In their presence we're not in any situation that makes us doubt: 'maybe this is also an aspect of you immolating yourself.' Yeah, right... Before you think *aspect*, think function. You will hit the mark with that more precisely.

The logic of significators

Let's take *the* question in cartomancy, 'does he love me?' as this question remains an unchanged classic. For instance, what used to be a very frequent question about inheritance some 200 years ago, now is more a question about winning the lottery.

You will find that there is very little practical value in what some old cartomantic manuals prescribe — not to mention the heavily loaded bourgeois symbolism of the Lenormand cards that also feature playing cards on them— for the way in which we relate to money and property issues today. So, therefore, let us look at the perennial love question instead, as otherwise we would need to do some serious cultural adjustments.

'Does he love me?' To demonstrate a point, I'll read for this question that happened in reality with two different sets of cards, the second draw intended as a commentary. For the first reading I used a predetermined significator. For the second reading I chose none. Now, what interests me is how we make clear who is who in a spread, what they do to whom, how they do it, and why.

Let's look at the popular 9-card again. Here we have two options: to pick the significator card and dump it in the middle of the tableau, or pick it beforehand, but let it stay in the deck. If it shows up in the spread, we can read all the relations around it according to where it lands. If it doesn't show up, then we must decide with ourselves that all the other court cards that may fall on the table will relate indirectly to the significator. Or, depending on what we see, we can infer that if the significator that's still in the pack is impacted on by the cards on the table, then we're talking about a subtle kind of impact, not a strong or direct one.

Now, court cards are generally seen as either family, helpers, or enemies, all according to their suit and the way in which they interact with the cards surrounding them.

So, the other court cards landing in your spread will not be seen as 'aspects' of your significator representing the querent, as is often the case in tarot readings, but rather as others who are with you, against you, or who act as neutral agents and messengers.

Which card in the center? Let's make a preliminary, yet crucial distinction, as we come up against a first dilemma that beginners often confront. Let us have the question again, because it always starts with that: 'does he love me?' Insofar as *he* is the subject, we must place the card representing *him* at the center of the spread. Not the other way around. So although you may think that you need the querent in the center because she is the one asking the question, it makes more sense to reserve this place for the person the woman wants to know about, so *he* gets the central spot. Why in the center, some want to know? Because visually we're drawn to that place when we need to focus.

I've seen readers placing the card representing the querent wanting to know in the center, but surely she is the object of the man's interest — or disinterest if the cards suggest that — not the subject, so it's a fallacy to think that the cards must answer a question about *her* when all she wants to know is *his* thoughts.

In other words, before you lay down any cards, you must always think of how the question is phrased, what the topic is, and who the subject of interest is. You must always pay attention to what the querent is saying and to what you're saying.

For my first spread here with a significator, I picked the card of the King of Spades. Let's see how I went about it.

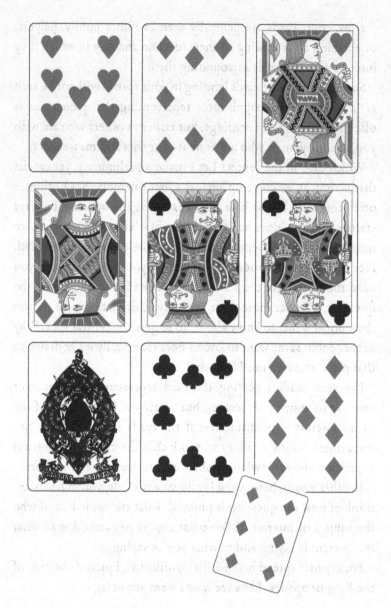

The woman significator, which we must also decide on in advance, did not show up. In this context here she is the Queen of Spades (though we don't need to create consorts; another Queen can also do, as we pick the significator according to physical characteristics; traditionally however, lovers share the same suit, unless otherwise prescribed).

From this we may infer that the answer to the question, 'does he love me?' will address more the ways in which the King of Spades loves or doesn't love the Queen of Spades, rather than say something about a direct contact between the two.

As it happens, this spread turned out quite beautifully, with the first card, the 9 Hearts, suggesting two things: the heart's desire – traditionally the primary meaning of the 9 Hearts is to express the heart's desire – or a change of heart (the nines stand for change; with the heart, a change of heart). Sticking to this simple rule: red good, black bad, we can say the following: the King of Spades wishes strongly to love the Queen of Spades, with whom he communicates and exchanges love messages in public via the electronic media (9H, 8D, JH), but he *decides* not to (9H, JD, AS). Note here the nod to the Ace of Spades to suggest a decision, here, against the wishes of the heart. Now this is quite interesting, for this seems to be in complete contradiction to the intent. Either you love or you don't. How can love be up to deciding either for or against the heart's desire?

A look at the first row and then the first column discloses, however, and painfully clearly too, that while the King loves the virtual love messaging, in person he himself delivers crap (9H, JD, AS). As I actually know people who do this, I'm beginning to wonder what the cards are telling me, statistically. But let us keep this reading on the demonstration basis, and leave the gathering of data out of it. There is also another interesting aspect to the 9 Hearts moving vertically into the Ace of Spades I can point to.

If we assume that this is about the heart's desire, then we must conclude the following: in spite of the King of Spade's desire to decide *not* to desire the Queen, he can't help himself. How? The 9 Hearts moving into the Ace of Spades simply means that this wish will not be granted. Logically speaking, and based on this alone, we must thus infer that the answer to the question is yes, the King does love the Queen even though there seems to be a strong indication that he decided not to. Psychologically speaking, why does he have to make an effort not to love? Because he loves.

Is this a moron we're dealing with? See, that's the question, the reader's question, I might add, insofar as this follow-up question also happened. Remember that the Queen of Spades herself didn't show up in the spread. In fact we have four males on the table, out of which two are either children or messengers. As there are no 3 Hearts in the spread, which would indicate that the Jacks are the children of the two, we must go with the messengers.

The first Jack is clear, as he enters our sentence unambiguously. The heart wishes (9H) to communicate (8D) a message of love (JH). The second Jack initiates the string in which two Kings face each other. Here we could say that the King of Spades *might* wish to cut a deal with the King of Clubs. The Jack of Diamonds here indicates a message of negotiation or at least the intention to consider the other King.

So we can infer that the King of Spades is thinking (8C below him) of how to get through to the other, the King of Clubs, or how to get past him (JD, KS, KC). Looking at the two nines in the significant diagonal relation, we could say that the love of the King of Spades for the Queen of Spades is conditioned by an exchange of place (9H, KS, 9D modified by KC).

From this we can infer that the reason why the King of Spades desires not to love the Queen of Spades is because she may already be in a relationship with the King of Clubs. Ergo, there is love, but this love is conditioned by a change.

For a bit of variation here, we could say the following: given that the 9 Diamonds card is associated with the top of the line in terms of value, 9 being close to 10, perhaps the Queen of Spades represents a trophy that two Kings are in an indirect exchange about. We can further say that since the Queen is not present in this spread, we can imagine the two men in a competitive conversation about her behind her back, as it were. Though it looks like the King of Clubs is lovingly winning this one (he is in the future column below the Jack of Hearts), simply because the other one decided to give up (Ace of Spades below the Jack of Diamonds, the King of Spades' calculating thought) and love from the distance. The surprise card, the card from the bottom cut deck, the 6 Diamonds tells us precisely that. Tough luck.

Now, let us turn to the same question and use the exact same pair, but this time I let the cards fall on the table without getting the main significator out of the pack. At the time of playing this game with the significators (present and missing) on the basis of a real reading first and then for the purpose of teaching, my expectation was that the two spreads would be closely related or that the second reading, indeed, could be seen as a commentary on the first, while at the same time telling us something about the dynamics of reading with no significators on the table at all.

Now, we saw how in the first instance that the love of the King of Spades for the Queen of Spades was conditioned. The King had decided not to wish to love the Queen for whatever reason — here probably because she was with another. In the second spread, neither of the significators showed up. So they remained in the background of what story emerged here. What didn't show up either was any single heart card. Quite disheartening.

This is always very telling. What is blatantly missing from a spread, when there's a clear expectation for a topic to be heavily represented one way or another, is very telling. In a question about love, hearts usually show up for better (with more hearts) or worse (with more spades).

Now we want to know: why such insistence on 'no heart' involved? We get an idea already by looking at the first card, the 8 Spades. This is a card of high measure of negativity. With great pressure nearby (10C) as an insistence to find a new opportunity (AC), a story emerges already very nicely.

So we can say the following: the King of Spades succumbs to his negative thoughts (8S) and obsession with the Queen of Spades (5S) with whom he is in a mental relation (2D). We call a mental relation platonic, unless other signs of mental disturbance are present. Remember that although neither of the significators, the King and Queen of Spades, are present here, we still read for them.

Because we have another Queen smack in the center of this tableau than the one that represents our querent, we could argue that the King of Spades is now one step further away from the possibility to love the Queen of Spades; he is no longer occupying the initial center position in relation to our Queen of Spades where

133

we forced him to be. Another woman is in sight, and she has hers to say. The Queen of Clubs here seems to offer an invitation to partner with her and her enterprising child (2D, QC, JD). The insight for this line is based on our basic principles: Clubs indicate work relations; 2 Diamonds almost always suggests an invitation or a call, and the Queen of Clubs indicates a pragmatic woman; Jacks can stand for both boys and girls.

Here it seems also that a 'fix it all' Jack of Diamonds facilitated this Queen's interest in our King of Spades, missing from the spread (JD with AC above and 2C below). We can even say that this was his idea (again, AC above 2C via the JD), and that the young person has done this before. The 2 Clubs card can represent a repeated act, or a doubling. All this is actually a plausible scenario, as I already know that many single mothers experience that their children want a father role model. Consequently, they want nothing more than to see them find a man to marry again.

So, with the new Queen of Clubs on the table the King of Spades moves from being depressed to changing his situation (mainly financially, however) and accepting this new deal. The surprise card here, the Jack of Spades tells us, however, that there is lot of suspicion involved in this whole set up. The Jack of Spades may, on the other hand, be the son of the King of Spades. So, the King of Spades relinquished his agency to the young ones, and went off with the new woman. Kind of... he is still not in the picture, but since a pragmatic woman can force things through, we can easily see how even the most resisting types can yield if some pressure is applied. Here, lots of it, as testified by the 10 Clubs above the Queen's head.

Now, however, how does this answer our question?

Does the King of Spades love the Queen of Spades? The cards insist on not telling. Can we then say no, simply because there are no hearts here at all? Or do we take the missing hearts as a sign of just how romantically uninterested this king is in this other woman that snatched that focus, the center spot here? We *would* have to have some hearts in this spread for these questions to be answered unambiguously.

What we got here is an indication that the King of Spades *might*, indeed, still love the Queen of Spades, since they were both hiding from view together with all the other hearts in the pack. Also, the 'bad' cards we got here refer more to the mental state of the King of Spades, rather than his emotions (8 Spades for negative thoughts and bad communication, and 5 Spades for the afflicted body). With pressure culminating (10C) and the inexperienced ones cutting deals (JD), we could say that the King of Spades was left rather emotionless. Conversely, one might be tempted to say that with these cards on the table the King of Spades definitely does not love the Queen of Spades, because as established before, he decided. But also before we established that, we know from the first set of cards that his wish to not love was not granted.

If there are no hearts in this equation here, it is because the cards show us beautifully the consequences of going against the heart's desire. You go against the heart's desire, there'll be no heart left for you to feel the world with. Again, tough luck. On the other hand, if pragmatism is desired, then good luck. Not all of us need to feel the sublime anguish of the heart in love. Being normal, that is to say, married with children, and getting down to business is also a kind of happiness. As we can see then, it pays off to think very clearly about how we delineate the significators, and how important it is to *not* go with the temptation to associate the court cards with random aspects of the self à la 'but that court card can also be me, as I'm also like that.'

The court cards are *not* about the *relatable*. They are about relations. Just because a situation looks familiar, it doesn't mean that it is connected to the question at hand. There is thus no need for embellishing beyond what the cards tell us and show us, even when we have to venture into unknown territory and speculate about love triangles when, to begin with, we're only asked to describe the thoughts of two people at odds with one another. The job of the significators is to tell us something about how desires are negotiated against what is available.

The odd card interprets the double

As with everything else that changes all the time, so with the method. A method is only as applicable until it no longer applies. Determining when that is the case is the art, and I find it extremely pleasurable to bust my own solid perception of just how pedestrian I want to be when I see a flying opportunity with the cards. I like flying.

Let's have a look at this 9-card draw on the opposite page. This is a spread that might have excited Etteilla, what with its insistence on three sets of doubles.

Two threes at the top flanked on the right by the Jack of Spades. Two Aces in the middle flanked by 2 Spades on the left. Two eights at the bottom flanked by 5 Clubs. So, do I go about this the pedestrian way, where I look at rows, then columns, and then the diagonal lines that cross the tableau? Of course not. Let's see.

136

What I look at is the way in which the odd card out in every line modifies the double. So the important cards here are not the doubles, but the ones that disturb the symmetry.

The threes, one of gain, one of loss, influence the Jack of Spades. What he is saying is, 'WTF?' The Ace of Hearts in the center is no happy house, with conflict and strife sabotaging all new working plans and strategy that have to do with the Jack of Spades, a nasty young man. Good intentions (8 Hearts) turn into negative efforts (8 Spades) under the sign of forcing (5 Clubs).

Is this reading fair? Why, yes, says the surprise, the card of 9 Spades looking on. Whatever is going on here is taking a turn for the worse. The upshot is that the emerging picture spells out a futile insistence of having everything doubled. But why? This is the question that we must pose. Why this forcing? What is the querent, a man, trying to achieve or tell himself by deluding himself that as long as the effort is doubled, then all is well? Since when is this logic good logic?

So it goes. Try flying with the cards above your own radar next time you see odd cards on the table aligned in such a way so that you can 'see' where to start, namely at the odd end. That's where the meaning is. Doubles are fascinating, but if the odd cards present disturb their symmetry, they trump the doubles. That's when we know that then we're in for a real treat, as the odd touches the heart in surprising ways.

STRAIGHT UP STORIES

I T IS DAUNTING TO LOOK AT 9 CARDS, LET ALONE 40, which is what we'll be doing here. In the face of a daunting task, what do you do as the first thing? I hope you listened up and started registering the importance of making preliminary observations before you launch into interpretation. Seeing what you see must come before you start unpacking and advancing your argument. When many cards are on the table, instead of getting cold feet, simply notice what is missing from your spread that should be there representing the topic at hand. Is the question about money and you see no Diamonds? Ask yourself why.

Generally students can feel that there's something missing in their attempt to nail an interpretation. If this happens to you, it's best to shift the attention from you to the cards. If you read for others and they don't get your point, look at the cards. Start with a focus on a three-card string, whether it's alone or part of a larger set. Point to the obvious. Let me give an example. A student posed a health question and her answer baffled another. She asked: 'will my wrists get better soon? (I injured both of them after lifting something really heavy at work).' For this she got 9 Hearts, 7 Hearts, and 9 Diamonds.

She went like this: 'yes, they will get better and the swelling will go down (9H to 7H) but only after you follow expert advice (9D). The healing process may be slow but I'll get there.' As this reading was solid, I nodded in the student's direction. But another was baffled: 'how do you interpret the 9 Diamonds as expert advice?' The first student offered her reasoning based on more context. She said the following: 'I was thinking of Diamonds representing the sanguine type – ruled by reason and cunning. And then the number 9 often symbolizing change. Knowing that I'd be going to a doctor I figured they would be my source of reason/change. So, I rounded that all off to mean following expert advice.'

I pointed to an even simpler way of seeing here, when we don't have access to a more specific context. This simpler way is called observing the obvious. If you have a problem that needs solving and 9 Diamonds shows up, what are you going to think? You need a brilliant idea that will solve your problem. Who might have a brilliant idea that's also close to the top? How about an expert?

To an extent all fortunetelling has been informed by learning the system by heart – quite an arbitrary system at that – and then finding confidence in the set symbolic meanings of the cards. If no one tells you that 9 Diamonds *means* expert advice, you get suspicious when others fling a different notion at you. But consider what the aim in cartomancy is, namely to address a question and its context on point. As people ask about all sorts, it makes little sense to meet them in their specificity with generalities. As I like to repeat in cartomancy courses, generalities move no one. You don't want to know what is missing from the system of divination at card level. Look at what's missing at topic level.

Let's now look at a different 'missing' case in a 9-card reading.

141

142

It is commonly the case that when people can't formulate a concrete question, it is because they feel something is missing. What is missing is often the core coherence that we all need in order to make sense of how we can live on a daily basis. Feeling disconnected is more common than uncommon, which is also the reason why, on occasion, it's a good idea to ask the cards about what is missing in your life, before you can ask how to fix a problem that you cannot even identify properly to begin with.

Here is a reading that addresses what is missing at the existential level, and not just at the level of what we find is challenging in a method of reading the cards that steers away from making presumptions about just what 'meanings' the cards can cover.

A woman, Queen of Spades, wanted to know what was missing, so that she could get a sense of what she would need to do to re-establish the flow. Nine cards fell on the table and I proceeded to read the cards in trios, first the rows, then the columns, and then the diagonal lines crossing the square in an X, just as we've seen previously. The significator didn't show up in the tableau.

At first sight, the cards indicated that what was missing was emotional stability (4H), perhaps due to failure to recognize the need for a woman friend, or a close relation (AS, QH). What was missing was also a concrete link and exchange between practical work and practical vision (7C, 7D, 2D). What was missing was the ability to ditch (6S) virtual ideas and communities (8D) and do something good for the body instead, such as eating out with a girlfriend (8D, 5D modified by QH). What was missing was thinking more positively about work (7C, AS, 8D). What was missing was clarity on the familiar, yet bumpy road (7D, 4H, 6S). What was missing was an invitation from a good friend to enjoy a meal with (2D, QH, 5D). What was missing was an emotionally stable, yet more exciting way of engaging with peers (2D, 4H, 8D). What was missing was turning boring work into a magical feast (7C, 4H, 5D).

The surprise card, the Jack of Clubs, was looking on to the drama of the missing link. While he was not the one that was missing, he wanted to remind the querent that she could turn her gaze unto him if she wanted to. A practical young man in need of learning something could easily contribute to concretizing our woman's plans for recovering an emotional core that ended in a *cul-de-sac*. What is she doing? We went looking for her in the pack. We found the Queen of Spades gazing at the King of Diamonds. Is this the reason why she was not present in her life and cards?

Thus, you can see how this type of information may bring about more clarity when you want to consider the way in which you can pose a good question. Asking to know what you don't have can easily be the answer to what you need to have.

Let's look at a third case of missed shots, and what happens when the basic principle in choosing significators is not observed. Before we say anything, let's have the significator principle again: skin color when you pick them, function when you read them.

A student asked: 'can we change significators during the reading?' and then gave an example of how she went about it in a question about a reconciliation with a lover. She accounted for her process thus: 'designated significator: Queen of Diamonds, me, King of Clubs, him. Quick answer: Yes, there is reconciliation. Long answer: none of the designated court cards showed up. Oh well, I'll just switch significators. We're both brunettes with dark eyes – that's Spades, right?'

After changing lanes with the significators, the student then proceeded to unpack her reading in this way, having an eye on the King and Queen of Spades as her new representatives, and because these cards showed up in her spread: 'a month ago, he (KS) gave some sporadic effort (3C) to me but he was focused on work and other things. We bickered and... he suddenly blocked me (3S). The following hasn't happened yet... but he's thinking of me (6H) and unblocks me, sending lots of texts (8D above QS). This is a big change of heart (AS, 9H), going from blocking me to texting me (3S, 8D). Meanwhile, I need to make a serious decision whether the effort of reconciliation is worth it (3C, AS). And what does his change of heart (3S, 9H) and texting me (8D, QS) lead to? What big step does he take (KS, AS)? He lives 90 miles away, but he comes to see me (5H). The real question is: Who is this mystery King of Hearts I'm eying in the wings, the surprise card?'

I intervened here according to the book. I said, 'I'll make three points: [1] In the middle of a reading it's not a good idea to change significators – or the whole question – on a whim. You'll only muddle the waters. There is a reason why neither of you popped, and it may well have to do with the fact that in reality you're just not that much into one another. This being said, you can still read the cards according to the possible outcome here, one of reconciliation, but I'd see the other courts as participating in this reconciliation. Perhaps you have common friends that will facilitate the reconciliation. [2] No, the brunette is the Club, not the Spade. [3] Since the last card in the spread has much to say in a reading, it goes without saying that when X'ing the *carré*, you start with the top right to bottom left and end with the top left to bottom right. For the last word, as it were, you must land on the last card.'

   The student then posed an essential question, while making a remark about the status of the relationship, at least from her perspective: 'I certainly am into him, so I'm surprised I didn't show up. And we don't have any mutual friends. Does this mean this reading is not for me and I should start again with new cards? Or do these cards represent ideas, rather than people?'

   I offered this personal practice and comment: 'I never re-do the cards. If there are no common friends, then we must think of the couple, King and Queen of Spades, as some official channels. In this sense it's conspicuous that we have the Ace of Spades in the center. The body (5 Hearts, your body as you're the one who asked the question) fancies the man for sure, but the question is, can we take this fancy alone as a sign of reconciliation? Fancy is not action. The 8 Diamonds card indicates connection via the internet (for many wires), but they are mediated by the Black Queen. So the task for you is to figure out what this means. In other words, there's some policing going on. You said he blocked you. That may well turn out to be a situation that stays. While the 5 Hearts card 'ends' the spread, and we may think this is enough testimony for a positive outcome, there are other central cards in play that may overrule the personal body heat. The last diagonal line in the X'ing here goes to the card of 3 Spades.' After these remarks and probing the situation further disclosures were made.

The man was from North Africa, and presumably of dark complexion. Why was the King of Clubs picked as the significator? Technically this was sloppy work. When the King of Spades did pop in the spread, could we have a change of heart about him on the spot? How would we justify it? This student did. But then she also changed her significator to the Queen of Spades. Why? Because she couldn't think of another who may interfere here, so it's easy to do the other thing, change lanes.

I suggested that the Spades couple must be the man's parents, as I still insisted on going with what was picked as a significator to begin with – culturally speaking it's fair to assume that there may be resistance to a 'tall, dark stranger' getting involved with a freckled Queen of Diamonds. What was worse, if we accepted that now the King of Clubs, the significator picked initially, was the King of Spades, then the Queen of Spades may be his consort. Ergo: This man is married already, which may explain his behavior.

Now you can see how quickly the waters muddle when you don't stick to the basic rule: the significator follows the rule of skin complexion, not theme, such as 'love,' and not function, such as 'controlling boss.' Once the significators are picked, stay with them, whether you see them in your spreads or not. If you don't like the idea of reading for 'random' people represented by the court cards, instead of the ones you picked but which didn't show, decide that the action or the plot is more important than these significators. Consider the subject represented by the court card on the table as secondary to the topic you're reading for.

148

In French cartomancy the Clubs are the most fortunate. If there's any association at all with the cunning folk cartomancy where we think of clubs as logs you use to build your house with, then it's in the idea that it's fortunate to have your own house.

But this is thoroughly implicit. Explicitly the French associate the Clubs with the luck of Clovers *(trefiès)* when it comes to money. Luck trumps working for your possessions, as it's better to do nothing. If there's any spark in the diamonds, then it's the kind that highlights the worst in human character. That's why the French see the Diamonds suit as the most unfortunate, the *carreau* being associated with tiles you labor to arrange and death.

Which system is the best? They're all equally random. The method is always arbitrarily invented to fit a specific cultural vocabulary. Your interpretation is not. Ideally it is the result of a spontaneous response to what you see *and* free associative thinking applied to the linguistic framework of the method constrained to a set of rules. If you think: 'I feel something is missing,' I can assure you that what you're missing is not method, but cultivation. What you need to cultivate is staying true to the constraints of the method, while exercising freedom in working with what presents itself as nuance. It's pointless to *think* 'death' when you *say* 'diamonds' just because 'it's French.' Consistency is the first rule. Changing your mind about what you say that doesn't make sense is one thing – remember the idea about filling the gaps by revising your hypothesis as you develop your argument presented in the previous chapter? Changing your mind about the method is another thing. You do this, you're an amateur.

The only thing that will ensure you stay on track and not lose yourself in the wilderness is your ability to remember the essential moves. Therefore I insist: 1 is little, 10 is a lot; 1 to 8, a fast progression; 2-4, a slow progression Hearts love, Spades kill, Clubs build, Diamonds buy. Reds 'give,' blacks 'take.' That's it.

Don't look for fancy books and expert explanations. Divination operates with simple, fundamental ideas. To give an example from the oldest divination system we know of: the I Ching. You'll find countless, elaborate commentaries and decodings. Ninety-nine percent of them are useless. Why are they useless? Because most forget the essential. The I Ching consists of two ideas: positive and negative energy, each symbolically represented via a continuous line and a discontinuous, or interrupted line. The continuous line suggests connection; the discontinuous line suggests disconnection. Let's look at a simple I Ching divination when it's done according to the essential way, rather than the complicated way.

I ask this question: 'Will my trip to the country be joyful?' I toss three the coins. I get the trigram called *Gen* (Mountain). What do you see? A continuous line at the top and two discontinuous lines in the middle and the bottom. I answer in the following way: 'your trip will be shitty. The enthusiasm you put into it (top line), lands on broken terrain (bottom line), and is unable to recover (middle line).

In contrast, let's divine with the playing cards for the exact same question, and keep it simple, rather than loaded à la French, German, or cunning folk schools, all labels for arbitrary systems.

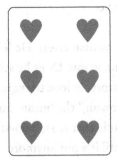  

I toss the cards, 6 Hearts, 7 Clubs, 8 Spades, and answer in the following way: 'your trip will be shitty. It starts out well, hearts are rolling, but then, sticks in your tracks. You invest 'black energy' in fixing it. This means that whatever the Hearts had to give to begin with is now absorbed by a pile of frustrating shit, without any possibility to recover the initial joy.'

There you have it. Divination the simple way, which is always the way that no one can argue with. You demonstrate your true justice, so to speak, by simply pointing to what is the case. That is to say, you point to the cards, not to some secret system that's also layered with occult mystery. What you see, the other can see. That's the beauty of it. In my cartomancy I'm quite happily Zen which is something that runs counter to any occult positioning. My divination is of form, as that is the premise I start out with. I pay attention to form, not grabbing the nearest symbolic inter-pretation that happens to fall into my head. I transact in surfac-es, transparency and the obvious, not depth, the hidden, and the occult. Nothing is hidden here, as you can't hide the obvious. The obvious needs no revelations. The only condition for seeing the obvious is paying attention, not selling a secret key to knowledge.

Love triangles are always entertaining. A woman cries: 'He left me for another. But we had this cosmic connection. Does he still love me?' We start with picking the significators. In love triangles, the Queen of Spades is always 'the other woman,' the 'mean' one stealing men. So here we deviate from the rule that says, 'go with the physical traits.' The method is rigid, until it's not anymore...

Queen of Spades: the 'other woman' (regardless of looks). Queen of Hearts: querent, blond woman (we stick to the rule). King of Spades: dark man, the object of desire; we also stick to the rule of complexion now. The King of Spades is not picked here because he is now the 'consort' or lover of the Queen of Spades. He is picked in accordance with the rule of following the physical traits.

Now let's try a new layout, a classic, and a variation on the 9-card spread. We cast the cards in a pyramid form; a pyramid of 9 built from the bottom to the top. The cards in the 3 points describe the connectors between the 3 people. The card in the middle is the core. The base: we go from left to right to get a sense of a temporal progression going from the past to the future.

We start scanning the pyramid: what is missing is the Queens! The man in question is on the table flanked by 3 cards of one suit, 7, 2, and 5 Clubs. This is a man of action, one who likes to formalize (KS) his relationships, (2H ending his line). At the center of this is 3 Hearts. Well, that's obvious, there's one too many hearts here. We deliver the answer to the question, 'does he still love me?' thus: 'yes, but there's also a distancing (6C leaning on 8S, with 3S repeating, or rhyming with 3H for the worse).

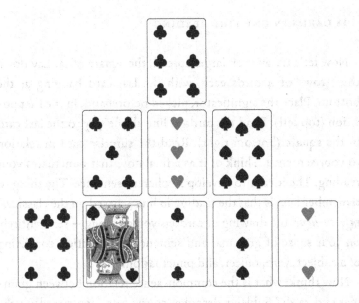

What did I just do here? What happened to the bloody method? Oops, sorry, my eyes went wandering through the cards... You're welcome to curse me, but what do *you* think? Could you arrive at a different answer to the question of love, if you were to follow a more rigid strategy, for instance start with reading the points of the triangle, cards 7, 6 and 2, and then move inwards? Which point would you start at? The thing about triangles is that when the line gets going, it becomes circular. In the absence of a start-point and end-point, what would you rely on for direction? The point of this question is to get you to understand that an essential reading relies on method only instrumentally, not fundamentally.

Fundamentally, what leads your reading is not method alone, but the question and your cognitive ability to recognize a pattern emerging that you then place in relation to what is plausible.

Now let's try an even larger spread, the square of 13. Lay down three rows of 4 cards each, with the last card hanging at the bottom. Place the significator, picked beforehand, in the first position (top left). Read the cards in line all the way to the last card in the square (bottom right). Read the surprise card in relation to your sentence. Think of it as a final note that punctuates your reading. The idea is to develop a coherent sentence. The thing to remember here is that the reading in line — based on the classic *tirage-en-ligne*, the drawing of cards as you go along — rests entirely on your sense of grammar and sentence construction consisting of a subject, verb, object, and punctuation.

Now think: what is the common-sense relation between grammar and cards? Subjects describe (courts or a theme card); verbs act (look at active cards, or the odd-numbered cards); objects show the status-quo, a goal to realize, or a deal to land (look at passive cards, or the even-numbered cards); punctuation stresses tone. What we want is to have an eye on the continuous and the discontinuous, expansion and contraction, increase and decrease. These sets of binaries belong to the category of from, not symbolic conceptualizations of random mappings. The point is that we start with looking at the cards, not 'interpreting' them before we notice the obvious when we connect image to context.

A woman wants to know: 'how can I increase my business and at the same time conserve my energy?' The preliminary thought here is what is implicit in the question, namely knowing how to be efficient. Ideally, you attend to growing your business, while thinking of strategies of decreasing the very work that goes into it.

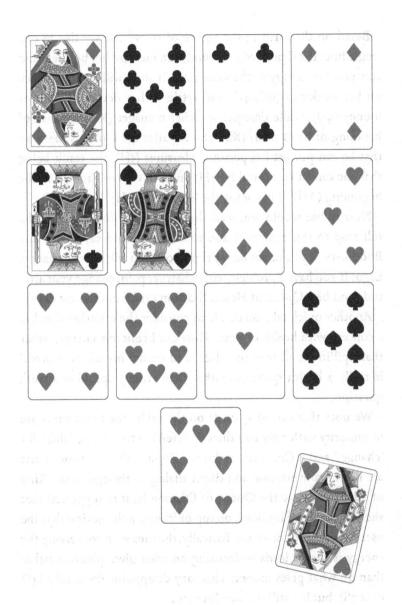

Based on the cards in the square of 13, we can say this in one single line: the Queen of Diamonds can increase her business and conserve her energy at the same time, if she's willing to cut back on her workload (9C, 4C) and settle with a decent amount of money (4D), while delegating to her manager (KC) the task of handling difficult rivals (KS) who are after the Queen's ideas, so that he can protect her personal pleasures (5H), the result being that she can sit comfortably (4H) on both the end (10H) and the beginning (AH) of just what she likes to do (7H). Period (9S).

Now think: would you read the 9 Spades differently than the full stop to this sentence? You could. You could say it with the Buddhists: if you're not happy right now, you will never be happy. Ergo: If you have a problem with whatever pain, change your attitude and be a Queen of Hearts (bottom card from the cut deck).

Another quick take on this is to consider the question that has a concern with health in view. 'How can I conserve energy, rather than spilling it all over the place, and render myself exhausted,' is really a health question, rather than strictly speaking a work question.

We note that out of 13 cards on the table, the black cards are in minority with only two directly referring to work, 9 Clubs for 'change,' and 4 Clubs for 'stability.' Visually the two male courts are not in conversation and direct dialogue, though as the King of Clubs is below the Queen of Diamonds, it is suggested that she's in charge of his head, on top of it, hence the notion that she uses her power to delegate. Basically, the idea with conserving the energy is that it leads to focusing on what gives pleasure rather than on what gives money. This may disappoint financially (4D over 9S), but it's still the way forward.

Always pay attention to involved questions, to how many questions a querent is really asking when formulating one sentence. For instance, people ask: 'I want to know if my manuscript for my novel will be accepted, etc.' I ask back, 'what does *etc.* mean to you, what do you imagine it covers?' In this case the woman said, 'well, you know, I just want to know what the next chapter in my life will be.' Whoa, that's some departure from the very specific to the very general. It pays off to know what range of interests you're dealing with so that the reading and expectations are made clear.

40 CARDS: A FINE ELASTIC

Let us now move into an even larger spread. Lay down 40 cards in rows of 10 each (you take out of the pack the Jokers and the cards from 8 to 10). You read each row until you get to a Clubs pip card, the Clubs being your full stop to the sentence that you will be creating as you go along (in some other variations of this layout, the suit of Spades fulfills this function, as in, 'you dig that, right?' basically because what you do with a spade in your hand is stabbing first and digging next).

No 'meanings' are assigned to the cards or the numbers other than the common sense that dictates: 1 is little, 10 is a lot. What you must observe is intensity, the move going from expansion to contraction. This is the basic bone in traditional cartomancy.

The quality of each suit is considered, but not beyond the bare essentials: Hearts are good will, Spades are bad will, Diamonds are transacting will, and Clubs are working will. In other words, you go with the mundane intentions to love, to hate, to assign value, and to collaborate.

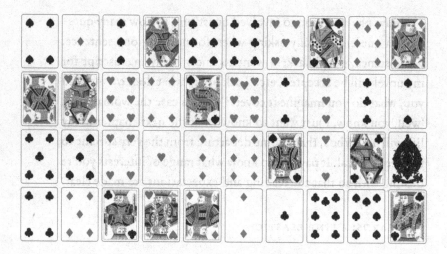

For this 40-card tableau, we're going to do something different. We're going to see how the simple is the advanced. We'll read this with no pre-selected significators. Only context.

Get ready to read in line, that is to say, form sentences starting with the first card and don't stop until you get to the first Clubs card, which is your full stop. The idea is not to get sharp on the cards but to get sharp on the context. This is what saves you from inventing things.

As usual, we have a question, this time from a woman querent, 'how can I help my partner in his desire to become a professional writer?' to make sure you actually stay on track – the question is even more significant than when you perform a standard reading with 3 cards or more. Since you have no predetermined significations, or meanings, you may want to take a moment to consider what is at stake in the question. Now consider immediately what suit would represent the line of work, besides instantly resorting to the list: clubs=work. Sure, but what kind of work? Gender, rank, and identity are also fluid; the querent can be all the Kings *and* the Jacks and sometimes the Queens too. And why not? Context will decide who's who and what's what, not lists of meanings.

As usual also, we engage in making some preliminary observations. The basic premise here is this: man wants to be his own boss. There's writing involved. Ink on paper may not even be metaphorical. You will think this because when you get to the Spades, you don't want to see blood all over the place, when you should probably just think 'ink' as part of the metier. The woman's intention is to offer a helping hand. Now think: is that the Clubs for practical issues, the Hearts, for emotional support, the Spades, for urging the man on so he won't procrastinate, or the Diamonds, for buying him a website domain name where he can publish his writing as a test first? It can be all of them.

What you want is to aim for flow. Develop a sense of urgency when you look at your 40 cards. The best advice I can give you here is through this image: you get kidnapped. Someone points a gun to your head, and says: 'unless you give me an answer in 30 seconds flat based on these 40 cards, I'm going to kill you. Don't dilly dally and don't give me crap. Only the truth.' Well, I like that. I hope you like it too, as this is exactly the type of urgency you need when you stretch your cartomancy elastic.

Now let's see what we can say. In this case here, it happens that we have 5 sentences determined by the number of full stops. So we go: [1] As the writing needs a sharp focus, you can help your partner discard the irrelevant (4S, AD, 3S, QD, 6S, 6C – the last Clubs card here is the first full stop). [2] There's pleasure in making it clear who the audience is, what they like, what value they get out of it, and for what emotional purpose (5H, QS, 7D, JD, JH, QH, 6H, 4D, JS, 7H, 2C). [3] But beware of too much focus on the emotional direction, as it can lead to conflict (3H, 3C, 2S, 5C). [4] Your partner can take your support as a personal affront, and before you know it, the good household harmony can turn into a nasty point (5S, 4H, AH, 3D, 6D, KS, 2H, QC, AS, 4C). [5] It's clear that the man prefers to assess his own value, whose image is raised to the power of three kings. That is to say, a nice tune can be played, but only as the man sees fit, and not in accordance with whatever you may have to say (5D, KC, KH, KD, 2D, AC).

Note here that the last cards after the final full stop, the Ace of Clubs, are not read, as there isn't another club to end the string. So although we have more cards in the tableau coming after the full stop, since we can't have a complete sentence after it, we disregard these other cards.

In this case here, the final answer is neatly given in the last row. The Queen wants to help (she's early in, occupying a position in the first row), but the King insists on self-reliance (there are 3 appearances of kingly status in the last row alone. Ergo, we say to the woman querent, 'help him to help himself.'

More concretely, we you unpack the first line, we can observe how we basically get a summary of the first three cards that gives us an indication of how the topic at hand is validated, and where this is going. The card of 4 Spades represents the partner's work, but there is trouble with it (Spades always indicate this), so something needs to be done to make it less rigid (numerically 4 suggests the most stable structure among the pip cards, and hence posing a potential challenge where flexibility is concerned; 4

Spades being at odds with the creative mind. Imagine a writer sitting at his 4-legged desk, and not having a single original idea... Ah, can we have some Diamonds here, please? A Diamond appears in the first row, but not before 2 Queens have a say in it. As the first Queen that shows up here is the Queen of Diamonds, we take her as our significator. She makes sure to infuse the dull writer with some inspiring notions. As the red cards are benefic, we can expect the trouble with the writing to be reduced.

Here the Spades most definitely stand for writing. As the question was about writing, and the spread started with the Spades, we can take this as a nice omen that corroborated the theme. Secondary to that, the Spades (when not associated with impaling and cutting objects) resemble pens. Their blackness makes us think of ink.

We can thus go on: in the first string of cards that forms a complete sentence, there is one court card, the Queen of Diamonds, so she is the subject. She is doing things for her partner. We therefore get this idea: the Queen of Diamonds (remember that reds give, and the blacks take away) helps reduce what is irrelevant in her partner's writing (there's movement from 4 Spades to 3 Spades via the Diamond as a single drill, with the Ace of Diamonds indicating the focus), so that what remains in this reduction from 4 to 3 is a straight line of three sharp spades. Taken together: a sharp focus. Are Spades not sharp? Don't Diamonds focus? – there is only one right here: it's the Ace of Diamonds.

But since the Queen of Diamonds discovers that there are many more Spades coming in after the 6 Diamonds, she realizes that there is much more to discard. The surplus of twice the 3 Spades in the first reduction also needs to go. The card of 6 Clubs is only here as a full stop and hence it's not read as carrying information. Or, in another version of what I like to call the master sentence, we could say the following based on just this first sentence with the cards: there is a structure to the work. It needs a spark. What could it be? 'A sharp focus,' thinks the Queen, who is now ready to discard everything that will disturb the already settled focus.

In other words, what we find here in the first sentence is the gist of what the querent needs to do precisely in order to help her partner on his path towards becoming a professional writer. It's fine that he got his writing desk and his ink ready, but he also needs an idea on point. Or indeed, as professional writers are characterized by writing a lot, the danger here is that if one is too creative, one may lose track of the writing tasks, which may not always be part of what a writer would like to express creatively. If one has to write on commission, the inspiration for the writing may vary. Hence, a first step towards not losing one's nerve is simply to focus on the act of writing itself as a craft, rather than fantasize about what philosophy to invent for the ones suffering from existential crisis.

When that is said, be prepared for a final answer to your query to also come in the last moment, in the last row, or in the middle of the tableau. The cards have a way of revealing what needs revelation according to rules that exceed our rule of thumb method, such as the general idea that the first card down is either the querent, or a representation of the topic at hand, both in its explicit and implicit manifestations.

Generally, however, the whole point with scanning a spread is to get a sense of the tone of the reading, as the tone helps you unpack the information in relevant and useful ways.

An essential system is essential, not complicated. You have two options: to keep it simple, or to develop a habit of sounding like meaning-spitting machines. You may fool some people some of the time, if going for the latter, but it won't last. What lends you competence is seeing things as they are, not this way of putting it to a client: 'I know everything, your situation is very complicated, but guess what, today is your lucky day, I'm going to demonstrate to you how this works because I'm so clever, and not to mention, I'm backed up by a special spirit court that only I have access to via my illustrious lineage that no one heard of.' How many words did I just use here to say all this? Too many for exactly nothing of substance. Did I actually hear this line delivered by someone? You bet. Alas...

Keeping it simple discloses your deep understanding of the question, the explicit and the implicit in the question, and how the cards can address both. Whether you can read 3 cards, 40 cards, or the whole pack in one sitting, depends on your ability to know which type of reading is called for.

Often people ask: when do I read the 3-card, when the 9-card, and when the 40-card? When the fancy pyramids, the string of a 5-card line, 21 steps, the fan and the horseshoe, all names for positional undertakings? My answer is this: whenever you want. But if you remember the first chapter here with its emphasis on the various interpretations we can extract from the cards, you will know that there may be different points of entry to a reading. Sometimes you want quick action, other times you need to understand the premise for your predicament, thus calling for a thorough description of the situation, reflection, analysis, and final evaluation.

A 3-card draw is dynamic. It can be prescriptive and predictive. A 9-card draw holds a lot of descriptive information, giving you something to think about. A 40-card is an ample story, from business to fairytale. Visually the 3-card has a better sense of direction than the 9-card layout. The 9-card is a box, describing the status quo, inviting to reflection and evaluation. What's happening, why did this happen, what are the relations I can point to that are tensioned, or crossed? – the X always marks the spot. A 40-card is freedom that can also be as sharply disciplined and polished as a diamond.

🐾 ASSIGNMENT 1: GENERAL PRACTICE

Fling your cards, following my examples of layouts here: the 9-card in a triangle (assign significators beforehand); the 13-card in a square (assign the significator to the first position in the square); the 40-card in 4 rows (reduced 52-card deck and no significators)

The task is to train your elastic. Pay attention to just how much need you think you have for lists imported from other cartomancy systems. Assess to what extent what I'm teaching here at the essential level actually gives you access to the main method, *read like the Devil* and its chief mantra, *read the damn cards*, summed up neatly: form is content; the red cards give, the black cards take; 1 is little, 10 is many; 1 is bottom, 10 is top; tension/release; contraction/expansion; function has more value than the symbol; the essential qualities of the cards follow what nature teaches.

ASSIGNMENT 2: THE CORNERS

Sticking with observing the basic rules of living as these rules fall structurally into two categories, [1] there's pain and [2] there's pleasure, lay down 13 cards in a 'square' (use the 4x3 layout I showed before), with the 13th at the bottom for the surprise, and ask this question: 'when do I feel most cornered, as in, what situations corner me to the extent that I only see pain in my undertakings rather than pleasure?'

Look at the corner cards and take them as representatives of what you must do, but you prefer not to. How do they corner the core of what you'd rather do, but you have no option to do? The core is formed by the 6 cards in the middle, that is, the two middle columns. Look at the 13th card as the card that makes you free of all obligation. Can you see yourself *released*, if you *performed* that card?

ASSIGNMENT 3: THE GYPSY SPELL

Now that you know what power is beyond belief, you're ready for a magical tool. In the next chapter we look at the playing cards from a magical perspective, so you need one such.

Lay down three cards and ask this question with view to crafting a self-enhancement tool: 'what is the one object I can create for myself to remind me of my connection to the craft of divination?'

Based on the cards you get, think of an object suitable to your magic (the idea is to keep it close to your cards when you divine). For instance, if you get Clubs and Hearts you may want to go to the woods and pick a twig that you will then baptize in some holy waters; if Diamonds and Spades, you may want to create a sigil, ink on paper — remember the sanguine scribes being the representatives of the merchant caste? Then, next time you read the cards, have this object by your side. Can you notice a difference in our reading? Remember also that the purpose of this magical object is not to enhance some occult excitement, but rather bring your attention to the task of divination at hand, which is all about seeing things clearly, not getting lost at the crossroads, hoping that the Devil himself would show up to rescue you.

COMPREHENSION: FOUR ESSAYS

In this section we're going to look at another 40-card example to consolidate the points made regarding the benefits of reading such a spread. In order to not forget that you can read large spreads if you grasped the reading of three cards, we're going to look at a short essay on tricks and treats with the court cards in a simple 3-card draw. The third essay will demonstrate a point about present and absent court cards in a spread, while the fourth will give an example of preponderance in a 'red spread.'

Kill your neighbor's children

Once I got up in the morning and I went: 'there's nothing more I'd rather do today than kill the neighbor's children.' I had different sets of playing cards on the table. I looked at them and said: 'Give me a second to get my coffee, and I'll be right there, reading all 40 of you in the fastest wheeze.' As said as done. It took me no more than 30 seconds to get through a narrative.

Over the weekend prior to this episode I was fortunate to have a fellow cartomancer and former student in the house, Miguel Marques from Portugal. We did what we do best. We read fortunes to death. We exchanged variations on reading with the playing cards, and looked at the value of keeping it even simpler than some more sophisticated methods.

For instance, the French love to count cards à la Etteilla, and create mirroring pyramids, while the *hedgewytch* cartomancy, based on a compilation of classical texts, relies on using a cunning folk approach that enlists the 'common-sense' of nature and its cycles. I myself use modified versions of these, with an added love of the *tirage-en-ligne*, or linking cards, straight Romanian/Gypsy style – read this also as Yiddish style.

What we did when Miguel was here was to lay down 40 cards in rows of 10 each, just as in the earlier example, and we had fun with my reading about the neighbors. We read each row until we got to a Clubs card, our full stop to the sentence. Same procedure as the last. Now consider this. Sometimes the first sentence starting with the first row can easily stretch over three rows, or you can experience that you have three sentences in the first line of 10 cards. The determining factor for your sentence break is the Clubs pip card. You read the Clubs courts as you do the other cards. The first court card is your main subject. If a King when you're a woman, then take this card as a sign for who you're dealing with and vice versa, then pay attention to what court card is likely to represent you, topically.

In addition to the pips in the Clubs suit counting as full stops, they can also function as a comma, or ellipsis, if that turns out to be the case. As explained earlier in the mechanics for reading this spread, it may also be the case that, depending on where the last Clubs card falls towards the end, you will be left with a number of cards without a full stop. You discard these, and give them no further attention.

No 'meanings' are assigned to the cards or the numbers other than the old style of common sense that dictates: 1 is little, 10 is a lot. What you observe is a simple move from what is increasing and what is decreasing, numerically speaking. You consider the function of each suit in a very rigid way, as these functions participate in the creation of a solid structure. As you don't have the significators picked in advance, the only ground you have is function and choice: what to keep and what to discard is your main focus. That's the method. Nothing more, nothing less. The art is to go through the cards while maintaining a sharp eye for context and coherence. Nothing is more important in fortunetelling than context and coherence. I stress this a lot in my writings when I insist that people not only formulate a clear question, but also answer it. The reason why you want to keep up with context and coherence is because when you encounter a cluster of court cards, then you can easily get frustrated and ask: 'who on earth are these people?'

When you do *tirage-en-ligne*, what you look at is how you maintain the focus on the subject, seeing how the subject changes position and attitude. What this means is the following: you can read three Queens as one person changing position and attitude, until all of a sudden the fourth Queen is someone else. Now, the art is to recognize that when this shit happens you need to calculate quickly what is plausible and what is possible in terms of assigning agency so that it makes sense to the querent.

When Miguel was here we also did a few readings together for other layouts, and one of the 9-card layouts featured 5 court cards in it, one next to the other. Miguel went: 'fuck it, I hate it when this happens.' Exactly. For you see, making sense of who is who is completely contingent on your genius as a reader. In my readings what I strive for is this: to stay as far away as possible from formulating lame generalities. Generalities kill the very spirit of this high contemplative art, which reading cards is all about.

But let's keep it simple, and give you here yet another taste of this game, based on my desire that morning, namely, to kill my neighbor's children. Here's how I read my 40 cards.

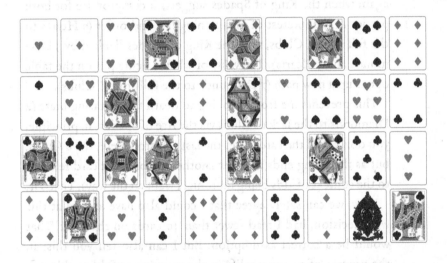

The heart of the house contracts in facing instability due to the unruly behavior of the black-haired kid; I, Queen of Diamonds, clearly intend to put a stop to it (Ace of Hearts to the full stop, the Ace of Clubs). The red-haired kid is not any better, as he attempts to maintain the conflict by enlisting the mischievous deeds of his blond brother (Jack of Diamonds to 4 Clubs via the Queen of Clubs who lovingly tries to address the pain). I can elect to turn towards the three boys and talk some pragmatic common-sense into them, kindly showing them the error in their behavior (2 Hearts to 4 Clubs). The manager, King of Clubs can't do much. Full stop. But the landlord King of Diamonds is already on top of the situation, urging the mother, Queen of Hearts, to collaborate on education with her husband, King of Hearts.

Not much comes out of it, however, other than escalating anger (3 Spades, via the Queen of Spades to 5 Clubs). Things calm down again when the King of Spades suggests a compromise for both parties in the interest of maintaining law and order (3 Hearts to the full stop, 3 Clubs, with the King of Spades flanked by 5 Diamonds and 5 Hearts). The value of what is being put on the table opens up a new path (7 Diamonds to the full stop, 6 Clubs).

This prevents me from stabbing to death the irritating brats (2 Diamonds to the Jack of Clubs via the Ace of Spades; in principle, you don't read the cards after the last full stop, here, the 6 Clubs, but as the string ends with yet another Clubs court card relevant to the context of kids being moronic, I went all the way). That's it.

Now, we can safely agree that I could also have arrived at this wise decision, had I read fewer than 40 cards on the table. That would be a correct assumption. But I can also tell you this: in the process of seeing my life in the morning unfold in this way – spending time on cards – I got to consider how I avoided turning my anger into aggression. The cards showed that high standing officials were already at work on it, so why waste my breath? Taking time to put down 40 cards saved me from overreacting.

There's a lot of value in anger that's put to creative use, like reading the cards and testing your abstract sharpness against the concrete image. Now you know why I find reading the cards the highest and the most rewarding of all the contemplative arts.

Trick or Treat

Someone wanted to know how to make others want what she had to give. Strange request, I thought, but then, upon thinking some more, I realized that desiring for others to want what you have to give is not so strange. Marketing empires have been built on making others want what you have to give... The cards, King of Diamonds, King of Spades, 7 Spades were blunt about it.

To the question, 'how can I make others want what I have to give?' the answer was 'you can't, unless you trick them.' Materially speaking you can't give the King of Diamonds anything, as he has everything already. So if you have something to sell him, you'd have to don your magic cloak.

But since the question came from a woman, let us stick to the classical tradition of fortunetelling and assume that the two Kings in the picture are not about her, but about how they affect her in their own relationship with one another.

I can see how the King of Diamonds *may* be receptive to the King of Spades – his back is turned but his ear is as sharp as an ax. The latter King having his own suit in sight – the magical 7 Spades indicating all things hidden, trouble, or tears – comes across to the King of Diamonds as a more mysterious King, but therefore also as a more untrustworthy King than the Kings of merry-go-round of love and labor that we associate with the other two suits not present here, namely the Hearts and the Clubs. 'Better to just listen, not face him,' the King of Diamonds thinks...

Simply put, what the cards are saying is that the woman is up against two men, one of money and one of war. When the King of Spades is not a magician he is someone who is either alone, working for the government, an enemy of the querent, or all of the above. So we can safely presume even without having the woman say a word about it that what she has to give is something she would like men to want. A tall order, as, by implication, I can further presume that the reason why she asked that question is because she didn't find that there was congruence between what she wanted to give and what the men wanted. In other words, they were not on the same page. Tough luck.

Meanwhile, however, it also looks like the two men are too busy being each other's rival – the pesky 7 Spades is in the picture – and there is an indication that what the woman is called to consider is who she wants to side with. The money-man is good to know, though he may be a conservative bore. The war-man may be interesting to know, as you never know where you have him. It's better to be close to him also in case he turns against you. War-men are known for intricate and calculated strategies, so there you have it. You'll never be bored with one such.

Love is not an option here, nor is negotiating. We're thus back to the first assumption, especially if a neutral stance is desired. I said it again: 'you can make others want what you have to give if you trick them, or if you pretend.' A classic, really.

I have to say that this scenario made me feel sorry for our lot. Most of us, both men and women, have to sell things all the time to people who don't want it, or pretend to want it. How many of us can claim to be in a job or a relationship that is entirely satisfying? How many times can we swear that the ones we have to deal with are also the ones we are on the same page with? Not many. We can get very pessimistic here. The pragmatists, however, know better: the meaning of life is all about selling: our looks, credentials, fantasies, you name it. It would be nice for a change if what we had to sell was actually also what others want in all truthfulness. Perhaps some are lucky, but the day I read these cards for the woman, her luck was tough.

Yes, but...

A few notes on how to read the court cards in connection with yes/no questions. You don't. As you're here to read like the Devil by using your logical brain and deductive faculties, you know already that one of the first rules you obey is that of color. If the card in the final position is a red one, then the answer is yes (for the most part).

So, what if the final card is a black court card? Is the answer no? Not necessarily. Court cards are people, not relations, so depending on the nature of the question, the court card in the final position will always tell you something about an other person influencing the 'yes' or the 'no' of the situation. Take the example below featuring 5 Spades, 3 Hearts, the and Queen of Spades.

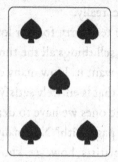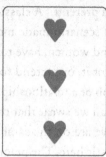

If the question is: 'does this woman love me?' then the answer is yes, especially if the significator is the Queen of Spades herself. The 3 Hearts card tells us that there's a sharp interest in the querent coming from the woman in question, and she is responsive to the querent and to what otherwise can also be perceived as a sick infatuation with her (the 5 indicates the body; here, an illness that the querent suffers from; with the 3 Hearts, presumably an illness due to the impatience of love).

If the querent is a man whose significator is the King of Clubs, who wants to know whether the Queen of Diamonds, the other significator, loves him, the answer is still yes, but the following would need to be said: 'the Queen of Diamonds (not present in the spread) is quite interested in the King of Clubs (also not pres-

174

ent in the spread), but she listens to the advice of someone, the Queen of Spades who is present in the spread, and who is not in the King's corner.' In the case of no significator for the woman, the answer is also this: 'yes, but she responds more to your own projections of love' – we say this because of the presence of the 5 of Spades in the spread.

Now, if we had a different question coming from a woman who wants to know: 'is my mojo working?' – in the sense of her wishing to hold someone specific in her power – then the answer would be yes, because of the nature of the question *par excellence*. Here we look at the function of the Queen in general first, and then at her function as the Queen of Spades, in particular. Generally the Queens represent truth (the Kings power, and the Jacks the go-between, hence by extrapolation, thoughts). The Queen of Spades, by virtue of the power of her suit to cut through everything, may represent a truth that disturbs or one that questions truth. Here, insofar as 3 Hearts precedes the Queen of Spades, we could argue that the truth of this Queen is dignified.

Given the nature of the question falling more under the magical realm where we deal with projections of fantasy that are not only willed but also become real, we take the Queen of Spades, the Lady of Fate herself, as a strong affirmation of the possibility that the mojo is indeed working. If anyone can hold someone else in their power the magical way, then that would be the Queen of Spades.

Now, as in the first scenario, given also that here the string begins with 5 Spades indicating a case of illness related to the querent, we may question the truthfulness of the extent to which our querent's mojo is working in her best interest. Magically speaking, it's definitely working, but is it good for her? While the Queen holds power over the other, she is also tied. Consequently she is prone to making herself sick by obsessing over it.

Now, this would be the sort of thing that the reader, if she wants to help the querent, would have to bring into question. But some readers prefer to stay neutral and not ask anything beyond the scope of the reading. I admit that I'm one of those. I don't like yakking too much when I divine with the cards. However, as we're dealing with a red card here, we could also argue that there's pleasure involved in exercising this otherwise unhealthy power and keeping it in line, as it were, if we consider the visuals on the cards of the 3 Hearts.

To keep it simple then, and given the indication from the cards, the final answer would be to say, 'your mojo is working, but you're also a (sadistic) victim.' So the basic rule of thumb for the color code is upheld. A black card ends the string, bad outcome. My advice for tricky situations such as these, when we have to figure out what to make of the court cards in the final position particularly for yes/no questions, is to think of the court cards as appositions, as if saying, yes... but, or no... but.

In this sense, the court cards in the final position can be seen as full stops to a sentence, just as we've seen in the earlier example when we assigned the Clubs the punctuation honor. Or else we can think of what kind of gravity they might carry, that is to say, the gravity in tone, when we approach a point we want to make and lower our voices for it to mark the significance of what we're saying. But this situation is mainly relevant when we have many cards on the table. For the quick 3-card draw, we stick with the most obvious and urgent.

Two red spreads and one black

People don't just try to find themselves, but they also want to find others, or to find out what's happening to them. Let's have an example of a 9-card reading for the latter situation that also demonstrates a point about preponderance. Someone wanted to know what was happening to her friend, a public figure, who started to behave strangely.

A 9-card spread quickly suggested a plausible answer as this was an easy reading that settled the matter in 2 seconds. In spite of 'no challenge here' – and I like to write about challenging cards – I want to make a quick point and emphasize the following: although we generally tend to perceive a reading as fair when we have a preponderance of red cards over blacks, the rule of 'if it ends with a spade, bad news' will keep us in good stead, just in case we want to go rampant and herald that all is well in this country – except for some minor trouble.

Before we look at the cards, here's a point about the choice of the 9-card spread over the other possibilities, especially since I've mentioned already the idea with dynamic versus static readings, and the prescriptive and predictive versus the reflective and the evaluative. Whenever someone wants to find themselves, others, or check the barometer of a situation, it's good to go with the 9-card draw, and think of the architectonic structure of it that's able to offer several planes of perception at once. The reading of the rows can be likened to the reading of a landscape. The reading of the columns can be likened to the reading of a temporal sequence, past (first column), present (second column), and future (third column). The reflective starts with the descriptive picture.

Let's see what we can say here: the querent's friend (5D) has a grand wish (9H) to take the path of money (6D) and surround herself with friends that have it (8D rhymes with 8H; a group of jovial people with money; 9H rhymes with 9D; more luxury, please...) She goes for it full throttle (10H). The path (6D) to friends with money in this public space is clear (8D, 6D, 8H).

But, although our friend thinks she has just gotten there, where she can have her fingers in the sack of money (5D, 8D, 9D), things take a turn (9D) for the worse (2S) with the party splitting for good (2S, 4S). Or rather, to be more specific, our friend here, the one inquired about, gets thrown out of the party (2S, 4S). Looking at the surprise card (7S), there is hardly any surprise in learning that greed often leads to trouble.

My point is that although we often dance with and around the cards, we also tend to read towards some point of gravity, where we gather the threads. What I mean to suggest by dancing here is that although no court card appeared in this spread, I took the first card down as a representative of the topic at hand: 'what happened to my friend?' 5 Diamonds happened to her, meaning, she followed her own self-interest (5 for the body of the inquired about).

As mentioned earlier, usually the last card in a 9-card spread has much to say, as it ends both the vertical and horizontal lines we read. It also colors the description of the situation and its temporal sequencing. We can think of the last card as our gravity point that pulls the reading towards a resolution. But bear in mind here that the last card doesn't signify the final answer, as the whole spread participates in moving towards the final verdict. But the last card stresses the overall tone, adding gravity to the answer.

Here we have 2 trouble cards pulling the reading down towards the grave in our otherwise 'red' spread, with the reds indicating all good news, as it's nice to have both friends and money. Since they fell strategically towards the end of the spread, we're going to have to deliver a nasty message, and say something like this to our querent: 'perhaps your friend is not so close to you anymore. The fives indicate closeness, the 5 Diamonds here suggesting an inner fire or downright hunger for something. She seems to have gotten herself lost in a sea of wishful thinking about cash and adulation.' The cluster of 9, 10, 8 Hearts in the top right tells us that this person is seeking public company because she thrives on flattery. In other words, it takes more than lots of red cards to make a spread fair, or a person nice, or worthy of their friend's concern.

The point here is that although we may have many 'good' cards on the table, just one or two trouble cards thrown into the mix can cancel what the others are saying, especially if these cards land in a position that holds significance for the final resolution.

NO WORRIES

Now let us look at yet another example of a 'red spread' where the situation is the opposite of the above. In this case, although the 'bad' cards land in the central position that holds the focus for our reading, they have minimal impact on the final verdict that here acquired a positive tone.

There are certain cards in classical fortunetelling that have a special status: Ace of Spades, death; 9 Hearts, everything you wish for; Ace of Hearts, the house; 10 Spades, worries; Ace of Diamonds, a letter, and so on. The sevens are always trouble even when they follow the most benevolent of the suits, namely the Hearts, so we have 7 Hearts for a heart problem, or a heart ache, 7 Diamonds for a money problem, 7 Clubs for a challenging task, 7 Spades for trouble with detecting trouble itself.

Now think: what happens when we have several of these 'special status' cards aligned in a spread that has no more than 9 cards in it? How do we read their 'locked in' signification along with the other cards?

Here is an example of a snappy reading that I did for a writer who started entertaining paranoid thoughts about what others might think of his writing, the fear of theft of intellectual property having also been expressed. As a writer myself, I can see how debilitating such anguish can be, but as far as I'm concerned, I have learned that both praise and criticism last equally long and they end up meaning equally nothing. Unless hailed a classic, any creative work will interest no one after the three days of marvel and wonder have passed since the big novelty announcement. Classics tend to stay relevant and hence in print for ages.

As to having one's work shamelessly stolen, there are other ways of dealing with that than reporting the theft to the courts of justice, especially if one is magically inclined. As to some people's actions that gave my writer cause to worry, judging the man's book on account of what others had to say about it, doesn't strike me as very intelligent. Why, indeed, worry for the dull? Generally, opinions are not very interesting if they have no foundation whatsoever. Consequently, worrying about people who can't make a distinction between an opinion and an argument is not very useful. But as not all are willing to listen to the voice of reason, thus avoiding wasting time, some want to ask the cards.

What we observe in this tableau is that there's nothing to worry about. Worry features prominently in the middle of the spread, and we have here aligned quite nicely 3 of the cards with 'special' status. 9 Hearts over 10 Spades in the house of the Ace of Hearts, worry being a 'familiar' to this writer.

But the cards say that our writer will get on top of it, becoming mentally confident over what he already established (10D, 9H, 3D). Visually, as the 3 Diamonds card suggests shooting straight to the target, I don't see the progression from 10 Diamonds to 3 Diamonds as detrimental. In this context, 10 Diamonds can indicate an overly excited writer, with excitement being of the worrying kind. The writer, Jack of Spades, clearly worries all the way to the top (10S), as he feels (8H) that his assets in the form of ideas (10D) are nothing but trouble (7D). However, the truth is that, in spite of the suspicion of what others might think of the written word of our writer, he's quite stable emotionally (4H), regardless of his mental projections. Why is this writer actually comfortable when worrying is so central, one might ask, what with all those spades at the core? Because he knows that his love story template works (4H, 8H). A Queen of Hearts is also in the wings, giving him her support and making sure that whatever doubts our writer might have about himself, they amount to nothing.

Here is the point where I myself secretly entertain the idea that the cards enforce my philosophy about what to make of evaluations, namely, keep a cool head, and never get exited either way. My advice to this author was to take it easy, but if he thought that the worrying situation couldn't be helped, then he could try turning the 10 Spades into a central plot, thus creating some tension and a counter point to all the hearts already in the picture.

183

There's no such thing in life that's not called 'selling.' From the minute you step into life, the steep climb that's called 'learning how to sell yourself' starts. If you're a sweet baby and learn to grace your mother with a charming smile, you get a lollipop. The whole premise for the existence of schooling also rests on learning how to build an identity, and skills and competences that you then sell to others. I'm thinking of all this because on eclipse days, both solar and lunar, I read the cards for the situations when my mind goes opaque, the consequence being lack of clarity. When we don't have clarity, our actions can obscure and downright eclipse our initial intentions. How do we sell skills if we don't have clear vision about what we do?

There's a marked difference in the way we use language to emphasize what we sell, even when we don't call it that. As a former university professor, my biggest sell was defined in terms of competence in research. As a fortuneteller I get enticed to define what I sell in terms of reading and consulting services. As a writer of non-fiction books I sell formal knowledge, and as a visual artist I sell art. One way or another, much of what goes into figuring out the meaning of life is figuring out how we all serve by selling. Whereas universities serve by selling education to students, yet toning down the selling part, businesses serve by selling useful products, heralding the tangible and concrete solutions, toning down the skills that went into the process.

Many of my friends and colleagues in the interpretative and contemplative arts, from divination to Zen and other such related branches, also refer to their offerings in terms of 'services and products.' But why? I see that, in reality, what they sell is very much skills and competence, often of educational character. Why not think of it in those terms? The point that I'm trying to make here is that, via language, we often eclipse what we do to our detriment.

If you're a diviner, how might your website look like if you started calling what you sell knowledge, skills, competence, and originality? If you're with the university, how might your sense of worth change if you admitted the reality that as long as you sell your knowledge to students, or go out and beg the rich corporations for a large sack of money for your research, you're in no way more special or intelligent than the merchants of the world? We find culture wars everywhere, but what is the point to these wars when all the soldiers wear the same uniforms? Only the banners and the logos are different. Banners and logos can impress and make people believe in causes and ideas. But what are they really, when essentially, they're all about selling something?

In my own description of what I do these days, I've refrained from calling what I sell 'services,' 'products,' 'skills,' 'knowledge,' or 'competence,' as I see all this as a unified pack already, part of my constructed identity that I don't even bother to identify with, as it changes all the time. What I find most reassuring these days, precisely due to the constant changes that we all undergo whether we like it or not, is that along with the selling pack, what informs our existence is a whole lot of clueless bumbling about.

If I were to ask you, 'what do you sell today?' what would you answer? Is your serving and selling clear, or is it eclipsed by a fashioned identity that you don't even like, or empty words that sound relevant?

Eclipses in the sky are good to watch, not apply to your life unwittingly. Take your cards and ask them, expecting also a whole lot of black cards to populate your spread: 'how do I eclipse what I do, and what might be a better strategy of coping with the darkness that I create around my activities than the natural waiting for the eclipse and my confusion to pass?'

Perhaps your cards might say something of this sort: 'if you're too concerned with what the bad and power-mad kings of the world have to say about what you do, you can be sure to eclipse not only your activities, but also your good health. If an eclipse happens, make it magical, by calling on the good King to preside over your troubled waters and restore the flow of things. Make what you have to sell mysterious and erotic, pulsating with fresh blood through the heart. Be joyous with the partner who has your best interests at heart, rather than succumb to your fascination with the dark veil spread over your face by what brings misfortune to your business.'

COURT CARDS AS PEOPLE, EVENTS, AND FORCES

As you've seen from these examples, the court cards have been read in various ways, whether in spreads with a red or black preponderance of cards, challenging us also with the question of agency. Students often get challenged and provoked when seeing many court cards in relatively economical spreads of 3 to 9 cards. 'Who are all these people,' they ask, for good reason, for the court cards represent primarily people, the querent and others alike, before they stand for something else, all according to what occasions a specific reading and interpretation.

A useful rule to remember when in doubt is this: in a question about prescriptive action, you must read the court cards as participating towards the realization of that action. Thus you're not reading for people, primarily. You're reading for the action: 'what can I *do* to score this job?' For this you need to think of the function of the courts in tandem with the intensity of the numbers.

For instance, if your problem is with procrastination and you want to know what you can do to fight it, you follow your significator if it's in the spread, and read all the other court cards present not necessarily as representations of other people that can help you with it, but rather as forces, events, or even objects that can help you. The King of Spades can be seen as a force that might help you kill your procrastination by virtue of the function that this king performs. It's up to you to decide just how 'killing' might manifest for you. If you can't sit down and write your 10 pages of text per day as you planned, then seeing the King of Spades in your spread might remind you of the benefit of killing all distraction. So the King of Spades in this case would not be another person.

Given the question about procrastination, you must also see it as significant if your significator doesn't show up at all, and instead all you get to look at is 4 Jacks. You must admit it's ironic that your significator is procrastinating too. So here I'd say that what you then need in order to manage your procrastinating tendencies is do some research, read more and learn, before you sit down only to agonize about having to write 10 pages. Think: what do the Jacks do? They are curious. They study, and they learn. They follow their inspiration. So what you need is to activate that force. Be open and be curious towards something that's relevant for your writing process. In other words, in contexts that amount to existential questions, it doesn't mean that when you see many court cards on the table, they all represent 'other people.' The same applies to questions of reflective and evaluative nature. As is the case with what we make of the stylization of the numbers, the 'meaning' of it all is only settled by the question and its context.

Another example of reading the court cards as participating in or towards an event that requires action is in the situation when you must think of the courts not only in terms of performing a function, but actually being a function, especially when the question doesn't occasion any encounters with people.

If you're a Queen and all you get is Kings in the picture, then, in a prescriptive question, that is, a question about what to do, you see the Kings as events embodying their respective suit functions. Generally, when I say that 'the courts are other people,' I refer to the method theory I present you with here, not concrete situations, as there's no way I can address specific questions other than via concrete visual examples of cards and contexts on the table.

Consequently, it's always up to the reader to assess which case applies. That's why I find lists of meanings useless, as they only hold the promise for the illusion of a concrete answer. As to the popular idea that the courts are aspects of the self, I always want to know: what does that mean? An aspect of a whole, or an aspect of a set of attributes that make up an identity? Are we transacting with separate parts – and if we do, what's the motivation for it – or are we transacting with wholes? As this is not a question anyone can answer, insofar as we all perform our desired identities, rather than know our true nature, the 'aspect' notion remains a flat cliché in the face of the realization of truth, which is the realization of the now, that is to say, the moment when we predict a future or an outcome in the now. So, what does an 'aspect' of the main significator mean, when the main significator already comes with it own set of functions? It means nothing.

Therefore it's better to stick to the rule of identifying functions first as that's what comes closest to your own specific context.

Is this function embodied by a person? Fine. There's no person? How about a force or an event that's plausible in context? If you read for metaphysical and intangible questions about how you 'grow spiritually,' it's likely that you'll have to read the Jacks in the picture as an indication that you grow by being curious and open, by studying and learning, and by cultivating tenaciously a skill. In this sense the Jacks will not be representatives of other people, nor will they be representatives of some vague aspects of you.

For the nuanced and more advanced reading, you also have to think about how shifting the rank notion is. While at method theory level we have a neat distribution, with the King at the top, followed by the Queen and the Jack, think about the times when they all want to be King. The Court cards are not a democracy. They are an anarchy. The King rules until he's usurped by the 'chancers,' here most obviously the Jacks, or by the famed Queen of Spades who will only rarely accept any sign of abuse from any King or Jack. I'd also have no trouble slashing the throat of the King of Hearts if the quality of his natural inclination for love that he performs is delivered unto me as a bucket of 10 Spades. I'd show him who is boss. As to the recalcitrant children, Jack of all trades, master of none, I'd teach them a measure of hard core discipline, without succumbing to any manipulation.

All this to say that a rule of thumb is exactly that, a rule of thumb. The stories we create with the courts are dynamic, and we have a lot of freedom. The only condition for our precise reading is that this freedom actually goes somewhere and makes sense. Otherwise it's just the hippie commune lost in impressions having missed the memo on how form is everything

190

CARDS AND MAGIC

SOMETIMES I LAUNCH INTO MAKING unexpected analogies, yet useful enough, when I compare cartomancy to mathematics. Just as mathematics is more about patterns than about numbers, so with cartomancy. We have number cards and court cards, and you'd think that all you need to do is put two and two together, like in arithmetics, a branch of mathematics that studies numbers. In any deductive process of interpretation there's that, indeed, putting two and two together, but we gather the visual clues and analyze them according to a number of set principles that have to do with quantity, structure, space, and change.

The mathematicians reading this will have recognized just what mapping I'm doing here to number theory, algebra, geometry, and function analysis. Just as there's the myth that mathematicians like numbers, there's also the myth that cartomancers like systems of correspondences. Wrong. In both disciplines, mathematics and cartomancy, what we're after are patterns, semantics, analyzing the integration of the visual symbols into the larger sets, also called contexts, and decoding the differential value of functions against the background of chance.

When we predict an event, or tell someone we've never seen before that they are *like* the Queen of Spades, or that they'll encounter the tall, dark stranger at the crossroads, a place they're never inclined to go to by night, what we do is offer an analysis of an emerging pattern. While we don't know the people we read the cards for, not even when they're our family, we know what the cards have to say, because we learned their language. This language is the language of function analysis, cultural semantics, and change. When a pattern emerges right under our eyes, because we have a question and a formal system of interpretation for it called 'playing cards,' what we do with it is apply some pressure. This pressure is called formalizing what is happening, how it's happening, and why it's happening.

As a general principle, we don't operate with any significance, or 'meaning' of the cards before we internalize the more basic tripartite structure of what is happening, how it's happening, and why it's happening. The context of the question gives us the area where what is happening, how, and why it's happening occurs and unfolds. Also as a general principle, the pip cards give us a sense of what is happening, the court cards show us how it's happening, as they exercise controlling agency, while the pips and the courts taken together give us a sense of causality: it's happening because the King of Spades impaled 10 times the Queen of Hearts, the woman he loved in spite of himself.

What we also look at is space. How something takes place occurs in space, geographical locations, or geometrical triangulations. What is happening in a love triangle is very much a case of figuring out how each involved in the relationship triangulates their positions vis-à-vis the others. In a love triangle, the querent wants to determine the location of their standpoint, as the simple question, 'does he love me,' has just turned complex. 'The other woman' often wants to know what the function of the wife is when she is no longer the lover, while the man may want to know what to do about each of the two hags he is involved with.

'What is the structure of our relationship?' same sex people involved in polyamorous affairs want to know, while the ones climbing ladders are all about quantity: 'how much can I make in my next leadership function?' As long as fortunetellers answer such questions and conundrums, what we do is math, calculating risks, analyzing odds, and offering statistical and probabilistic resolutions. What we don't do is read the cards mechanically, or engage in meaning-driven babble.

The point that I'm trying to impress on you is the necessity to shift from the perception that depicts the role of the fortune-teller as a dispenser of truth, 'coaching' people, to considering the function that she actually performs, which is to notice patterns and the complexity of their formation. In this sense, we're not consultants. We're analysts. We work with visual data and the identification of functions in a particular space and time.

What I've done so far is to demonstrate that when we hold ourselves to the questions asked, and then provide the evidence from the cards for what we're saying, what we do is perform magic. But before I explain more, let me start this chapter with a round of examples based on student readings, where we can observe how attention is actually given to how we create space between the reader and the sitter, and within that space how we assess the solidity of the structure of our readings against the background of form, the abstractness of numbers made concrete, and the agency of the court cards in dynamic exchanges.

WHO TAKES THE TRICK

Depending on what card game you play, if it involves taking tricks, you want to know which card holds the most power. Card games come with rules that are not subject to interpretation. In cartomancy we have similar rules, as we consider rank and numerical progression, but other rules apply here too. These rules are called trumping and taking the trick with the question. In other words, the question rules the rules. I must stress this in every chapter so that any misunderstanding about it can be eliminated. Let's look at some examples. A client asked: 'does the Jack of Diamonds trump the 10 Diamonds in a reading?'

My answer to this was 'no.' They are two different things. 10 Diamonds is assets, money, valuables and other possessions. The Jack of Diamonds is a person who either has access to the assets, manages the money, loses it, or adds more value to it. So there's no 'trumping' here. If there's any 'trumping,' it will be due to agency. A person can act, money cannot. The point is that it pays off to keep agents and objects apart and not confuse their functions. The court characters act *in relation* to their objects and tactics to use these objects. The King, Queen, and Jack are not subsumed by their suits. They represent their suits to the best of their ability. I say, 'to the best of their ability' because if they happen to be afflicted by the suits contrary to their nature, we'll have a situation when we can see that the courts act in detriment.

The court cards also act in relation to the overall context of the question, whether this context is about a direct, indirect, or meta dimension. Let's have an example of a meta-question posed by a student that gave rise to a discussion about methodologies in divination and how a specific tactic fits one's temperament. Said the student: 'I had reservations about taking this course, as Camelia's method sort of went against my grain. But I could see the benefits of her method, and every divination I did prior to class encouraged me to join. I cast the cards in a pyramid for it.'

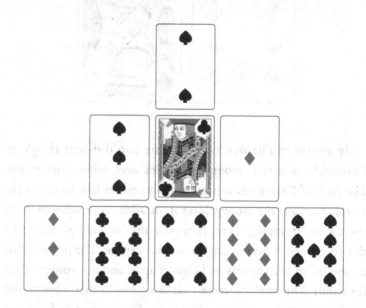

The student then went like this: 'going up the left hand side of the pyramid, I see the little bit of knowledge I have is troublesome, and I need to divest myself of it (2S at top). This has required a lot of work to change (9C). The middle column is in-

196

teresting with 2 Spades, Jack of Clubs, and 6 Spades. My significator would be the King of Clubs, which did not appear. I tend
to see the Jack of Clubs as my discernment, for certainly there is
a need to separate the wheat from the chaff inside my head. The
Jack turns towards what is troubling in the past and doesn't look
to new knowledge in the future. With the 6 Spades below there is
obviously a lot of shit to dig up and discard in conjunction with
the 2 Spades... So more understanding comes in (9C) and it is a
painful process (7S). I like the symmetry of the two 9s flanking the
6 Spades. The hard work of digging and discarding makes room
for new knowledge and understanding, at a price. And I think *it is
worth it*' (student's own emphasis).'

I offered my contribution, pointing to the essential steps towards interpretation. As this was a question of methodology
framed by a meta approach, that is to say, by divining with the
cards about the act of divination and its related disciplines, I
started with a few observations. I said the following: 'here is a
basic application of what is fundamental in my teaching in the
form of a question: 'what is the best tactic in divination?' Note
how I didn't give any priority to the idea of value, or worth.

Then I pointed to the significance of making a preliminary
opening, followed by scanning the cards. So I said: 'since the
question is about a modality of doing things, all the cards will
speak towards that, not something else (such as value or worth).
In other words, the reading must reflect the position of giving
advice, *do this*, not something else. When scanning the cards, we
note this: 6 black cards, 3 reds. Conflict at the top. You against the
other. Who or what is this other? The previous method, obviously, as that is what was implicit in the question. You want to test a

197

new method against an old method. What does the top card say? War. Next. The advice. Since it's pointed out that you look at the past, turn your back on what has a propensity to still creep up, as the old method insists (from 2S to 3S). You can fuck it by turning towards something that's rather brilliant (Ace of Diamonds with 9 diamonds below it). Thus, put down the trite, however valuable (3D, 9C, 6S) and get on with the program of sharpening your knife (9D, 7S). Indeed, do this: follow the brilliant current and cut through shit like a master detective.'

As you can see from these examples, it is not method or a card's presupposed inherent value that trumps the so-called 'intuitive,' but the question itself. If you ask a question about value, then give an answer that has value in focus, not one that is descriptive of what *you* want to hear.

TACTICS AS MAGIC AND THE ENCHANTED CARDS

Speaking of tactics, any strategy you engage in towards the solving of a problem is a magical act. How? Let's begin with this axiom: magic is all about tactics, strategy, assessment, analysis, reflection, performance, design, implementation, and power. You think this sounds like life, no? Like the stuff you do on a regular basis? You're right to think that. But now think some more: you get up in the morning, freshen up, put on clothes, some perfume, maybe a lipstick, or a tie. Do you think you do that because you're rational? No, you do that because you're magical, and because you understand what magic is at the fundamental level: magic is a form of constant enchantment of yourself and the world. When that is said, don't think for a second that magic is reality, or that it creates your reality. Reality is reality and it has zero to do with magic. Magic creates magic. If you want the real, you join the Zen masters who point to it, and don't let yourself be afflicted by the self-help plague full of thoughts of supremacy: 'I, the empowered bad witch, am not to be messed with.'

When you stand in front of the mirror getting ready for the world, donning a specific face of seduction and trying on gestures or a precious costume that go with it, what you do is conjure Venus, the goddess of love and money. You may not be conscious of this, but that's what you do, conjure mojo to boost your confidence. You may be the most rational person on the planet, but if you think about it, when you go wooing, you'll carry a red rose with you as an offering, not a spade, unless the spade is something that your lover happens to like, in which case you give it to her in an encrusted form, with a diamond in the shape of a rose on the handle, or a sigil in the form of a heart on the blade for good measure.

Now think: why do we engage in and perform acts of magic? Here's my theory: we engage in and perform acts of magic because magic itself is all about the healing arts. Even what we call black magic is a healing art. Why? Think again. When we heal, we get rid of a problem. What is the purpose of magic? To get rid of problems. We don't fix things. We get rid of problems. So I like to think about the ways in which magic participates in our refining of this particular awareness.

Now, how can we make the leap from this idea to using cards as tools that enhance our perception and skills of what the healing arts are all about? First, it's a physical fact that there's nothing that has inherent existence. In other words, nothing has substance. Problems have no substance, money has no substance, love has no substance (sorry to bust the myth of this one), we have no substance. Ergo: what we have left, if anything at all, is the immeasurable potential. Have you ever thought about what it means to step consciously into the immeasurable potential? I have.

Let's think of the suit of Spades for a moment. If you like my theory that focuses on getting rid of problems, rather than fixing problems, then you'll see why you need the Spades for magic, rather than any of the other suits. With a spade you cut. You use the blade and the sharp point to cut through things, to discard, to kill off, to cauterize an open wound, to perform surgery, to tattoo sigils on your body, to keep order, to connect, to draw down natural forces.

Think also about what is implicit in the idea of stepping into the immeasurable potential. This sounds great, but what does it mean, especially since there's also a catch? Detachment. That's the catch. You must sever *all* your clinging if you want your magic to work. That's where the immeasurable potential lies within. An attached magician is an amateur. This simply means that unless your desire to effectuate magic is greater than your desire for a specific outcome, you will not experience much, other than dabbling in the occult. So we're here with the magic of form. You do magic for magic's sake, which is another way of saying that you acknowledge what the whole business of being in the flow is all about. Magic for self-interest is neither interesting, nor does it work. Occult practices that are not anchored in seeing things clearly are neither interesting, nor do they work. In my book of life and magical practice, we don't dabble in the occult, or the cult of personality. We're happily Zen, which means that we lean on the obvious, and chase it diligently in order to catch it in all its evasive glory. There's nothing occult in the clear form.

When reading cards, we look at what stares us in the face in the now. We think we look at the past or the future, but this is not real looking. It's speculation. Real looking is not speculating or inventing, but rather, seeing how what stares us in the face reflects our perception of what we *think* is the past or the future – which is never reality. Cards are mirrors of this process, of looking at the now. Without the ability to look at the now, which is something most people cannot do, you cannot perform any successful magic.

If we say, 'I recognize this as a past trauma,' we say it out of the perception of how we experience working through the trauma in the present, but without any effort. If we say, 'I can see that my wife is going to leave me for another man,' we say it out of the perception we have of the present experience of the situation.

Now think: is there a time when we are not in the present? Even as we assess the past or invent the future? No, there isn't. The question to ask, then, is this: how do you attend to this present, without coloring it with your past or future imaginations? A witch's power is in her ability to stay present *in* the present. That's why we can read fortunes to precision. Just as there's no separation between question and answer when we provide a precise reading of the cards, so there's no separation between magic and a projected desired reality. There's no separation between the heart's desire and the flow of life as it happens.

But there's a catch again. The condition is that you recognize the flow of life for what it is, while seeing also that if you 'fix' a problem, what you fix is your own circulation in the flow, or the circulation in the flow of the ones for whom you work. Magic works if you do it. And by 'doing it' I mean experiencing it on a plane that has little or nothing to do with how involved and invested you are in yourself. Magic is a symbolic act that you perform with view to effecting a tangible result. The experience of this result as a synchronous event is neither *you*, nor *reality*. Magic just *is*. Magic is mind that creates a personal experience.

The way in which we speak about magic is informed by the negative value in language. We understand magic in terms of defining it according to what it is not. We say: Magic is *not* (physical) reality. Magic is *not* mainstream culture. Magic is *not* interacting with the invisible world. Magic is *not* a symbolic order. Magic is *not* a system of correspondences. Magic is *not* the body. Magic is *not* sitting around and waiting for divine and oracular inspiration.

What magicians of old have figured out is that although we use the binary codes in language to describe our experiences – (black/white, male/female, strong/weak, red/black) – in magic the idea is to get to the point where we enter the pervasive flow of what *is*, which is to say that we position ourselves as neutral vis-à-vis our conception of self, and hence desire. 'I, the fortuneteller as a witch,' doesn't exist beyond the shape of the construction I give to my proclamations. Try waving your arms around in a funny way, and conjure yourself into just the existence that you fancy. This is called self-enchantment. In order for this enchantment to work publicly, however, you need others to recognize and consecrate your act. For a 'how to' manual, consult the classic *1001 Nights*, or go read my book, also hailed as a classic, *The Oracle Travels Light*. Meanwhile, magic is above causality. While magic operates with inherent intention, symbolic action, command, prayer, and gesture, it is above causality. Why? Simply because magic is non-dual and power is non-dual. Magic is neither black, nor white. Power is neither good, nor bad. The art is in observing how your magical ritual (intention + decision + gesture) finds manifestation in synchronous events.

When we cast a tableau with the cards, from the 3-card to the 52-card draw, what we do is embark on a journey towards the realization of what is obvious. Often clients prove this rule when they say, 'I knew it,' about a reading that casts their lovers as infidels. Of course they do, know it, but what they don't realize is that due to their various attachments, they can't see the obvious until you point it out to them. We start with their intention for clarification, and then move through the decision for a resolution that we then enforce or implement via gesture or a speech act.

THE 4 SUITS AND THE MAGIC OF LOCATION

If we look at the four suits in the playing cards set, we see that all these moves towards clarity and its manifestation are not only clearly represented, but also made available to us. Let's see how.

Hearts. Now that your head is cool after all this theory about magic, rather than hot and hence unable to distinguish between passion and drama, think location. Context is still king. You want to do magic. What kind of magic? Home is where the heart is, and where your body dwells. Think of this possible scenario: you have diabetes on the table. The cards tell you that there's an increase of the insulin level (3 Hearts goes abruptly to 8 Hearts). What magic will you do to prevent a disaster?

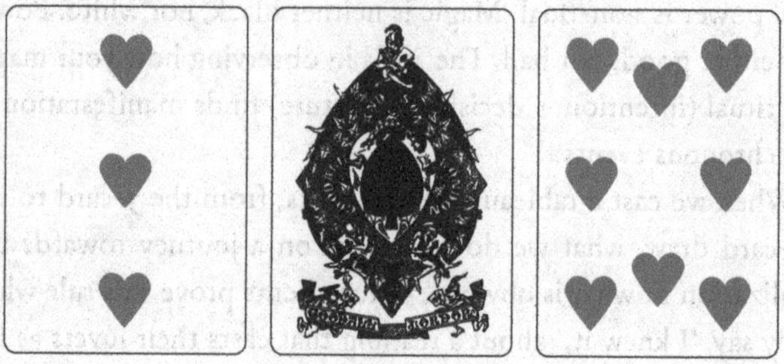

How about placing the Ace of Spades in between the 3 Hearts and the 8 Hearts? You'll do this with a cool head, not one that doubts: 'what if the Ace of Spades creates more damage, as it means death, after all?' Exactly. Think: not all increase is good. When cancer cells grow, how is that good? We would only insist on the idea that 3 Hearts means 'increase' (in the *hedgewytch* system) and because we're with the hearts it's 'good,' if we have no regard for context and how it rules everything. So much for 'meaning'... If you perform a reading with magical intent, then the idea here is to use the Ace of Spades as a gesture towards interrupting the insulin levels going high. After the Ace of Spades does the job, you then see with your magical eye that the card of the 8 Hearts now signifies a restoration of the good flow.

¶

Spades. Think location again. What magic do you need to perform? Raise the dead? How about you go to the cemetery, armed with willingness and a cool nerve to perform magic with all the court cards in the suit of Spades. Who will show up? In classical fortunetelling the Jack of Spades is the Devil himself. Maybe so. Try to conjure him at a crossroads, while holding the Jack of

Spades in your hand. It's easy to make petitions. But how involved are you when you do that? You may think that inflaming your passion is a good idea because it worked for Aleister Crowley, but do you know what he paid for it, what he paid for having a hot head? Making pacts with legions is only fun if you know exactly how 'empty' you are. You make pacts with a full heart and a head full of ideas, you get fucked.

Clubs. Nature teaches you magic. A student asked this assignment question: 'when do I know power beyond belief?' She got 10 Hearts, the Queen of Clubs and the Ace of Clubs on the table.

Her answer was the following: 'I act with power when my heart is full.' As you can see here, the student is reading the cards from right to left. Sometimes that makes sense. But what if there's another, sharper answer? It starts with thinking about what power is beyond belief. Where do we locate power? What *is* power? Power is our nature. Power *is* nature.

You find the clubs in the forest. They provide you with a magic wand that points to what you need, or a walking stick that you use to tap the ground with 3 times. I made this remark in context, pointing to a linguistic slip. Earlier I had this question as part of a 'trick' assignment, but the phrasing there was not about 'when,' but about 'how' we know power beyond belief. So I said: 'When? If you put it that way, then you must account for the Ace of Clubs in the last position. Clubs are with autumn; the Ace marks the beginning of autumn. In an extended reading, when you look for analogies that give you a sense of how you work with concepts such as power, you must search your brain for what comes close to the mundane idea of seasonal cycles. What happens when we're in early autumn? We see the fruits of summer giving off what they've been growing into. The Queen of Clubs has the knowledge of what happens in autumn. You will know power the minute you understand what happens when things come to an end and a new cycle begins. So, it's not so much about your heart being full, but about how familiar you are with endings and beginnings.'

Thus for a magical reading you must consider how the Clubs put you in touch with a natural force. You may want to design a garden, but the way a tree grows will still follow the rules of nature. Therefore in magical applications the Clubs highlight all the things you associate with trees and their nature on all levels, real and symbolic.

♦

Diamonds. Here comes the ritual. Ask yourself: 'what kind of magic do I need?' One that takes place in public, one that follows a script, a book of shadows, or a grimoire? Think: who are the scribes? The scribes are the ones who handle the diamonds and the polishing fire. We're back to the plain common sense we started out with: if you want to understand essentially what things mean, you look at what functions they perform. The suits perform the exact same function in magic as they do in the mundane. The only thing that changes is the context. Therefore, let us intone again, 'context is king.'

It may well be that we can agree on the suit of Spades representing all things magic, or the 'Craft' itself, if we need a concept that's not even particularly specific and concrete other than in a Hollywood setting, but when it comes down to performing a ritual by the book, you don't call on the Spades. You call on the Diamonds. Without the Diamonds no one will see just how sparkly your black coat is, how brilliant your invocations, and how powerful your words. Spirits in the dark don't want more darkness. What they want is to follow the light. Diamonds lend energy to your working, whatever setting and context you're in. Diamonds spell out for you what the purpose of what you're doing is. Without being crystal clear about this purpose, there's no magic.

In making your own considerations about how you use the cards for magic, or how you compose your own book of spells, if you must create lists, then let them be of your own imagination. What is obvious? What makes sense? How does what is obvious and make sense activate your common sense? How do you know that what you call common sense is not already contaminated by culture and projection? Are you free of clinging (to lists, other people's ideas or their recipes for magic?) People say, 'I received a secret Hekate transmission and got permission to share it with you all.' Right. I'm so excited...

Here's a list of some magical traditions I'm familiar with: Western Esotericism, Tibetan Buddhism, Shaivism, Quimbanda, Palo

Mayombe, Vodou, Balkan magic, Norse magic, Arctic shamanism, Zen. On occasion I design custom rituals with cards to mirror these traditions. Do you think I assign to the Hearts another function than to heal, make things familiar, and empower potions in any of the magical contexts I happen to move within? I don't. The Hearts perform a 'heart' function in all of these contexts, not something else. What does this tell you, then? It tells you I don't have a habit of clinging to notions of what tradition is. I perform magic according to what is possible and plausible in a context according to the functions that each suit embodies. Period.

HOW TO GET THERE

Some want to know, 'how do I get there, to performing magic with the cards without clinging to anything?' My answer to this is to urge you to check the following in yourself. What possesses you? – for instance, compulsion, addiction, repetitive patterns. What rules you from the 'inside?' or more specifically actually, from the place not sanctioned by society? – for instance, rage, hatred, lust, jealousy, greed. What limits you? – for instance, fear, desire, judgment, self-importance, or lack of confidence.

Being successful at magic is entirely dependent on your ability to detach from whatever binds you, for good or bad. The successful fortuneteller as magician is in the flow, not entangled in the modifications of existence as dictated by cultural labels and preconceived divisions: good and bad, high and low, hot and cold. The point is to know that culture operates with structural binaries: man/woman, heaven/hell, success/failure, Self/Shadow. Magic

208

sits in taking this knowledge beyond all conceptual hierarchies. Some magical discourses, aka as marketing strategies, promote the idea of 'hell,' 'shadow,' 'witch,' 'failure,' and 'vulnerability' as part of the success program, but what is all this? A sovereign magician will not be caught in any ideas, however popular. Power as the thing itself is more interesting than concepts.

Reclaiming power is all the vogue, with marginal groups being invested in restoring justice. This is a fine political project. But magic is cruel. It doesn't care about politics. Magic doesn't operate with endorsements: 'women didn't have a voice, let's give them a voice. Let's endorse their actions.' Who is this 'we' we're talking about? Some occultists are raving activists with strong convictions. Playing prophet is seductive. I often feel like telling them to make up their minds. Are they performing a projected persona, an avatar, a deity, a demon, or are they performing magic? The power to identify is a tactic, not magic. Powerful magic doesn't work with distributive pronouns, gender difference, race, and age. The figure of the Crone is not more powerful than a 5-year old if they both know how to make an invocation. Now, granted, although magic operates with image, glitter, and self-enchantment, these 'modes' are not 'the thing itself.' A desired, enacted identity is just a prop, not the thing itself. The thing itself is embedded in the art of acceptance. Things are always thus. Either you know that, and act in accordance, or you don't.

The condition for performing good magic is to develop attention. Kick yourself into the practice of shifting your perception, and with your perception, your consciousness. Imagine this: your boss is insulting your basic intelligence, again, simply by pretending that he values your contribution at work, when it is as plain as daylight that he has no intention of following his words with appropriate action, or match what he says with what he does. Not only is there no promotion in sight, even when it was promised, but he stabs you in the back. In case you didn't get the pecking order, now you do. How indignant!

Now feel it, the rage coming up inside of you. You have three options (the third applies if you already understand the basic premise for a magical working): [1] to let rage ruin your peace of mind by making you say and do stupid things; [2] to let rage ruin your health by making you keep it inside your body; [3] to look at rage, calculate it, and then ask yourself proactively: 'if I let rage ruin my peace, then what? If I let rage ruin my body, then what? How can I use rage as fuel for going against my boss the magical way?' You can decide the following: 'I will scribble on the face of the Jack of Spades words of cursing power, X-ing the card out too in cancellation. I will put the card inside my shoe when I'm at the office, and walk all over it. This act will make him apologize or better yet, resign his position.'

Note here how for this piece of magic with the playing card I considered the rank of the court card. I didn't take the King to scribble on, and then walk all over his face. Through this act alone, I demoted the imbecile boss to a lower position. This face is easier to squash. Note also that I didn't get bogged down by any cultural idea of what is 'responsible,' 'fair,' or 'moral' to do. In magical acts you go beyond the conceptual. Perhaps now you begin to understand the insistence on detaching. If you're attached in the slightest to any ethical justifications, then performing magic is not for you.

Let's have a comparative example of magic with the cards.

First we read a set of three cards for a mundane question: 'will the new counselor be able to strongly influence my investment in the company?' We get these cards: Jack of Spades, Queen of Clubs, 5 Spades.

  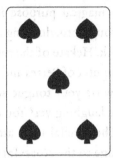

We can say the following: 'the Man in Black' will not influence strongly your investment, perhaps because there's someone higher in rank than him, preventing him from performing in the interest of your own wicked pleasure.'

In contrast, for a magical operation we'd have to answer in this way, if the same set of cards were on the table, keeping the intent to have the new counselor act optimally in our interest: 'the new counselor influences my investment by showing the boss his most intimate signature (a tattoo on the body, or his personal sigil that can be as simple as a personalized business card)' — here we take the function of the suits and together with the visual cues in the cards, we create a story as a spell. Thus, what I did here was to formulate my intention, and then cast the cards with view to reading them towards the realization of the goal. Also here I didn't get bogged down by the appearance of 'black' cards in a question about financial enterprise. I read these cards as an good omen via making a clear statement on how I saw the outcome.

The magic that we perform with the cards is in the images coupled with the skill to create a channel of manifestation for what is desired. Reading cards is an analytical process. Reading cards for magical purpose is about projecting the analytical process through broadcasting and proclamation: 'I, Radiant Spark of the Dark, Hekate of the three known dog heads, plus the secret ones, daughter of Perses and Asteria and third-generation Titaness, will now tie your tongue so you'll stop spreading false rumors.' Are you laughing yet? You could, as this is laughable, but I'm serious.

The general rules are the following: [1] you proceed from the image to the story; [2] you know that the symbol is only a representation of reality, not reality itself; [3] you take this knowledge to create a narrativized image of the self: 'I, the fortuneteller as the greatest magician...' [4] you open a path through mapping: 'I, the mere mortal' is projected as 'I, the mighty immortal.' Pick any grimoire of old, and you'll see how every magician achieves their aim through the use and manipulation of hyperbolic speech. You want to impress the demons, not let them run you over. You establish a lineage, call on Solomon the wise and threaten to have him preside over your transactions. Finally here, [5] you further the archetypes of experience in their moment of dissolution, not in their moment of solidifying 'your' self that presupposes a continuous 'fixing.'

The thing to remember is that merely proclaiming things, does not a magician make. So the catch here is that while you use language to your advantage, you also detach from its traps. That is to say, you don't end up identifying with the higher powers you invoke, if your magic uses that ritualistic approach, unless you're interested in ending up being cast as a madman. What you do is make speech acts that you back up with your spells derived from reading the cards for a purpose. This purpose can be of any nature, physical or metaphysical alike.

All spellcrafting with the cards rests on a premise of embodied fictions, and it works because you know already that it's fiction. Without this knowing, you'd be participating in deluding yourself with the consequence of your magic not working.

A LUCKY BREAK

Imagine this: you're at the office with others and no matter how much effort you make, you still get it 'wrong' from the perspective of the manager or your colleagues. Think of this possibility: nothing is wrong with your activities. You're competent and know your stuff. But something is wrong with your body as a container: it has holes in it, or it's 'up for grabs.' Imagine your colleagues in a meeting taking your idea from you before you even finished your sentence, one that proposes a great solution that brings with it a lot of recognition. What we're talking about here is body snatchers.

This is similar to the situation when someone takes something from you with a gesture that gives you no choice: 'give me that, will you?' Before you know it, your pen, a mug, paper, or some other thing is snatched from you. This is a case of others 'stealing your luck.' People may not do it intentionally – remember your Venus conjuration every morning without even realizing that what you do in the mirror is conjure? – but in a magical context, they're considered body snatchers, people with bad energy absorbing your light. What do you do? How do you get your luck back? Let's try some 'black magic.'

Think of the idea of containers. What happens here is very simple: we operate with the notion of the body as a vessel. You contain energy, and so does everyone else. You feel depleted of energy? You feel that your luck has run out? Fine, repair your container. You want to restore justice to yourself? Try this: next time you're at the office, or in a context where you suspect your body is vulnerable and prone to being pricked by others, place a black mug on your table next to your Ace of Hearts. Let the mug be large enough to contain small objects. Now go around and pick 'stuff' from your bad colleagues, something that belongs to them, a pen, their business card, or some other such small thing. Think: 'I'm stealing.' This is your intention followed up by your speech act: 'I'm stealing a pen.' Once you get the pen in your hands, you drop it to the ground. Why? Because you need to ground it. You need to let the ground absorb it, free it of its negative energy.

If you need a metaphor, think of the sky with all its luminaries: the sun, the moon, and the stars. They all give off themselves that which 'enlightens.' The earth receives this light. The earth absorbs the light. Any bells ringing? We're back to tension/release, contraction/expansion, negative/positive, continuity/interruption. Nice dualities. In polarity, black has a wind/earth energy and red has a fire/water energy. Let's cheer for the symbolic obvious for once.

Now, we're not done yet. Pick up the grounded pen, and place it in your container for all to see. No one will know what you did. But you will know that you now have the other person's luck.

The next step is to pay attention. A sorcerer pays attention. Without this attention your magical act amounts to zero. If you suffer from some modern diagnosis bearing the names of ADHD or some other such intricacies, I suggest you get rid of these labels. You will never be a magician if you suffer from attention span deficiency. Sorry for the bad news. Conversely, if you feel the tiniest bit of apprehension here, then you'll know why 'Gypsy' magic works, and why you are not a magician.

Now that you're done with your Black Mug and the Ace of Hearts calling back your luck (or soul, in some shamanic traditions), what do you do next? Do you hurry to read the cards and ask about how successful your operation has been? Bad idea. You do that, you're an naive magician who doubts his entire premise for working magic. What you might do instead is a ritual to keep calm and grounded. How might that look like? Let's take the draw below, Queen of Spades, King of Hearts, and 7 Hearts, and see how we can read the cards first, and then think of a ritual.

For the reading proper or the straightforward reading of the cards, we could say this: 'you can keep calm if you stay sovereign in your magic (QS) while also sharing your experience with a partner who is well disposed towards you (KH). You have faith (7H). You don't *lose your religion* because you can't help yourself but pose irrelevant questions. For the magical ritual, we can now advise: 'don the appropriate Queen of Spades robe and find a partner to kiss. Turn to him and kiss him 7 times for peace.'

SOVEREIGNTY AND OWNERSHIP

Magic is about sovereignty and ownership. That's why we associate it with the Spades. With a spade you can conquer territory (see how handy the association with the earth comes in), and gain respect. Respect is a strange notion, as it often rests on fear, other people's fear of you. When the Queen of Spades shows up in a magical reading, you can be sure to feel something. You let that sink in, but you don't attach to the idea. That's the catch: to see what you see and to work out of that seeing without attachment. Getting excited about how cool it is that the Queen of Spades represents you in a spread is a very bad idea.

What do you see? Always ask yourself that question, before you interpret the cards, before you deeply understand what you see, not what you think you see because there's a symbol to represent it. Here's a list. Add to it your own logic and ideas, then own it.

9 Spades:
Magic in general, and black magic in particular
Location: the cemetery, or deserted earthly and ghostly places
Time and season: nighttime and winter
Material: earth, bones, and iron

♀ Hearts:
Healing, spirituality, religion, and white magic in particular
Location: the home
Time and season: noon and summer
Material: liquids, spirits, perfume, libation

♀ Clubs:
Practical magic, talismans, herbalism (the poison path includ-
ed; it's not like you poison someone with a Spade, as other
magic practitioners suggest)
Location: the forest, or the country
Time and season: afternoon and autumn
Material: wood, cloth, herbs

♀ Diamonds:
Divination and the clairvoyant arts, sigils
Location: the city
Time and season: morning and spring
Material: gem stones and ink

What about numbers and magic? Let's see what we can make
of that. 'Why are the 7s magical? students always want to know.
You'll find countless attempts to explain, especially in occult and
esoteric books; the books that like to present you with a box of
correspondences on every page, as if boxes can stand for arguments. Fortunetellers of old don't bother with any explanations,
which is why you hardly ever stumble over a fortunetelling manual
that will tell you where all the associative ideas come from and
why. Now, all of this structuralist or not so structuralist approach
is fascinating, simply because within a given context what people

propose can actually make sense. But let's see if we can make sense of the 7s in our own context of keeping it to the bare bone, when we start with acknowledging that there's tension and release. This is our basic line on which we layer all other levels of significance. I hope we can all agree on that. If we don't, too bad. We're still in a classroom where 2+2=4, not a desired 5 or better yet, a symbol. Then, 1 contracts, 2 expands, 3 contracts, 4 expands, 5 contracts, 6 expands, 7 contracts, 8 expands, 9 contracts, 10 expands.

What do magical folks do? They think. By the time you get to '6 expands' you already got the spiel. You can also expect that by the time you get to the next contraction in the 7, some new shit must happen. And it had better be mysterious; you're tired of mundane contractions, so you need something out of this realm. Make it big too. You can sense the immeasurable potential…

♀

You have renewed faith (7 Hearts). You swear this new step is the new work written on the body (7 Clubs). In your visions at night you get instructions on how to activate your new tattoo (7 Diamonds). You then fling it to the public (7 Spades). You sit in a diner, and let the black ink do the talking: 'don't even think about messing with me.'

This is how you make up a story. 'A story? Aren't we suppose to divine?' some ask. 'Yes, a story, as divination is no different than what we imagine otherwise.' The only difference is that whereas in our mundane lives we use the door to walk through when we need to go out, in divination, when we need to go out of a rut, or see a new vista that can inspire us in our actions, we use windows to walk through, or a door in the floor, leading us to a rabbit hole where we can find alternative solutions. So yes, it's all stories. And what of it? If somehow you think that reading cards is not about making up stories, I urge you to think again. If somehow you think that the occult books you've been reading are not made up of people making up stories, I urge you to think again. Talismans, grimoires, sigils, and accounts of personal gnosis are all stories. Astrology is a story about the stars. Cartomancy is a story about 4 suits and 10 numbers. The I Ching is a story about the heaven and earth and the stuff we find between them.

Number 4 is deadly in some Asian cultures. In Western esotericism and shamanism 4 is about the corners of the universe. When we see 4 Hearts in a string of cards concerning a question about health, we urge the person to regulate their medication. A Korean diviner might urge the person to prepare for a funeral. These are all stories. And so it goes. 'Thank you human imagination. You're great... and full of shit. But that's precisely why you're so great.'

Is there a 101 magic application of all this? Indeed there is. Just think again: black has a wind/earth energy; red has a fire/water energy. There's increase (red cards) and decrease (black cards). When your heart energy is decreased you feel unmotivated, drowsy, depressed. Too much black energy eats up your vitality. In tantric esoteric traditions, black energy is also called ghost energy. The Romanian 'strigoi,' the Haitian 'zombie', and the Tibetan 'hungry ghost' idea are one and the same thing. You wish for your enemies to die? Bad idea. Think again. They'll just enter a new cycle. What you want is to keep them close, so you have something to steal from them. If you take someone out, as it were, you'll be the one filling the void in their absence. In other words, you take over their luck *and* all the other undesirable baggage they possess. It's only from this that the idea of magic returning three-fold back at you comes. But I bet no one explained this to you in quite these terms. Yet not all acts of magic are open to you. The cards will sometime warn you against using magic. Let's look at a student example.

After her initial reading for this question: 'what must I do to create more space in my life for magic and ancestor work?' focusing on the loving nature of the Queen of Hearts embracing the Jack of Spades, we had this conversation about my objecting feedback she received. I made the following observation: 'the Queen of Hearts makes her offering to the wrong man, unless we want to go with the idea that the Jack of Spades is the Devil.' She then asked: 'why do you read this card as *the wrong man*? And in the context of the question *what must I do*.... wouldn't this mean I'm supposed to give my cup to this Jack?'

I offered this idea in turn: 'when the Jack of Spades is in the picture, he calls for assessing what you're asking for. Why? Think. This Jack is not the loving Jack of Hearts, who says yes to everything. Nor is he the Jack of Diamonds, ready to cut a deal, or the Jack of Clubs also open to negotiation. This one says no. His inclination is towards refusal. So think again. You have a big cup, and say to this one: *here you are. It's yours.* What makes you think he will open up his arms and say, *thank you dear, I've been waiting for your love?* The Jack of Spades is not interested in that. He's a closed off young man who will tell you to go fuck yourself, or worse.'

We come to the end of the formal teaching here, and I cannot stress it strongly enough: what makes a good reading is not the number of set phrases you can manage to remember, but rather your ability to think back to the essential fundamentals and then make your own creative permutations in such a way that it's convincing. What you want is to be able to demonstrate with evidence from the cards why what you say is so. Context rules, and the question drives the narrative forward towards a precise answer. Therefore, let's have it again: with the hearts you love, with the clubs you build, with the diamonds you negotiate, and with the spades you dig. There's increase and decrease in numbers, but not all increase is good and not all decrease is bad. There's speed, tone, temperature, tension and release in both the court cards and numbers. If you're in doubt as to what is what, why it is so, how it is so, and when it will happen, I'll stake my head on it that if you simply went back to the question and reassessed, the true and simple answer would stare you in the face. Basic knowledge is real knowing, not sophistry.

As to your own speed and how fast you either get it or you don't, there's a reason why they say, 'practice makes perfect.' Find situations to read for. They're everywhere. Train yourself in asking questions, any questions. Then ask yourself: how can I see the bigger picture for this particular concern? They say, 'trust the cards,' but I prefer, 'trust your eyes' — though indeed, in order to see clearly, you must make sure that you don't cling to any emotional, intellectual, affective, cognitive, or other self-induced pre-programing. It's not difficult to see things as they are, but if you're 'in a state,' then there's no method on the planet that will accommodate you: you're either in a mood, or you have clear vision. Free yourself of 'being in a state' — whatever state — and read your cards with zero degree involvement (personal or other-wise). We could be fresh and call this 'reading with two minds...'

When that is said, in reading cards for magical operations, think about sympathetic relations. How likely is it that the Queen of Hearts would be comfortable with sending someone to hell? But if that's the only one you get in the picture, then how do you create a story in which the Queen of Hearts, while honoring the quality of her suit, also knows everything about the consequences of having a hard heart? A hard heart is a serious condition. For instance, you'll find in esoteric Buddhism a lot of insistence on magic that softens the heart. But if the Queen of Hearts needs to perform black magic or have an efficient encounter with the Jack of Spades, then she'd have to access the hardness of her own heart before she starts touching any of the necessary *materia magica* for her intent.

These considerations that I'm asking you to contemplate here are part of context. This means that what applies to your mundane readings, applies to your magic. There's no solid magic with the cards unless the structure of the context has been thoroughly pondered. A magical act is thoughtfulness, not impulse.

ASSIGNMENT 1: THE OBSERVATION

Put down a 3-card spread for a mundane, everyday question. Glance at the cards, and jot down 2-3 notes containing your initial observations. Then walk away from the cards and do something clear your mind — have a cup of coffee, take a walk, do a bit of yoga — anything that clears your mental state. Put the cards and your notes about them out of your thoughts.

Return to the cards after a while, and read them. Remember that any 3-card string that answers a question can and will generate a neat sentence. Write down your sentence and then go back and look at your initial observations. Compare. How different are your notes from your final sentence? Are there traces of them in your final reading, or did you succeed in 'reading with two minds' — the mind of the void and the mind capable of producing thoughtful and powerful speech acts?

Part of the cartomancer's lot is to answer this question without judgment: 'Am I cursed? What can I do?' Once someone who confused my service with an iPhone divination app, soliciting an answer to 5 questions in the 30-minute session that she booked, insisted that I addressed the cursing situation. She gave me exactly 3 seconds for that. This was a face-to-face reading. My samurai self loves this challenge, especially when the premise for answering requires exactly one precise cut performed out of what Korean Zen master Seung Sahn insists is always the case: 'not-knowing.' I answered her, and then looked at her bleeding.

There's never anything other than 'not-knowing.' There's never any, 'I know this because of lineage, psychic ancestors, 40-year cartomantic experience, clairvoyance, intuition, or esoteric scientific approach.' All we've got is seeing what we see in the moment. The other 'arguments' may well be present in the way in which we end up drawing on heritage and experience, but if you care to pay attention to what you do when you read the cards, you'll notice that your best readings will spring from your seeing for yourself, not from going to this or that doubtful and dubious source.

Let's have an example, so you know exactly how to approach this assignment. A client wanted to know: 'am I cursed? What can I do about it?' I laid down 5 cards in a cross and started to describe the situation. I used the 3 cards on the horizontal line for this. I then took the card on top as a significator for the appropriate action, 'do this,' and assigned the card at the bottom the opposite value: 'don't do this.' This spread is excellent when you want to keep in balance what need to do and what you need to avoid.

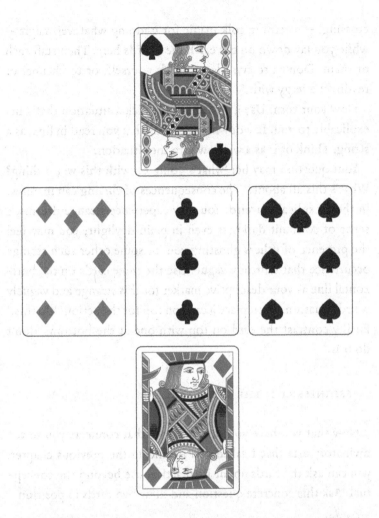

Thus I said: 'It looks like it. There's envisioning it (7D) and a concrete cursing *work* set in motion. Nothing too serious, but enough. I suggest you do this: go to the 3-ways crossroads armed with an iron dagger and a pack of cards. State your wish for 'uncrossing' – a term in folk magic for undoing whatever magic – while you lay down on the earth the 3 cards here. Then stab each of them. Don't use crystals to purify yourself, or to channel or re-direct energy with.'

Now your turn: Use a 5-card layout. Pick a situation that's inexplicable to you. Lay down three cards that you read in line, as a string. Think of it as a window into the situation.

Your question may be: 'what's going on with this weird thing? What's this all about?' The consequences of cursing can manifest in the inexplicably weird. You may experience strange dreams, a sense of constant darkness even in plain daylight; you may feel the presence of others ghosting you, or some other such strange occurrence that's already vague. Use the three cards on the horizontal line as your descriptive marker for this strange and vaguely weird situation. Then place a card on top for the action: 'do this.' Finally contrast the card on top with one at the bottom: 'don't do this.'

ASSIGNMENT 3: THE GYPSY SPELL

Now that you have your magical tool that connects you to the divinatory arts that I asked you to find in the previous chapter, you can ask the cards about its practical use beyond the conceptual. Ask this concrete question and draw two cards in position.

Card 1:
'What does my magic tool affirm in my magical undertakings?'
Card 2:
'What does my magic tool negate in my magical undertakings?'

226

Place the cards side by side and create a synthesis phrase that connects the 2 sides of this magic 'silver coin.'

Here's my example based on the cards above: 7 Hearts and 5 Hearts. I went like this for it: 'my tool affirms the spiritual and negates the personal, pointing to non-identifications with the body.' How very apt, given my tool, a twig that I found in a water. I baptized it after Nāgārjuna who was an Indian Mahāyāna Buddhist thinker, widely considered one of the most important Buddhist philosophers working on the notion of nonduality and practices of non-identification with the self, body, and other.

🐾 COMPREHENSION: FOUR ESSAYS

In the following, we'll look at four essays dealing with some aspects of card magic, or magic with the cards. As magic is contingent on having a vigilant eye and 'I,' we start with tales of magic and a consideration of our fear of words and love of labels. We then read for the power to fly, and round off this comprehension section with an essay on dreams and magic with the Devil's card.

Tales of magic

The cartomantic community like any other community is invested in a set of beliefs. These may be common across the board in eclectic or conservative ways. But a belief is a belief. According to the dictionary, 'a belief is an acceptance that a statement is true or that something exists; trust, faith, or confidence in someone or something.'

Now think about why people come to fortunetellers or why we perform magic, with or without the cards. Everyone wants transformation. Now think this too: insofar as everything is transient and nothing stays the same by virtue of the law of impermanence, we don't experience anything *but* transformation. So what *kind* of transformation are we talking about, when we ask for the redundant? Controlled transformation. No one wants to feel powerless and at the mercy of the tides changing as they do. We want to control change. And if we can't, then we ask the fortuneteller magician to intervene.

The belief in the transformative is big. As all beliefs have a strange way of selling, or rather I should I say that selling beliefs is a magical act, transformation as the vehicle for all transactions is big business. Think of how much pagan and occult oriented folks like folklore and fairytales, fantastic tales and abracadabra. There's a reason why we like these tales; because they're marvelous; because they operate with the promise for transformation.

Here's an example of such tales: 'yesterday I was Cinderella, today I can fit the glass slipper. Yesterday I was the ugly duckling, today I'm the hottest chick in town. Yesterday I was a carnivore, today I save the world. Yesterday I was sweeping NASA's floors, today my starship lands on lucky Jupiter. Yesterday I was cursed, today I control demons and djins. Yesterday I was eating old food in my friend's fridge, today I make 7 figures.'

What these tales have in common is two things: [1] belief in transformation and [2] the promise that 'you can also...' The classical tale 'from rags to riches' is a fantastic tale, a magic tale. As such, it doesn't mean it's not 'true,' but rather, that this potential veracity doesn't render the tale any less fantastic than it already is. There's truth in fiction, and you can perform all sorts of magic, especially when your performance is not one of repeating others' beliefs.

The point I'm trying to make is that the transformative, if it exists as we fantasize about it, is always somewhere else than where we actually think it is. The space between the rag and the riches is covered by an investment that's not the result of maintaining grand enthusiasm for the proclamation that 'you can also do it,' no matter how much you work for it. The space between the rag and the riches is covered by emptiness, the space where 'real' magic occurs independently of your efforts, rituals, sacrifices, and devotion.

If the transformative is big business, it's because it's anchored stubbornly in the idea that you absolutely 'need this.' No, you don't. What you need is to relax about all names, read some cards, and have a good laugh. This is particularly important if you read other people's fortunes. You could go the classical way: start with a first layer of cards, or order of signification, then you stack another layer on top of it. You stop there, but then you also ask the client: 'do you want me go deeper, but it will cost you extra?' The client says yes, as they believe in your secrets. By the time you get to the curse that only *you* can undo, you're in for the magical ritual that will be worth all the money in the world. But you don't want to do that, because your business doesn't hinge on threats as you don't believe in them, even if there's a clear history of success when such tactics are employed. You are the type of fortuneteller who is analytically Zen. This means that you don't fall or the temptation to read the cards for the beliefs of others. You read the cards because they give you an opportunity to see a few ingrained habits knocked off their throne. There are other alternatives.

As a way of practicing seeing the obvious and sticking with the obvious, which is never about belief, try for a day not to let your actions be informed by any belief whatsoever. It won't be easy, but you can do it. You'll feel liberated. I hope you believe me, cross my heart. When I teach cartomancy in a classroom, I always ask the students to read like the Devil according to the rule of commonsensical exactitude I lay down here, while suspending their beliefs that I can deliver the very thing. I'm always curious to see how it goes for them, and what transformative power that has, which is the inverse of the promise that 'you can also...'

As for you here, ask your cards if transformation is still something that occupies your mind: 'how can I live the magical life, when this living is not based on belief in anything whatsoever?' Let the premise for this question be one of curiosity, as in 'can I perform magic without making recourse to a whole arsenal of other people's ideas about what magic is and how it works?'

Here's an example of what the cards might say to you. This is a completely random draw, as usual. Although this question could be answered in nuanced ways by a 9-card layout, let's go for the urgent and the quick, the 3-card draw that packs a punch.

 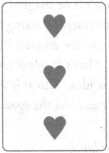 

Look at these cards and love them to pieces: 2 Hearts, 3 Hearts and the Jack of Spades. If you know anything about the 'meaning' of the Jack of Spades, then you'll know this: apart from designating the tall, dark stranger, also known as the Devil, or closer to home, the dashing young man ready to fuck you, but also only reluctantly – oh, the paradox of playing hard to get – you'll know that the Jack of Spades here calls for total skepticism, also known as the dictum, 'believe nothing.' Amen to that.

But that wasn't what the question was about. The question was about 'how to...' You can live the magical life that's not based on any belief whatsoever, if you're skeptical about how your emotional core intensifying by one degree, going from 2 to 3, is not the thing itself.

'What is an emotion?' the cold Jack of Spades wants to know. 'Is that something you fuck yourself with?' Pardon my language, but we're not here with using the language of the senses, emotion, and enthusiasm, because the vague, although full of promise, has a history of how cults are created. What the Jack of Spades asks you to do is investigate into how you go from B to C, without even knowing where A is to begin with (we're here with the progression 2 to 3 – wouldn't it be magical if 1, the Ace was on the table as well? Damn, this story is missing that element...)

Never mind. You can live the magical life, if you let your heart transform into a spade. That's it. Now let me close here, before we move on to a similar idea, with this Zen thought: is there a difference between the heart and the spade, or are they the same?

Fear of words, love of labels

A sharp reading like the Devil and magic with the cards share the same starting premise. You approach both cards and magic from an empty platform. You are not attached to beliefs, schools, or rituals that worked for others and you hope will work for you too. They would, if you made sure to tread the void first, before you jumped at interpretation or made resonant invocations. As I cannot stress strongly enough the necessity to stand detached, here's another thought towards placing you at the zero point of neutrality, as this is the point that holds clarity for you.

For my cartomancy students I sometimes watch YouTube videos featuring fortunetellers that can prove this claim: if you're afraid of words, you won't make it as a card reader. I'm thoroughly amazed at the flood of words that can come out of these videos, having no substance most of the time. Shallow thinking abounds even when a genuine attempt to be informative and useful is made. But the most fun is seeing Romanian gypsies making boisterous claims that sound more like the worst marketing campaigns than fortunetelling or magic. This leads to the irrevocable desire to ditch all card 'meanings' and simply go with what you see laid bare right in front of you. There's no secret in the obvious.

However, this is easier said than done, as most of what we see is actually the result of habitual patterns of thinking. Seeing is an actual art, especially when it's based on displacing the idea that there's meaning. And this is exactly what we do when we read cards: we displace meaning, not co-create it in our own image. There is no such thing as meaning. Meaning is not in the cards. Meaning is not in a secret encoded in the cards that only you, the reader, have access to.

From a cultural history point of view, I can see why the carto-mantic world, and for that matter the pagan world too, has been invested in meaning, insisting on it too. If you can't make it as a male Harvard graduate, then you must find meaning in being a witch, a healer, a shaman, or a 7-figure entrepreneur dealing in the magical arts. If you're denied being a woman, the time comes when you will want to reclaim your power. You *must* mean something. All these centuries of men having meaning... Now it's your turn. You think. In reality, just as the Harvard graduate is nothing but a concept, so are all the other societally non-consecrated and non-endorsed professions. Concepts are not reality. This is both a scientific and a 'spiritual' fact. So you can relax.

But why do we insist on clinging to labels? Saying that you are this or that presupposes a reference point that doesn't exist. My theory is that it's because we're afraid of words. We're afraid that if we lost the meaning of 'I love you,' or 'I love myself,' all would be lost entirely. But why are we afraid of what we all know is reality already? The ritual of 'I do' today can turn as easily into a ritual of 'I don't anymore,' with domestic war declared. The house wins. The courthouse, that is. We know what words 'mean' and what fictions they create. 'I love' myself' presupposes a body, or a body of beliefs about my value as a human being. But are these concepts not as shifting as the clouds? What body? What value? 'I am a witch' presupposes a reference that goes back to ritual, costume, and worship. But is sorcery also *not* a concept? If anything, the philosopher witch already knows that what she operates with at all times is a game of make-believe.

Let's look at the magic of RE (not King). When I hear carto-mancers telling others to love themselves, what I hear is a game of 'change your metaphor.' Yesterday you were bad, today you can love yourself, empower yourself and be something else. While fortunetelling is more level-headed and action oriented towards a tangible form of pragmatism, when it's done in the interest of giving the other what they want to hear, 'power and transforma-tion, thanks,' then it doesn't work. What the promise for power holds, however, is nothing but a game of re-naming, re-fram-ing, re-labeling, re-calibrating. Now you're empowered, you take no shit, and give no fucks... and you're still miserable. Of course you're miserable. You're miserable because you buy the idea of hope. Hope that by changing your metaphors things will get better.

The only trouble is that the 'I' is already a metaphor. The 'meaning' of the 'I' is always postponed, deferred to a next sta-tion. In the game of make-believe, it's actually quite entertaining to watch yourself going from station to station. Yet, this position is dangerous, of course, because it's a position that renders you completely beyond desire. Not having any desires, ambitions, and self-improvement projects is rather bad news for culture and society. In the absence of a desired identity that's embodied via self-enchantment, what ideologies of the self, redeeming the self, goods and stuff can culture and society sell? The answer to this is zero.

The point is, to also go back to the idea I started out with, that in order for divination to function at its highest, it needs to place itself beyond labels, beyond the fear of words. If you have a river, let it flow, but is there actual water in your river? YouTube videos are rather short on water supplies.

In the video I referenced that I was watching,[1] a young man of 33 approaches gypsies at a market in Romania. He wants to know if anyone can read his fortunes. No one admits that they can't. One of the gypsies offers instead an instant tirade based on zero context. I translate the gist of it here: 'you're a fortunate man, this year is filled with fortunes for you, you'll travel too, abroad, I think, yes, you'll travel abroad, this year you're so lucky.' Now the young man wants to know: 'you can tell me all this, how?' — referring to the obvious fact that the spontaneous act of divination used no tools, no cards to look at, no palm in exchange for a glance, no crystals. The gypsy then says: 'this is called divination by eyes. I can tell you all this because I'm looking at your eyes. Ah, yes, I forgot to tell you, you'll live to be 83, and you'll have a boy and a girl. How much are you going to give me?'

Now, while we may think that this exchange is hilarious and completely beyond making any sense, what I see happening here is something of the highest: this, probably illiterate gypsy, realizes something about words and their power that the highest educated don't.

---

1 *La Ghicit de Ochi* [Divination by Eyes], 2015 https://www.youtube.com/watch?v=A_S-OFw6zL4

After all, one gets a Harvard education because one believes that such an education will validate one's sense of worth. One proclaims to be a witch because one believes that such a label will validate one's sitting on the hedge, being radical and 'against the mainstream.' But this gypsy here just knows that words mean absolutely nothing. She lives according to the highest principle of seeing *what is:* if it happens, it happens (in this case here, her palm being crossed with silver), and if it doesn't, it doesn't. This gypsy goes with *what is,* not with what she *imagines* is the case.

I invite you to think about this now: who is the 'I' thinking that I'm thinking? In light of the fact that this question places us right there with the absolute and the limitless, what sense does it make to still be fascinated with the liminal, in-betweenness, and the hedge position often associated with cartomancers, witches, cunning-folk and other good magical folk? I like the limitless. No labels. Form is emptiness; emptiness is form. Says *The Heart Sutra.*[2]

DIVINATION BY EYES

Let's perform a divination by eyes according to our own rules. What might the cards say about the 'witnessing I' when we offer a deluge of words to the other we divine for? Whose eyes do we stare into? Do these words represent our own true justice? Let's cast a tableau in pyramid form with the notion of the 'I' at the top. We stare at that one first. Then let the 3 cards below the top card say something about the 'I' thinking that 'I'm thinking.' Let

2 For a further spin off, see my pocket book, *The Heart Sutra and Tarot* (EyeCorner Press 2020) for more inspiration on how we deconstruct beliefs.

the 4 cards at the bottom perform a magical act. The intention is to use words to represent your true justice, leading you to experiencing professional satisfaction: you read the like the Devil because you *can* and because you're skillful, not because you're invested in selling beliefs for the sake of labels.

The 'I' is many things. As we stare at the 10 Clubs we understand that there's no such thing as a singular identity. We walk a path anchored in the conceptual (6D) leading us to group-think (8C), to ultimate disappointment (9S). Are we surprised? No. Because we all know what we're doing when we live our lives according to precepts and beliefs.

What magic can we perform to get rid of our delusions? We must first address the culmination of both fears and desires. What a grand pair we got right there at the bottom with to tens, 10 Spades and 10 Hearts, spelling out exactly that. Let us carve a staff of natural justice (3C) to remind us of our beginner's mind (JD). The polished, clear diamond in the hands of a child is suggestive of the need to reach the zero point of neutrality in fortunetelling, if the service that we render onto others is to be of the highest skill and understanding. When we divine by eyes, it is the eyes of the void we stare into before we pass judgment. When the void stares back, it does so with the force of sheer clarity and precision.

The point is thus that you are the better fortuneteller if you're not afraid of 'a whole lot of nothing' as your starting premise, or in between your words. You're the better fortuneteller when you don't hold any promises of revelations of what amounts to insubstantial truths peppered with references to blood lineages or regular name dropping. You may be a Transylvanian witch and vampire, but why would that be the business of anyone? Read the damn cards, and perform your magic by keeping it simple.

THIS WITCH CAN FLY

Let us stay with the notion of labels just a little longer. I clearly have a distaste for them, any labels, but culturally speaking, a label is useful. It saves you a lot of time when you have to explain. 'Yes, I'm a professor,' and everyone understands that I must have the appropriate degrees and consecrations. I don't have to go into it and waste my time about the past and how I got there. 'Yes, I'm a cartomancer,' and everyone understands that I read cards for people as a professional, which means that I get paid for my services. 'But you're also a witch,' people say on occasion. To this

I often reply: 'if by witch you mean, I can cast a spell, curse, fix people's problems, and fly, then, sure, I'm a witch.'

People don't flinch when I say this, but by the time I get to the flying part, they make big eyes. 'What do you mean you can fly?' I give them an example. I spent 20 years of my life as a tenured university professor, teaching in all the programs, from the undergraduate to the PhD level. Once in a while I had to take measures against unruly behavior. When students would be oblivious to the class having started, talking over me, I'd keep quiet demonstratively. This would normally help, as the ones talking would quickly realize to their embarrassment that they were the only ones doing it inappropriately, seeing also that their yakking stopped me in mid sentence. Not good.

On the rare occasion I'd go over to the person, lay my hand over their shoulder, and say the following, while placing an inordinate amount of pausing between each word, so the gravity of each word would be felt quite accordingly: Only. I. Speak. In. This. Classroom. At. This. Time. Once I felt the gaze from the student in question charged with what is called in the witch world, 'evil intent.' How did I deal with the situation? This was the university, after all, and I couldn't provide an equally evil contra-attack, however much that would have entertained me. For all my Zen, I'm a warrior at heart, so help me – though my Zen masters would applaud.

What I did instead was to fly over the whole classroom, just like you see the so-called 'traditional' witches do when they're depicted in various paintings. It helps to wear what resembles a black cape, which I did on that occasion. I assumed the Superman position, arms extended so the full glory of the true black could be seen. Then the lift-off. The problem with the disturbance in the classroom vanished on the spot, and the rumor thereafter was that I was literally flying. Well, yes, that was the idea. I wanted to suggest to the students ever so strongly, that if they couldn't be bothered to listen to what I had to say, then they might as well pay attention to *that*.

My point is that what enables us to produce such magical effects has in fact to do with the very resistance to labels. When you resist labeling, what happens is that you live in a world of no distinction, for what does it actually mean to say that you're a witch, or a professor, or both? By no distinction I don't mean to say that you must eradicate your discernment. Either your students are listening, or they are not. And if they're not, so help them. You embody the appropriate role and that's that.

But think: what good would it do me to say to myself: 'I'm just a rational, ordinary human trying to keep order in my classroom. I can't possibly also think that I might be capable of flying through the classroom like a superhuman to everyone's amazement.' The way I figured, if you can't make people respect you, you might as well have them fear you. If you're in the teaching business, I can warmly recommend donning your black cloak of defying the impossible, and have all the students in a stupor, trembling...

Here's a short magical practice with the cards that starts with considering this question: 'what prevents people from performing all sorts of incredible, magical feats?' – that is to say, apart from the fact that, at least theoretically, I'll maintain that what prevents people from manifesting their power is clinging to labels for better or worse, as proclamations of self-empowerment fall into the same category of thinking that you can't possibly fly so everyone can see it. Both of them equally useless. Now let's take this string of cards to first answer our question, and then to suggest a magical operation. I got interesting cards here, but I can't say that I'm surprised.

10 Diamonds, 4 Hearts, and 8 Hearts speak precisely of this situation: it's not enough to think that you can perform brilliant magic, if you cling to what is familiar to you and the uniformity of how others feel about magic. It's not enough to think: 'I'm a witch, a sorcerer, a magician' – because supposedly it helps to have a distinct identity – if this thinking is not the result of utterly original thinking, the kind of thinking that the Zen masters talk about, the type that places you beyond beliefs and labels. Indeed a magician worth her salt is many things, not by virtue of what she says, but rather by virtue of what she does, when *doing* follows the singular act of manifestation, not the emotional core of what we imagine a 'blood' lineage is.

More simplified yet, we can say that, what prevents people from understanding what magic is and how we can use it, is overthinking (10D) charged with conformist (4H) indulgence (8H). Now, can we use these same cards towards remedying the situation? We can, indeed. Remember that what goes into the crafting of a magical operation with the cards is a simple rule: you state your intention, cast the cards, and then perform the line you come up with towards the realization of your goal.

If we take these cards as an example, we could go about it like this: first, 'I want to fly' (the intention). Then, three cards down: 10 Diamonds, 4 Hearts, 8 Hearts. You read the cards for the intention, and say: 'visualize (10D) flying from a squatting position (4H) while drinking a magical potion (8H).' You'd have to determine what ingredients your magical potion consists of, but you may think of something that rhymes sympathetically with what you have in mind, a bird, a witch on a broom, or a dragon. A witch may like a wormwood drink, a hot dragon, a blood concoction, or a bubbly champagne that makes you plane like a bird. The idea is to experience the cards in their tangible suggestion of the ritual.

Then get ready to fly. It's actually not difficult at all. You can experience others internalizing your act of flying at the suggestive level, as was the case in my example, and enjoy tasting the power of performing this magic out of the ordinary for your pleasure.

The Devil's dream card

I often get up in the morning with the sense of feeling good having had a particular dream. But I often also think about the good dream as one in whose participation I prefer a different role. For instance, I can have an excellent dream about satisfaction at work, reconciliation with past lovers, or one in which I'm not a disciple, but the Zen master herself.

242

But what I also experience in these dreams is that I can adopt an attitude that's more submissive than active. This means that while I get up with an immense regenerative power, I can also go through the day saying to myself: 'that was very good, but why do I have to subject myself to waiting; waiting for the other to recognize what I do, or waiting for the lover to figure out how to touch me without my having to spell it out for him, and thus forever ruin the magic that is called high sensuality? Dream state or no dream state, there's nothing more frustrating than having to tell people what you like and what you don't.

In dream analysis this is what I actually want to get at, the state of experiencing my unconscious desires without having to use any words to describe either what they are all about or how to go about it in order to realize them. Everyone having tried a magical conjuration will know that words are important, but have you ever wondered why most of the words spoken are utter gobbledygook and why abracadabra is not something that your conscious mind acknowledges as part of rational discourse?

The magic thing about dreams is that they escape the trap of culture. As culture is all about maintaining a state of fear and desire, dreams open up the road that goes beyond fear and desire. Why culture wants us to fear and desire is not a secret, as it has to do entirely with the economy of existence. 'How are you going to survive is if you won't buy my recipe for love, or if you'll never fear that no one loves you?' This is culture-speak. Dreams don't give a shit. There's no taboo that can't be transgressed, no love that's not fierce enough, no mastery that can't undo itself for the sake of demonstration.

Let's have a magical practice based on a magical square. Let us call it *The Devil's Card* in reference to the idea of a coven made up of 12 people plus the Devil. Our 'people' here will be 12 cards arranged in 3 rows of 4 cards each, with the last card, the 13th card designated as a magic token. Now dream something, or recall a dream that you once had and that you thought was significant one way or another.

Read the top row as a representation of the question that your dream presents you with. Read the middle row as a representation of the challenges that your dream presents you with. Read the bottom row as a representation of the key to both the question and the challenges that the question poses.

The last card is a representation of your magic token in the sense that you think of it as your Devilish intervention into your unconscious. If, for instance, you like your romance dream, but you don't like the position of the damsel in distress — who, while euphorically enjoying her lover's touch is also at his mercy, begging for him to never leave — you can use this token to reverse the roles. If your dream is a nightmare, same thing here. After investigating into the dream's premise and challenge (top and middle row), you can take the token card (the 13th card, or the Devil's card) to intervene, and thus tweak the solution to suit your end, especially if the solution is one that resists you.

For the advanced practitioner in lucid dreaming, I suggest the following: induce the repetition of the dream via meditation prior to falling asleep, and dream the same dream while being aware of having the 13th card, the Devil's card on you. Make sure that your meditation contains wearing a piece of garment that has pockets you're aware of, or else you can induce a dream in which you carry a magic bag that has this card in it.

Let me give a concrete example of a dream that puzzled me and also frustrated me. A perfect dream for magic intervention. A few years ago, while I was still professor and chair of American Studies at Roskilde University in Denmark, I dreamt that I was in a meeting with the philosophy department. In fact, in my dream I was the head of the department. I was the only woman in the room, along with an all-male cast, all elderly professors of philosophy close to retirement, judging by their completely white hair. I presented an idea when, in the middle of it, one of the professors interrupted me: 'would you make some coffee for us?' he asked, without even blinking. 'Excuse me?' I said, and then asked back, 'I want to make coffee for you in the middle of my talk, because...' I wanted him to continue my sentence, which he did. 'Because that's what a PhD student does,' he replied. I got red in the head, as I felt a rush in my blood. I was beyond indignation. Not only was I the head of the bloody department, something a PhD student never is, but as it also happened, I was also finished with my doctoral studies long before this conversation, adding to my academic credentials another doctorate on top of the first one. I reminded the 'gentleman' of my standing. 'But you're still a woman, aren't you,' he then said, 'and here we like a woman's touch.' 'Here?' I asked, as in, 'you own this place, and I'm just visiting?' 'Never mind,' he said, 'just make the fucking coffee.'

I woke up with my heart pounding very aggressively. I woke up with a sense of utter defeat. I went over my dream and wondered why no one was on my side. Obviously the coffee was more important than fair treatment and straight records. I yelled, 'where is the basic respect?' I can't remember now whether I also started crying, feeling sorry for myself, but I felt immense regret infusing both my rational and emotional core. This was a dream that made me think of a number of implications concerning the disadvantage of working in academia, from pecking orders that can't be challenged to women's plight that also can't be challenged. Some things have changed since the day when women were making coffee on command for no good reason other than because that was what women did. We have the rebellious feminists to thank for these changes, but essentially, the reason why I was overcome by sadness and regret was because I realized that my dream was not even a dream, but rather an accurate representation of my reality. On paper I had power, but in reality there was zero respect for what I did. I never had bosses above me who truly appreciated my skills and research competence. I was always just a woman...

So my dream was a nightmare. I decided to treat it as such, and remedy my attitude towards having a hard time overcoming the situations that simply can't be helped. Psychoanalytically my dream could be explained in terms of my own desire to conquer the philosophy field, but at the level of action beyond superstition and speculation, the reality is that I didn't have to do that, as I had already conquered the discipline. Although I graduated in literature, all my theses, from the undergraduate to the postgraduate were theoretical in nature, dealing with some philosophical aspect of reading and writing, looking as well at cultural, visual texts from a philosophical angle. So I couldn't explain my dream in terms of desiring to jump ship from literature to philosophy, needing only the old philosopher's stamp of approval for it.

While my dream started well, with me in a leading position, I was forced into the worst kind of humiliation. I armed myself with a magical square of 12+1 cards and then performed magic.

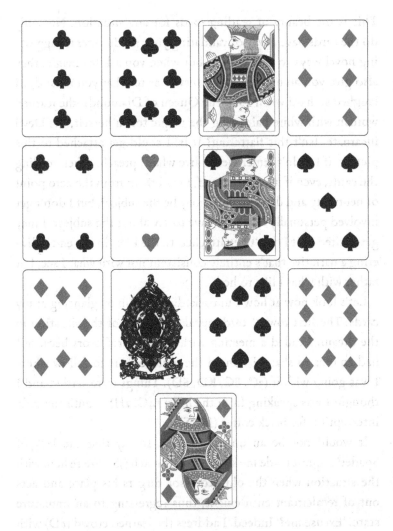

You're welcome to ask why I decided to share this dream, above all the others. Because I couldn't stop marveling at my significator, the Queen of Diamonds, landing in the Devil's magic spot.

This is the beauty of reading cards for any situation. Not only do the cards have a way of validating your predicament, suggesting novel ways to deal with it, but when you ask for magic, they also give you an unambiguous answer as to what you must do. I laughed so hard when I saw the Queen of Diamonds, the learned woman with white hair being the magic token herself, the Devil incarnate. Isn't this flattering? It is. I could get attached to this picture, if I didn't remember to live what I preach. When reading the cards, even if it be for myself, I read them from the zero point of neutrality and detachment. I may be the subject, but I don't get involved personally in what I have to say about the subject. I may get excited, but I don't get attached to the idea, in the end delivering a narrative that's entirely consistent not with what I see, but rather with what I like to hear.

Let's look now at how I unpacked my dream by glancing at my cards. The first row of cards speaks precisely of the situation in the dream. I called a meeting with the old professors because I had an idea to share. I wanted the philosophers to follow where I was going with it (3C, 8C, KD, 6D). Things were settled and I thought I was speaking from the heart (4C, 2H) — until the rude interruption for black coffee (JS, 5S).

It would not be an understatement to say that the Jack of Spades' request made me sick to my stomach (5S). We're here with the situation when the old professor forgets his place and acts out of recalcitrant entitlement, thus regressing to an immature state. 'Excuse me?' Indeed. I address the learned crowd (8D) with a sharp remark that demands explanation (AS): 'I have to make coffee because…?' The fair and rational mind wins, but the bad vibes send me off to rethink the tactics for this battlefield.

Then here comes the Devil's card to undo the trouble. Since there's a neat one-to-one mapping of the magic token and the significator in this case, I took it upon myself to instruct myself in the art of holding my ground. I did that in the dream, and it felt good that I did it, objecting to making coffee on reasonable grounds. I was not there as a secretary. I was there as the head of the department. But what wasn't good at all was the sense of futility and helplessness.

How do we face situations that can't be helped? Fighting such situations means death. Why would we be so stupid to do it on principle? I'm not a woman of principles. I'm a woman who risks her skin for survival, not for principles. Only fools battle with the windmills. I have no intention of imitating Don Quixote. Neither in dream, nor in conscious life.

The 13th card here had a simple message for me: be your own Devil. How? Perform all that which the Queen of Diamonds performs. Display sharp wit and a polished composure. Wear your best dress and jeweleries. If you come across as a sovereign, no one will dare to ask you to make coffee for them, so the costume is important. The lipstick is important.

Now some would say, 'that's contrary to feminism.' That may be so, but I'm not a woman of causes and movements either. I'm a woman of pure pragmatism. What works and what doesn't? Being sanctimonious and acting on principles and moral codes doesn't work for me. What works for me is sending out clear signals. What works for me is performing these signals too, not just sending them out.

The Devil is notorious for enslaving others. In this context here I might try to figure out how that can manifest. And I'm not talking about adopting the role of the dominatrix, no matter how efficiently that would work on old philosophy professors.

The Queen of Diamonds has a cultivated mind. The Devil always promises that too, whenever someone is trying to make a pact at the crossroad in exchange for all the knowledge in the world. I can easily see the seduction in that. Only a sharply cultivated mind can beat the smell of coffee and a woman's touch. Some are in for that ride, as they get how the cultivated mind can create all sorts of stories of suggestion, when, even in the absence of coffee, when the right abracadabra is said, then coffee appears by magic.

The point of performing magic with the cards is that in addition to practicing how to read the cards for their first level of signification, we can also ride with the subtle suggestions, with performance, and the conceptual idea of success that finds deployment in the tangible realm.

The point of checking dreams with the cards is also that we can start to think of the next time. Next time I'll meet a professorial crowd in my dreams making unreasonable demands, I may try to just snap my fingers and materialize the coffee, instead of getting all worked up about the injustices of the world. People are as people are. Some are incorrigible. Yet you still have to work with them. Wouldn't it be better to enchant them instead, and then roll with their admiration? If respect can't be conjured so it makes sense to the Queen of Diamonds who likes to think about what the purpose of going to war with idiots is, then there's always that, namely, coming up with something so brilliant and out of this ordinary world that even the worst philosopher can stare in wonder.

250

PERFORMANCE

ALL DIVINATION IS AN ACT OF PERFORMANCE. A spectacle. You dance with the cards at the tune of a question. A problem is on the table. The cards are on the table. You start pointing. The first act of captivating the querent has started. Second act: what do the cards say? Is there a teaching here? What's the advice? Good advice is instructive. The instructive inspires. If you have clarity, you know what to do. Third act. The sitter goes home enchanted: 'I know what to do!' Isn't this beautiful?

§

Consider these questions:

- Does he love me? (descriptive)
- When will he come back to me? (predictive)
- How can I deal with my broken heart? (prescriptive)
- What have I learnt from this love that's now lost? (reflective)
- Can I bind him to me? (intrusive)
- How can I curse him? (magically intervening)

What do these questions have in common? How about a desire for peace of mind? Does he love me? – I need to know so I can have peace. When will he come back to me? – I need to know so I can have peace. How can I deal with my broken heart? – I need to know so I can have peace. What have I learnt from this love that's now lost? – I need to know so I can have peace. Can I bind him to me? – I need to know so I can have peace. How can I curse him? – I need to know so I can have peace.

Given this simple desire, now think, what is the most useful: to check with the elastic that measures your answer on a scale that goes from expanding to contracting, or to engage in elaborate discourse, bringing in as many meanings as possible – sometimes conflicting meanings about what each card signifies and what it symbolizes? Whatever we do in divination, the useful is to see how cards stand in relation to one another and then in relation to what is asked about. I don't see where 'meaning' can enter this equation. There's meaning, to be sure, but when we match the creation of meaning in context to situations, we discover that the cards speak a very simple language. Black gives us goosebumps simply because we respond intuitively to the contracting and absorbing quality and nature of black, whereas red gives us expansive hope, making us joyful. Less work is better than a lot of work, and more money is better than almost nothing. We keep our emotions in check, unless we want to over-dramatize or appear indifferent. As for public office, we cut through that shit according to whatever program.

What you work towards establishing in any divination setting and with any divination tool you fancy is context and agency. 'What is this about?' – this is your context. 'Who is doing what to whom?' – this is your agency. These are your primary questions. You never go about identifying symbolic meanings in the cards because you're a fortuneteller and that's what fortunetellers do. No. First you make sure you understand the question and what's implied in its structure. Sometimes you have to pay attention to what's said between the lines. Not all confused sitters can formulate their concern in coherent ways. You need to make sure you understand what's asked. You put the cards down and look at who shows up. For the sake of your own safety, you choose a significator, though you can also read without one. You scan the visual text quickly, and pose the question of probability: how likely is it that,

253

given the context, a particular court card can be said to represent either your sitter, another person or agent, a thought, an event, or even an object? What is plausible? When you ask this question you demonstrate it to yourself that you're ready to risk something in your reading, while having exhibited precaution. This is your entry ticket to a robust performance. You never jump at conclusions. Why? Because a wise fortuneteller never does.

BLACK MOTHER, BLOND GRANDMOTHER

Let me give yet another example of just how convoluted things can get if you don't apply the basic rules to how you assign significators. Here is a square of 9 cards for a concrete look into how the Queen of Spades, as the significator for a black woman, can work towards bettering her relationship with her son who wastes her money. This example was offered in response to a student question as to why we want to assign significators according to the physical traits, rather than context, issue at hand, or even temperament. My first and main point was because we want to keep the function of a court card in play. Have a look at the cards on the opposite page, particularly the court cards.

The significators, the Queen of Spades is not in the picture, and her troublesome son, the Jack of Spades, is not here either. What I got instead is the Queen of Clubs and the Queen of Hearts. Suppose I would have said at the beginning of the reading session: 'here's a mother who is concerned about her son. She must be the Queen of Hearts (even though physically she is black).' Had I done that, I would not have been able to advise my sitter that the best approach would be to have her son consult, and perhaps even work for a while for his grandmother, who also happens here to be assisted by a professional. Since I already have a significator – the Queen of Spades – the Queen of Hearts can be read in this context as the Jack of Spades' grandmother. As the hearts indicate a blood relation, we go with this irrespective of the fact that we started out with the Spades as a significator for our woman.

The more agents I have in play, the more interesting the reading becomes. The Queen of Clubs here can be seen as a representative of a corrective institution; she is below the Ace of Spades and 5 Spades. Behavior being part of the body, with the Spades, a troubled body, we can assume that this is a woman who works with that sort of thing, correcting young men with a stick. 7 Hearts between the Queen of Clubs and the Queen of Hearts makes us conclude that the best for the 'absent' Queen of Spades is to trust that her blood relation, her own mother, together with a professional, will be able to help the young man stabilize his money issues.

The point is that, in practice, what you want to see is how 'actors' interact according to the function of their suits. Physical traits don't take that away from the court cards. Again, the rule of thumb is this: you pick the significators according to their physical traits, but in a reading, you read all the court cards according to the functions that represent their suits.

In a reading performance the function of the courts apply, not the physical traits. It's best to keep these apart, that is, color of hair at start and function during the reading, as they can be vastly different. This is also the reason why the Queen of Hearts can easily be read as the mother of the Queen of Spades, even though at the physical level they each indicate a different type of person.

Thus, if a person asks you a question, you look at them and say: 'you're the King of Clubs,' if their hair is dark. And that's that. Some sitters will want to object, saying, 'but my question is of the heart. I want to be the King of Hearts.' You have 2 options: [1] to ignore their indignation – you're the reader and you set the rules – or [2] to launch in a defense, giving a lecture. I prefer the first.

Part of what makes a context for a question interesting, but also tedious, is repetition. If you tried reading the cards for others, then you've already come across people who come to you to ask the same question over and over again. As I'm not in the camp of judging people's motivations for asking whatever question, even when it's the same question they're asking, I think of the fascination they might entertain when they go over the words of the oracle predicting the same as yesterday, or a variation of the same. As a curious type myself, I'm always interested in these new nuances or turns of the screw, as it were. So I read on, regardless of the seeming futility of it.

As far as the querent is concerned, if the same question is not asked for the sake of curiosity, as seeing a new variation of the same answer can be very entertaining, the simple explanation for the practice of asking the same question is rather obvious. Some people simply don't like the answer from the cards, so they'll keep asking the same question until the cards give them what they want to hear. This is hardly the case, in my experience, but as people are very good at rationalizing everything 'after the fact,' they are quick to point out just where they think that the Tower in the picture is not about the busted relationship, but rather about building a new tall house that has better heating. Fair enough, as such a remark can point to what may well be the case, but from what I've seen, such stretching belongs more in the category of wishful thinking, than solid deductive and analytical reasoning.

Let's have an example of such a case, when I got to read the cards for the same question on repeated occasions.

Here's a reading I performed for a man who kept asking variations of the same question over a stretched period of time: 'how can I negotiate with my ex-lover to give us a chance?' The cards kept saying, 'wait, don't negotiate.' But as he never could, he posed the question, again: 'has this relationship come to a close?'

As the cards are very clever, they decided to put this man's mind to rest, as he was obviously tempting fate, so I said the following: 'you're done. Move on to brighter projects, and don't cry.' Now, what I found fascinating here was the 'surprise' card, the bottom card from the cut deck. The 9 Hearts clearly states what this man's real desire is, namely to actually get closure, as per the presence of the King of Spades here, not a significator picked in advance. But in the way in which he formulated his question, he disclosed a lot of dodging of his heart's desire, because, 'what if...?'

Sometimes the cards will speak to something that you can clearly see is avoided in the question. If that happens you have two options: to put the person on the spot, and hence be confrontational, or let it pass, and hence address what he actually asked, not what he secretly desires. A good diviner uses her discernment, and knows at all times that whatever she has to say will be said at her own discretion.

Visually here we also have a clear message. As both the Queen and the King look away from the promise of the 10 Hearts, we're with a strong testimony that actually neither wants a reconciliation. What they both want is clarity regarding the message that they're done. The woman of the hearts is not compatible with the insistent king. As he knows this already, the only thing he has to lean on for comfort is his regret. In combination, 7 Spades and 9 Hearts can easily be seen as a representation of that.

While we didn't have an image here for the possibility to wait and see what happens, as in the previous readings for this man — the idea of waiting very much spelling out the status quo: the two are no longer together — there is yet a faint trace of waiting in the heart's desire, when you wait for your wish by default.

259

At the opposite pole of the repeated question, we find predictions. They are always fresh. Predictions also operate with what is urgent and significant simultaneously. Yes or no. These are the options. There's no space here for objections, for any 'but...' Therefore let's have a look at a prediction in two quick steps.

A student offered this context: 'when Arizona receives an abundance of snow and rain and the reservoirs start to reach capacity, water is released into the Salt River which is normally dry. This floods about half the roads that don't have bridges and diverts traffic to the bridged roads and doubles it. If it normally takes a person 30 minutes to get to their destination on the other side of the Salt River, it now takes them 1 to 1 1/2 hours. I have to cross the Salt River on Tuesday to get to an MRI.'

This student's question was based on 'The Observation' assignment in the previous chapter, so her reading for a prediction followed the rules of taking notes first. The question was phrased thus: 'will it take more than an hour to get to my destination on Tuesday, 3/12/2019 if I use Central Avenue to cross the Salt River?'

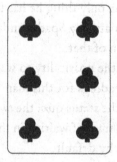 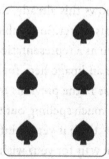 

The student offered this narrative based on observing what was happening in the cards of 6 Clubs, 6 Spades, and King of Hearts. She said, 'no, it won't take more than an hour, but there will be a lot of angry and frustrated drivers on the road (6C,6S), so keep your cool (KH). The 6s look like open roads and the cards look like angry, frustrated drivers. These were my initial observations. After walking away from the cards, and not thinking about it anymore, yet returning to them, I ended up with this statement: no, it won't take longer than an hour, but you will have to deal with some construction areas and angry, frustrated drivers; just go with the flow. I didn't deviate much from the initial observation other than adding construction areas and changing *keep your cool* to *go with the flow*. Both worked for my context.'

I made my own observation and said this in response: 'I'd say the following, especially since I read the court card as a representative of your doctor, rather than as a representative of the situation on the road. The situation is dreary. The roads will be blocked from bad to worse. So I'd expect delays. But you *will* see the doctor and that's the good news.'

As this was a prediction that was to be validated almost immediately, the student revealed how it all went. She told the following story: 'I got back from my test. It took me 30 minutes to get there. There was construction on the road, and one person cut me off. But, the MRI department was behind and I had to wait 3 hours to get in for my test. So I made it in under an hour but the clinic time was 3 hours over normal time. The doctor screwed up my appointment. And after thinking and looking at the cards more, I now consider the possibility that the cards were telling me not to go! *Don't go to the doctor's.* If they would have called me and told me they were running 3 hours late I would have rescheduled because this MRI was just a routine test.'

In hindsight we can say that the combination 6 Spades and King of Hearts means 'trouble that the King creates.' If we didn't know any better we could start writing a book where this combination meaning would feature prominently. Alas, however, this is not how divination works. The lesson to learn then is based on what I insist on, namely, the necessity to use the basic functions of the cards. Spades suggest trouble and the courts act. Together here we have the idea that the road to the doc's was still blocked, but not because of the flooding conditions, but rather because of the King of Flood's (Hearts) own behavior.

In their defense, lists are useful. When we categorize and make lists, we do so because we want to keep things in check, that is to say, we want to keep things concrete. When it goes wrong is when we forget the pragmatic aspect of literalism, and start privileging some symbolic order of things because there's money in the mysterious – let us not forget that what makes a symbol a symbol is the fact that symbols contain several layers of ambiguity. In the woo world ambiguity sells like hot cakes. But is ambiguity useful, however enchanting? Not really. Consequently, when in doubt, keep it simple, not involved.

As a visual exercise on the distinction I'm trying to make, here's an example of literalism combined with symbolic meanings, but one where the symbolism follows a measure of functional logic. I'm looking at these cards: the Queen of Diamonds/Woman of intellect; Ace of Hearts/The House; 2 Clubs/2 things. Note how I instantly assign both basic 'meanings' to the each card and a visual cue for the 2 Clubs, '2 things...'

I can say the following in a straight line: 'Be clever. Keep your house in check. You only need two things in it.' Practicing making such formulations is particularly useful when you have to make predictions and you don't have much to go on. If the question for these cards were this, 'will I renovate the house by the end of the month?' after the straight unpacking that I just did, you could provide the answer in the positive: 'yes, you will.' So here the affirmation would not be based on the reductive rule that dictates a negative outcome if the last card is 'black.' Rather, we operate with context and with what is probable and possible in the context. Going minimalist on the house sounds to me very much like a renovating project, a project that often starts with discarding things. Since the visual line ends with just two things dear to this Queen's heart, we can infer that she'll be on schedule with her plans. So our prediction will be 'yes.'

If we look at another example where we can talk about an extended yes or no in prediction, we could say the following: the essential idea that the blacks restrain or block the light and the reds expand it extends to how we can see the court cards being either in agreement or disagreement over it.

Here, what do you think: are the Jack and King of Clubs following the Ace of Spades in agreement or disagreement? Remember, just because looking at gazes and following their direction
is always a recommended option, mutual recognition doesn't
necessarily entail agreement. Would you take the fact that here
both court cards look in the direction of the Ace of Spades as a
sign of agreement or disagreement? If you said, 'yes, they share a
common view, so they're in agreement,' how would you back up
this statement, especially if I were to point to the function of the
Ace of Spades to signal discord?

Start nodding. Reading a string of cards, from a 3-card spread
to the 40-card and beyond should be an exercise in nodding. I
often find myself delivering messages that are no more than the
summation of recognizing what the reds are doing to the blacks
and vice versa — which is the reason why I insist on getting familiar with a deck of your preference, where the colors are never
more than 2, even when we have fashion in connection with the
dress code of the court cards. Once I baffled a client when I went
on summing up 17 cards and a follow-up question: 'Yes, yes, yes,
definitely not that, but this will work, yes, absolutely. Don't cry.'

In spite of being amazed, the client was nodding too, as he got the message at the internal level of the gut. What *can* you say in the face of 15 red cards on the table and only 2 black ones messing about? Not much. You nod, and get on with the program.

For a fresh prediction to work, it's also a good idea to be poetic about it. You'll hear that methods of reading cards divide into groups, with some prioritizing the language of poetry, or the language of the birds, over the language of corporatist coaching. In reality, when we speak of the poetic, I'd say that there isn't even a time when we are *not* poetic, no matter what group of people we target or prefer to work with. Any reading is a poetic act to begin with, the reading of a visual text making it even more so. We don't just read cards. We read principles and fundamentals of recognizing design and culture.

Here's another example of looking at the King and Queen of Diamonds followed by 8 Clubs. Just by noticing the odd scepter behind the king's praying hands is enough to make me go like this: 'when the King's power consists of praying that no one sees his ax and the Queen smells the flowers, they may both optimize their work for something that they don't really want.'

Perhaps at this point you begin to get the idea of dancing with the cards. Once the foundation for your reading is solidly laid out, all you need to do for a sophisticated *pasodoble* is to start layering what you observe. If you decide the number 5 stands for the body, then you build on that basic line, and move in and out of perspective from it. Sometimes students want to know: 'can the 5 Diamonds be about something other than the body?' Here's what I say: outside of the system that operates with the basic principle that the 5 stands for the body, 5 Diamonds can be about many other things. Will you be on target, however? Not very likely, as the foundation would be missing. You'd just be with pure arbitrariness at worst, and a fascinating idea at best. But is it enough for precision? No. But if you started to dance with the notion of freedom of the imagination and the constraints of the method, then you'd go somewhere: 5 Diamonds can be about cooking. How? Well think in terms of how you layer ideas onto your basic principle. Diamonds are fire. When you cook you need fire. What is the function of cooking? Nourishment. Without eating you die. So the body is right there in it.

The point is that when you dance with the cards, you're like the privileged princess who went to marry a prince and demanded that her bed be made of many mattresses. Her body was so sensitive that she had to make sure she wouldn't get up with any bruises in the morning. You may recognize Hans Christian's fairy tale *The Princess and the Pea*, featuring also the old queen who was not convinced. She stripped the bed of all its linen, and then took twenty mattresses and laid them on a pea. Then another layer of

266

twenty eider-down was placed on the mattresses. But the princess was true to her word. She was all black and blue when she got up. The analogy that I'm thinking of making here is the one in which the fortuneteller is so sensitive to her method that she'd feel it right through layers and layers of nuanced significations that she'd find or create from her cards in the course of a reading.

What I'm urging you to do is to get down with your method in a most solid way. That's your pea. No matter how imaginatively you may get about a string of cards, you must feel that pea through all the sophisticated palimpsesting that you're able to create. Adding more 'meanings' to the cards as you go along and developing your own vocabulary is a great idea, but if you get caught in mere repetition, delivering the same lines again and again simply because now they're yours, you will have noticed that you've grown insensitive to your own method that you now also only keep as background furniture. There's no thrill in the tediously decorous. Nothing to risk either. Boring.

A good dance with the cards starts with being confident in your steps. Once you know how to step, you can try some seduction, some mysteriousness, heralding the type of points that are always in your face. There's nothing more essential than keeping it close to nature. The suits are stylized to imitate nature: water flows, blood flows, the hearts pump up the blood, and so on... This is the basic line, the basic step, or, indeed, the pea under layers and layers of hard and soft feathers.

As far as the abstractness of numbers goes, do you think it makes a difference whether 10 is the top card (in 52 pack) or 7 is the top card (in a piquet deck of 40)? In either situation the top is the top and the bottom is the bottom. In the next chapter we'll look at how we can read with both a reduced and an extended deck, that is to say, all the cards on the table. Same procedure as always: 1 is little and 10 is a lot. Black gathers in, and red expands. You're welcome to flirt with whatever other system and theory, but I doubt that you'll achieve the highest level of precision if you forget to use these fundamental ideas here against the background of context, situation, and the question.

Again, when you think of 'function,' you can also think 'quality' via connotations. What would be the quality of the reds that expand and the blacks that contract? Enlarge your dualist vocabulary, but keep the essential in sight.

Reds: collaborative / Blacks: adversarial

Reds: eros / Blacks: violence

Reads: release / Blacks: constrain

Reads: gather / Blacks: split

Aim to create variations of these in a reading, as these variations will ensure that you deliver a fresh reading every time. Make sure, however, that you don't avoid the 'negative.' Practice. Here's another question: 'what can I do to work less? I'm looking at 9 Hearts, 10 Clubs, and 5 Diamonds, and I shoot from the hip:

 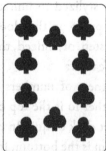 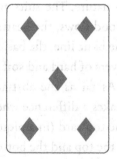

'First stretch it to the max, before you lean into a new mental perception, and then declaring that your strategy has worked according to your heart's desire.' Note that I wasn't tempted to invent a dodging story for how to avoid the heavy duty 10 Clubs. I said, first the pain... There's value in desiring to do your best first, and then relax. So the finer point of advise here is that the person who asks must be made to reflect on how to reach the satisfaction of having done their best before the resolve to work less is actually on the table. What we have on the table is a lot of work... The point is that you have to be able to weave into your final judgment even the contradictory, not just what fits together. In other words, keep it simple. But not that simple.

Besides these essential ideas here, I gave you something to think about that I repeat as far as divination practice is concerned: detach. I mean exactly that. Get involved, emotionally or otherwise, and your readings will be involved, exhibiting your own personal problems and projections. You have a brain. Use it. You have the cards. Practice thinking with them. Ask about everything, and see what the cards suggest that you look at when you check with that elastic of yours. Mastery comes when you're not attached to what you're doing as a diviner, how you're doing it, and how well. Divination is about seeing things as they are. Divination is not about power either, or about influencing what others think of you and in what light. It's about reading the damn cards, not getting caught up in what you already know, or you think you know. Reading like the Devil is a process that starts with simple curiosity, sincerity of the heart, and the acknowledgment that the premise for your start is of a clueless nature. We don't know the people we read for. But we know how to look at the cards.

We could argue that one of the chief constituents that go into the success of a magical operation or mundane work is focus. The ability to focus is a rare commodity, as many things distract us from performing a good job. Nothing is easier than to get side-tracked. There are two ways to focus: easily or forced. The first conserves energy. The latter loses it. If we don't quite know where to start when we need to focus, I propose that we look at a pyramid of 6 cards in order to establish what to focus on, how, and for what purpose. Let me give an example of questions that spring from the cards that you can then further use to ask the cards.

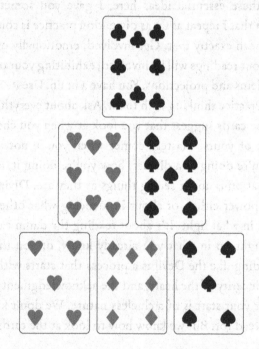

The card at the top, let us call it the leader, discloses the focus. What kind of work? 8 Clubs. How do I do the work? 8 Hearts, 9 Spades. I start to think already: does my work to please others lead to disappointment? I look at the bottom row, and wonder: is playing with my ideas a healthy approach, and will it lead to an unforced natural focus? 5 Hearts, 7 Diamonds, 5 Spades. This latter question leads to the reflection that unless I have a clear direction for my focus, I can easily experience being stopped in my tracks; by myself, others, or other things interfering. Play renders me vulnerable. I must focus without feeling obligated to do it.

As you can see here, this assignment is two-fold. First I laid down the cards and extracted from each row a question about focus. In other words, I let the cards formulate the questions, rather than come up with them myself. This is a game of cards I often play in my series of cartomantic prompts with the students of Aradia Academy. We put the cards down and let them formulate questions for us. Try it. Can you hold double vision on point?

ASSIGNMENT 2: THE GYPSY SPELL

Before going to bed tonight, pull three cards from a well-shuffled deck. Do not look at them. Put them in an envelope or pouch and stick it under your pillow. Sleep on them, literally.

Before you fall asleep, formulate your question very precisely. The cards you read in the morning will answer your question. If you dream during the night, read the cards with the dream recollection in mind, instead of your original question. For an extended reading, you may cast a pyramid of cards and follow my example of reading for dreams presented in the previous chapter.

271

In the following we'll look at the idea of performing choices when we divine with the cards. Each of the three essays here focuses on the aspect of performing a choice as the premise for the fortuneteller's work. This is to say that even in predictive readings the reason why people come to the fortuneteller is not so much because they want to know the future, or get a sense of an outcome and resolution for some event, but rather because they need a window into what choices they have available to them. Let's look at variations of reading for choices, with a note on timing.

Do it today or do it tomorrow

I don't want to say that occasionally I'm immersed in all sorts of projects, because it wouldn't be true at all. What is more true is that I'm immersed in all sorts of projects *all* the time. This requires some planning and self-reflection. I'm good at finishing whatever I start. I don't know the meaning of postponement, or of ditching whatever project if it turns out to be some shit. I still do it, if for no other reason than because I'm curious to watch my reaction: 'oh my, you wasted so much time on this?' my conscious self tells my unconscious self, or rather my fancy or the unacknowledged. In my book there's no such thing as the unconscious. There's only non-acceptance and non-acknowledgment. So this type of the so-called 'unconscious' has a way of retorting stubbornly in a rhetorical question, 'so what if I did, only capitalists buy the idea that time is money.' Now this would be right on the money, my unattached self invested in seeing the obvious, in seeing things as they are, would observe, but consider this: if you 'struggle' with time, give yourself no more than two options: 'do it today or do it tomorrow.' Note that I didn't say, 'do it today or some other time at a later point.' That's not an option if you want to get things done. I often put myself on the spot like this, and ask the question of either/or, using the cards to respond. If I'm tired of deliberating and playing judge between my competing conscious desires and unacknowledged aversions, I don't ask a question about modality, 'how do I do this?' or 'what does it take for me to do this?' I ask questions that force me to take a position.

Let's demonstrate with an example. What I do is perform a reading in two parts. Each option gets a set of three cards. I compare the readings and go with the option that looks most efficient.

For 'do it today?' I got 2 Clubs, 3 Clubs, and Ace of Clubs.

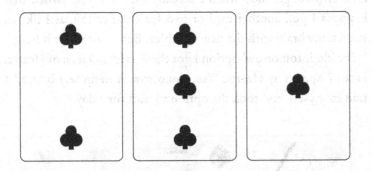

This is an easy one. With this line up, the answer is 'definitely not today.' While the Ace of Clubs in the last position speaks of initiating things, because the implicit idea in the question is actually about a situation when 'do it today' needs to be accomplished already, not just initiated, the Ace of Clubs is ultimately too weak a testimony towards a fair judgment. We can be tempted to say, 'yes, clearly, I'll do it today, as this Ace testifies to the beginning of action,' but what you must always think of when it comes to the Aces is exactly this: is the beginning of action also the end of it? Does beginning work also mean finishing it? It doesn't.

The reading like the Devil method is all about making such observations that often go against the first impulse when we start observing: a question about work, and an all Clubs cast on the table. Work. Ergo: get to it, do it today. But as you can see here, a finer analysis of what's at stake in the question discloses how semantics works, via logical inference and situated meaning.

What's interesting now is to see what the cards for tomorrow's option say, as I very much like as little contradiction as possible. On occasion, however, the cards play pranks on me, and give me an even stronger 'no,' when I actually expect a 'yes.' When that happens I pull another card or two for clarification, as I like to stretch my brain with the new variables. But no need for it here.

For 'do it tomorrow' option I got these cards: Queen of Hearts, Jack of Spades, 4 Hearts. 'Yes, tomorrow is definitely better,' I said to myself, and took the option to wait for a day.

Now, someone considering these cards with some measure of bewilderment may look upon my effort with reluctance, but it's been a while since I've seen a Queen of Hearts listening to what the immature and hesitant Jack of Spades may have to say about it. At the functional level these two cards share the same quality where slacking is concerned: they are against taking direct action; the Queen of Hearts for reasons of comfort – it's better to indulge than to accomplish things; the Jack of Spades for reasons of insecurity. A man of war with the wrong strategy and tactic is a dead man, not a hero. The Jack of Spades knows this already.

SIDE-BY-SIDE COMPARISONS

The usefulness of these examples is that it makes you realize that by comparing sets of three cards side by side when you have to choose between two or more options, with each option being represented by one of the sets, you inadvertently also answer your question predictively. Just think: if the question had been this: 'will I do it today?' or 'will I do it tomorrow,' the answer would have been the same. 'You won't do it today, as in comparison it's more likely that you'll do it tomorrow.'

Comparisons help us to deliberate when choosing resists us. Sometimes we prefer not to choose, in the process exasperating ourselves or those who are waiting to hear from us. While leaving everything up to fate is something I find very interesting, even when the outcome tells me that such an activity is pretty dumb, the best is to have clarity about the right momentum. Choices are resolved by clarity, not by postponing seeing the obvious.

The art of refutation

You know that there's a difference between generations because of the art of refutation. Most young people know jack, but they pretend that they know a lot. The consequence of this is that they hardly ever engage in refuting conjectures. This is another way of saying that they are not very good at prediction. They can't guess correctly what happens next based on observing reality, so they often end up in a depressive ditch, where they wallow in the attitude that's called: 'others don't understand me, I'm different.'

When that is said, it's also a matter of course that there are young people who are intelligent and thus able to navigate their environment, adapting to what is the case and not merely chasing after what isn't the case. The only condition for a successful navigation of life here is that the young take the time it takes to read the landscape, the atmosphere, and the available choices. When the latter is not properly installed, we experience a case of stubbornness that prevents the discovery of what actually works.

In contrast, older people are more capable of filtering information, and because there's less of it, it's easier for them to process information and turn it into applicable knowledge. This means that not only are older people better at figuring out what works and what doesn't, but they're also more able to refute the inessential, even when the inessential is part of the attitude that's called: 'I've always thought this, so there's no reason to change.' The danger with this group of people is that they stop discovering new things, the result being a form of conformism that's not the most inspiring. Let's look at some cards for this generational conversation of choice: 'be younger or older in attitude & mind?'

Let's see now. The Queen of Clubs zooms in on social relations, suggested by the presence of the 8 Hearts. The Ace of Spades and the Ace of Clubs align with the Ace of Diamonds on the vertical axis. I told the person I read these cards for the following: 'It's about refuting. It's not about what you're inclined to do by virtue of your pragmatic nature, which is to find a working solution.'

'Yes, but I'm worried about the people I work with,' she says. 'They like me to be social and participate in all sorts that the company comes up with for the sake of the well-being of the employees. I've been to these gatherings that have a fake flavor of company party. It's all a waste of time. They're all there for the meaningless gossip and to take the temperature of the internal, endless competitions.'

'What's your guess'? I then asked her, 'what would the consequence be, if you simply refuted socializing when you don't see a sharp purpose to it? Why is it preferable to sit in a contrived way, or listen and pretend to be interested in small-talk about work?' Note here the three Aces in line as a representation of the small; the Ace of Hearts in the wings calling for honesty to oneself.

The woman nodded pensively. I ended this discussion with telling the woman that she was old enough to know the value of honesty, assessing accordingly the pressure from her social environment to play a role that she preferred not to. Applying honesty to an environment that cultivates hypocrisy is always risky business, but it pays off to think about what one is good at, and hammer that to the table, whether this be the social table or a platform for the private expression.

The three Aces aligned in this way here gave us an opportunity to reflect on the notion of adaptability. Things are set in motion, as per the value of number one, the Aces being suggestive of starting things (AC), investigating the value of a transactional deal (AD), being resolute and making a decision (AS), and making things comfortable (AH). But motion moves with timing. If the timing is not right for the promise of the Aces to be realized, then we're there with a situation of difficulty where adaptability is concerned.

Adaptability is not about being nice or being a contrarian. It's about the ability to predict the odds and act in accordance, even when it's in your detriment to do so. You can step up to your personal courage, refute what's not real, and take the fall as a consequence. If you're not 'social' in the sense of doing what everyone else does as a matter of 'adapting,' you have slim chances at succeeding in a place where everyone is invested in making everyone else feel good in spite of what's actually essential to address.

Based on the cards here, a follow-up implicit question arises: who wants to succeed in a place that cultivates false interests? The art of refutation is a subtle representation of knowing your place, There's wisdom in this art. When the woman querent asked her question, we noted that the question had the flavor of choice: 'do I keep going to these company parties, or do I refrain?' The reality however was that she already knew what she preferred or what she most wanted.

The alignment of the Aces here, with the Ace of Spades in the position of advice, posited that where this woman thought she had a choice, in reality she didn't. 'Do the Ace of Spades and refrain from doing the Ace of Clubs,' was a clear message from the Ace of Diamonds. In other words, the cards here showed us that this was a singular choice for what was actually a singular preference, even though a question about a variation of choices was posed to begin with. The fortuneteller's task is to note what is the case when the context is loaded or 'involved.'

Choice and timing in ordinary and extraordinary questions

Fortunetelling with the playing cards is associated with reading the cards for timing to a much higher degree than the tarot or oracle cards. This has to do with expectation. What most people expect from the tarot cards is a combination of fortunetelling with spirituality, esoteric and metaphysical concerns. Intangible questions prevail: 'will I be happy?' This is a typical tarot question, the implicit idea being that if you can do something for your soul, you'll achieve exactly that, happiness. Even when people ask about a job, or about shifting lanes, what they expect from the tarot cards is advice that addresses not only the pragmatic approach but also self-understanding in context. So the ordinary and the extraordinary type of questions are equally prevalent.

In fortunetelling with oracle cards, such as the Lenormand cards, the expectation here leans on the pragmatic side, but there's also a high dose of intangible hope that leads the narrative that we don't find in fortunetelling with the playing cards. The Lenormand cards were very popular with the bourgeois women of the 19th century, the majority of whom being interested in hearing whether the right man would marry them. There was also an unambiguous implicit expectation here that the person inquired about be of high social standing.

The types of questions posed to the fortuneteller can thus be divided into two linked categories: descriptive and predictive.

To give a concrete example of what I'm thinking of, here's how we make a distinction between the sacred and the profane, the ordinary and the extraordinary, the mundane and the metaphysical. Whereas I myself don't give priority in my practice to either of these categories, classical fortunetelling with the playing cards focuses more on the tangible question, whereas in readings with the tarot cards or the oracle cards we may encounter a mix, with the tarot leaning on the spiritual and the oracle cards favoring the mundane.

§

Examples of ordinary questions related to work:
'What does it take for me to score this job?'
'How can I improve my skills?'
'I'm a jack of all trades and therefore I have a problem with focus. What am I best at, so I can cultivate it towards mastery?'
Examples of extraordinary questions related to work:
'What mandates me to desire recognition for my work?'
'If I work through my illusions, how can work itself take the place of my illusions? What would this work consist of?'
'Chop wood and carry water.' That's work. 'Integrate your shadow.' That's work. 'Make a pact with the Devil, so he can work for you' (hahaha, but let's pretend this is so). That's work. 'What is the reality of work?' Which of the three scenarios here is true? For fun, you can use a set of 3 cards for each, and then compare. Use the same cut, without shuffling for each.
'What is the one aspect of my work that can be used as a spell to enchant my boss with, by simply referring to it through the mundane channels of manifestation?' Example: 'Boss, my work cuts through shit like a Samurai's sword; you, thinking 'Ace of

Spades,' the boss hearing: 'Samurai sword.' The result: the boss sees you as the most efficient and valuable asset on board.

¶

Examples of ordinary questions related to love:

'Does he love me?'

'What can I do to make myself more appreciated?'

'How can I love in a disinterested way?'

Examples of extraordinary questions related to love:

'Is love sacred or profane?' You will find opinions equally divided, with some claiming the first and others claiming the latter. When you ask an either/or question, you can cast a 3-card side by side for each of the situations, as we've just seen in the first essay in this section. Compare the 2 scenarios.

'In what can I find the highest manifestation of love?'

'To what extent is love subject to what I'm capable of?'

¶

Examples of ordinary questions related to health:

'How will these antidepressants improve my life?'

'What is the cause of my fatigue?'

'What type of fitness is appropriate for my body?

Think again about how you can apply the functions of the 4 suits to what is asked, about a cure or about maintaining good health. Example: Hearts, swimming; Clubs, yoga; Diamonds, skating; Spades, fencing.

Examples of extraordinary questions related to health:

Mens sana in corpore sano, they say, and they are right. A healthy mind in a healthy body. 'What is the nature of what preoccupies my mind?'

'What is pain? Why can't people feel the pain of others, no matter how advanced they are on the scale of true compassion?'

'As there's no reality outside of my perception, what strategy can I employ to change the narrative around the demons of fear and desire grasping at my body? – the mind is part of the body. Example: 'I fear I'm going to die from this disease.' A change of metaphor would result in this affirmation: 'this disease has no substance, hence, I can vanquish it by dissolving the conceptual framework around it.' 'I desire this wine more than anything else in the world.' A change of metaphor may sound like this: 'at two glasses, *in vino veritas*, this wine enables the truth; at three glasses we're talking bullshit.'

¶

Examples of ordinary questions related to finances:

'How can I pay off my loans in the fastest way possible?'

'Which portfolio can I invest in?' A 3-card side by side describing each portfolio is a good idea, as you can compare them and then pick the one that promises the most.

'How can I negotiate a better pay for my work?'

Examples of extraordinary questions related to finances:

'Money is a highly symbolic, virtual thing. How can I apply this truth to the way in which I think of money as a material thing, thus being at odds with what money really is, always fucking with my expectations and therefore always disappointing?'

'Everything passes. This truth applies to money. How can I simply let go of my being invested in accumulating?'

'When people talk about increasing their *havingness* levels, what exactly are they talking about that's not sheer conjecture, theory, wishful thinking, self-help, and cheap validations?'

As you can see from these questions, the extraordinary type of inquiry arises from a reflection or a provocation. We think first and then ask, 'why is this so, and who decided?' The extraordinary question thus features an embedded deconstructive or meta approach to the ordinary. If an expectation of timing is present explicitly, then it has the form of acknowledging what is possible and what is probable within a particular time frame. Classical fortunetelling is mostly devoid of this acknowledgment, the preference being for the clock, as it were, whether the clock is precise or not. People aiming for this type of fortunetelling feel reassured by this sort of pronouncement: 'you will marry your intended on October 31, 2033.' While we may judge this type of superstition and the ones giving in to it, the reality is that it has its function: the ones hearing when exactly such and such will happen will stop obsessing. This means that while waiting for the prediction to pass, people may give themselves a chance to focus on things that are more urgent than what is merely imagined.

THE ART OF PREDICTION

Any observation on the art of predicting must follow some general guidelines or principles. I'll share here my own philosophy that cuts across the board in my fortunetelling practice with the tarot, oracle, and playing cards. There are a few important preliminary points that you need to consider, points that you will also find in the first volume of the *Read Like the Devil* trilogy. Thus I'll repeat again my own universal guidelines arrived at through reflection and evaluation, followed here by two examples of how we determine timing in fortunetelling with the playing cards.

First, prediction follows the law of statistics. It is a always a 50/50 thing, no matter what your desire for a 'better' number is. This simply means that now you get it, now you don't. Second, prediction works like a quick arrow. You have to have a very specific and immediate target if you are to get it right. The longer the time frame, the less predictable the outcome. Getting close to being right is not good enough. In this sense prediction is brutal. Either you get it right, or you don't.

Prediction also depends on the question. If you ask: 'will my sister get married before me?' you can easily have a time span that's as big as 30 years, not just 3 months. You can only assess the point of prediction to the extent that it aligns with the nature of the question. That's the art. Or rather, that's where the art of timing is.

Prediction is close to what happens in mathematics when we talk about infinities that tend to the margins of 'things' and then get weird. I won't bore you to death with what in math is called 'complex analysis,' but I will urge you to have a look at a Mandelbrot fractal. The longer the infinity stretch, the weirder it gets − 'weird' is a math term here − with the lovely symmetry to begin with getting all distorted once it departs from the center point. In extrapolation, the closer the time span for the prediction to the question time, the likelier it is for the prediction to have a beautiful resolve, when you get it perfectly right. We want some beauty here, because, mathematics…

Statistically speaking, it's more likely that you'll predict correctly when you address the 3-month frame rather than the 30-year frame. Within the 30-year time span, there would be a million more things that could happen to the sister, weirdly preventing her from getting married, than if we gave ourselves 3 months for seeing what is plausible and probable according to her current circumstances and conditions.

But here's also a comparing thought that may be more tangible: 'Enchant Long, and Divine Short,' chaos magician Peter Carroll said in his book *Liber Kaos* (1992: 25). Keep your long term magical projects for enchantments. Divination is for snappy things. You want that elastic to make it or break it. Or, if you're a practitioner of weirdness, such as it is also preached by the Dzogchen school of Buddhism, then you will get the notion that as the cards are never about you, but rather about all that you're part of already – which you know about, otherwise, no catch – you also understand that prediction runs counter-intuitively to all that which we call 'the future.' If you don't believe me, you can check with the Harvard trading bros on Wall Street, who happen to enjoy a better reputation than that of a fortuneteller for doing essentially the exact same job – minus her sophistication.

In another order of less complicated ideas, predicting is the art of seeing without prejudice. That's really the best definition I can personally offer. Suspend all your judgment when you predict, and see how far you can see beyond your habitual and cultural conditioning. People into esoteric tarot, rather than straight fortunetelling, hate prediction simply because they are not trained in the art of never taking anything personally. When I say 'never' I actually mean exactly that, for that *is* the catch. In performing cartomancy readings for prediction, if you think the cards are about you, about being personal, or about taking anything at all personally, then you're in the wrong line of business. This applies also to the idea that a card reader's primary task is to sympathize, encourage, and validate the seeker. Wrong. The primary task in fortunetelling, from strict prediction to psychological counseling, is to read the damn cards, which is to say that you follow the rules for reading a visual text. In light of the brutality of predictions that are always in the face of someone, if you can't take defeat – 'lord, my prediction turned out all wrong today, I'm so ashamed!' – then fortunetelling for prediction is not for you.

You can predict events accurately only when you're mad enough to strip yourself of all your masks; when you're mad enough to know the truth and stand by it; when you're mad enough to stay away from comparison and competition; when you're mad enough to stay away from the diplomatic blah blahs; when you're mad enough to make no distinction between your predictive skills and those of your unapologetic prophesying – to everybody's horror; when you are mad enough to transmit clearly what you see and at the same time honor your tools, be they gods, cards, omens, bones, your own flesh and blood, demons and devils, angels and fairies – no parallelism intended.

Now that this general scene is set, let us look at two examples that demonstrate why we want to apply the same basic principles of reading the cards according to their function, especially as these functions are culturally determined in order to address the closest correspondences and approximations to nature and social status that we can think of. I say 'approximations' because that's all we ever do in prediction. We approximate according to expectations. So we don't take the practice of predicting from the other (classical) end, where we start with praising ourselves for having learned all the rules and secret meanings of a fancy cartomancy school or an even more secret order. No. We don't get impressed by that kind of stubborn 'precision' whose guiding rule sounds to me to be more the type that can be summed up by this useful saying, 'frequently wrong, but never in doubt.' We leave all that to the ones who work for an ardent cause out of an inexplicable sense of sanctimoniousness – Freud would call it a grand fear of the inferiority complex: 'if I can't think straight, no one else is allowed to...' What we're interested in is approximations. How do we calculate them? As we don't operate with dumb certainties, we want to know what we can risk in prediction. That's where the actual thrill is. I don't read the cards for constructed certainties, for the future. I read the cards for the present and for clarity.

Let's see what I mean by approximating function to seasonal cycles, temporality, and causality. We start with a recent event prompted by the chaos in Britain due to Brexit. I ordered 10 books in early January. I got a shipping notification that all was well. I got a delivery date. Excellent. Then the disaster. I got notified several times over the course of two weeks that due to the fact that the necessary export papers were not properly signed, the books got returned. I called the seller. 'We *did* do the paperwork,' they claimed, and 'no, the books were not returned here. The courier still has them.' 'Okay,' I said, 'I don't care who did what. When can I have my books?' 'We'll look into this,' I was told, and then a whole month passed. As I write now, I've no idea where the books are, nor do I have a new schedule for when they will be delivered. All I have is a promise that they're coming. Or maybe not even that. I'm not sure anymore. All I know right now is that the delivery trucks are lined up at the borders and they can't cross because all the export paperwork needs to be checked. Food decays while everyone is waiting, the consequence being that all of it needs to be trashed. Where to? Meanwhile the hard stuff suffers in silence, with the general impatient European public considering dropping all business with the UK. As they say, 'they've had this one coming.' One pays dearly for allowing stupidity and populist ideas to rule the country.

I cast the cards for this question of timing: 'when will I get my 10 books?' Three cards fell on the table: 10 Hearts, Ace of Diamonds, and 10 Spades.

At first glance, all I could see is that while the books were sent in good faith (10H), they're not arriving (AD) any time soon (10S). What I can expect is a notification of more delay. So here the approximation of the predicted time takes into account the situation and what is likely to happen. The precise answer is thus, 'not any time soon.'

While the fortunetelling purists may object here, demanding precision by the clock, the reality is that there's no such thing, as we're not with a verifiable event at the time of predicting. All we have is a sense of timing as it unfolds alongside with the function of the suits. We start with the Hearts, for easy-going, and hence an indication of the opposite of expediency. We then move on to the Diamonds suit whose function is to suggest a fast unfolding of events, or, as here, delivery. I prefer to keep in mind the idea of unfolding, though, as the Ace of Diamonds here is followed by another card which already modifies the first level order of signification, I'm not holding my breath. The Spades with their connotation of earth suggests a killing of the fire. Fire without air is not a strong testimony towards giving myself what I want to hear.

So we're with two slow cards and one fast, with the fast one being sandwiched between the slow ones. Now, however, suppose that we do the work that others expect of the fortuneteller, namely to name the exact time. Is this possible? Anything is possible. But will it hold? It's not sure. Many adherents to classical fortunetelling by the book like to speak with a lot of certainty. But is speaking with certainty a valid argument? – especially when no evidence to support this certainty is provided other than via reference to the equally classical idiocy that holds some random book of meanings as high authority.

If one insists, however, then this is what you do in addition to offering an already sound answer according to what you can prove with evidence from the cards. You approximate the prediction to what is plausible. That is to say, in this case here, you think of what makes sense. Would it make sense to say that my 10 books will arrive in winter, because the last card here is the 10 Spades, suggestive of high or advanced winter? It will not make sense, if what I have in mind is the winter I'm already in at the time of asking the question. It will make even less sense to think of the end of December, as it's very unlikely that I'll be prepared to wait 10 months for a simple parcel. I ordered the books in early

January and I'm asking about when they will arrive a month later. January and February are considered winter months. End of December is also winter. So I use my brain and predict an exact date according to what is plausible and according to what I actually expect. I expect the books to be here by the end of winter at the beginning of the year, not the end of the year. Technically we're in winter time until the equinox, March 21. So now I narrow my timing to that frame, between March 1 and March 21.

Can I be even more specific? Let's see. If we take the 10 Hearts and the Ace of Diamonds on board here, we note that we're with 10+1. Shall we then say that my books will arrive on March 11? That would be a fair guess. But a fair guess that's based on making arbitrary choices of taking numbers, speed, and seasons into account is not certainty. A guess is a guess. It can work, though...

The point with this example is to simply demonstrate that you don't need Etteilla or a spin off, or what's worse, some book of secret meanings that purports to have exact delineations for timing in prediction, in order to be able to come up with a convincing argument of your own as to why a particular date is chosen over the myriad of other equally potential possibilities. What you need is to put two and two together leaving from the premise of your basic line: 1 is a little, 10 is a lot; we have fast and slow cards; there's red that relaxes and black that constrains; there's limitation of options in the Spades and largess in the Hearts; eagerness in the Clubs and cunningness in the Diamonds.

If we now take an example of the type of question that belongs in the category of the mundane as it mixes in with reflection of what to do that may even have a magical application or consist of a metaphysical approach to the answer, we can refer to this type of question prevalent with some women: 'when will my insane ex-lover stop stalking me?' While we may think that the situation in which people can be said to be obsessed with other people is more extraordinary than ordinary, when it comes to predicting for it, we realize that the distinction between the tangible and the intangible, the sacred and the profane is eradicated. This is something that the good fortuneteller will acknowledge, if she is to tap into the same universal guidelines for prediction as laid out earlier here. I'm looking at 7 Diamonds, Jack of Diamonds, and 4 Clubs.

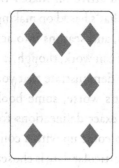  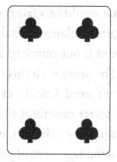

While I may be tempted to say here that the ex-lover will continue to do what he's doing now, with the 4 Clubs card finishing the line that suggests stable behavior, we note that such a remark would not answer the question of when. Granted, based on the initial observation we could say, 'never,' but are we really here with the 'never' situation? I'm not convinced. Let's see why.

We unpack what we see according to the basic principles of seeing presented at the beginning of this book, that is to say, we describe the situation according to what we know contextually.

292

The stalker, Jack of Diamonds, idealizes the woman. The single diamond between the two rows of 3 on the 7 Diamonds card is suggestive of that. He imagines that he's in control of his actions, as per the presence of 4 Clubs. Fair enough. But for how long? While obsessive stalkers can go on forever, their downfall also comes. We're with the fall here, so we begin our prediction with a pun. How about fall? Just around the mid point of autumn?

Now to the reasoning that accounts for the fall of interest. We're here with the Jack of Diamonds, a young man fired up by his sanguine disposition. Now think in terms of precedence. When was the last time you heard of a man of action maintaining a hot interest that is past spring – Diamonds time? We're not with the melancholic. We're with the mentally obsessed here. Imagine the leaves of autumn falling on such a mind. We're already with the wooden box here. His coffin.

Magically speaking, I told the querent that if she herself needed some action while waiting for the fall when we could presume that the hot interest in her will fade, all she needed to do is visualize the wooden box with its lid open to catch the breath of the other directed towards her face. 'Down,' I said. 'Use the metaphor of all things down, all stalking interest in you down, the vitality of gazing fading down. Capture it all in this 4 Clubs open box.'

Now, there's a condition here if the prediction is to pass, namely that the stalker will stop stalking in mid fall. This condition has to do with verbally ending the act of visualization, bringing it to a concrete resolve. What you hold open, you must also close. When you actively participate in a magical operation based on a predictive, descriptive, or prescriptive reading, you must also think of closure that you give to yourself. The magic word is 'I'm done.'

Fortunetelling with the playing cards blends concreteness with windows of opportunity via performance. We can only talk about temporal sequencing, causality, and projections into the future if we understand that what we do at all times when we tell fortunes is perform the present. Querents present us with a situation and we start reading with the help of the cards the landscape of their mental and physical state.

We can call clairvoyance our ability to extrapolate from people's predicaments 'a thing of the future,' but a more concrete label is available to us than the intangible and non-verifiable notion of seeing things when no one else can see them. Let us call it 'the theater of terror.' As no one is trained in seeing the obvious, it stands to reason that when we develop this capacity, we're right there with a violent act. Truth terrorizes. Giving people what they don't want to hear is an act of terror. Hence the history of fear of diviners. Fear and trembling. People seek diviners, but in reality they don't want to know. Most just want confirmation either of their own projections, their worst fears, as in, 'I knew this was a disaster,' or of their most heightened desires often manifest in proclamations whose aim is to elevate the self or to empower it: 'I, too, can be like the Queen of Spades...'

But all this is performance, a play with terror led by chance. 'What if...' is the question, even when an inquiry as innocuous as the desire to know if one gets the job or not is on the fortuneteller's table. 'What if I will be better off on the neighbor's greener grass?' We cast the cards in small or large tableaux, using three cards for it, the full deck, or a reduced, piquet deck. We act.

SCALE

W E WORK WITH APPROXIMATIONS not only in prediction, but also when we have to assess the interplay between form and content as far as the art of interpretation is concerned. While we can agree that it's just a matter of scaling if we used the full pack of playing cards on the table arranged in a grand tableau as against putting down just three cards for the same question, we begin to wonder to what extent our basic principles of reading might apply to the piquet deck that consists of 32 cards. So we sit with a question of form: how would this reduced format fit the numerical narrative of 1 to 10 that goes like this: 1 is unity, 2 is division, 3 is a new idea, 4 is consolidating it, 5 is the question of what else the body can come up with, whereas the 6 shows the way; 7 is a challenge on the new path, and 8 shows us our fears and desires. Why? 8 is a crowd. We wish to belong, and fear that if we don't we get fucked. If no one buys our idea, we're fucked. 9 changes all that though, proposing that we go beyond structural duality to a stage of totality in 10 that mirrors the unity of 1 we started out with. By the time we get to 10, we're already in a league of our own; singular in our individual expression. That's the beauty of it. Whether we scale up or down, the same applies.

But there's also a situation when we work with approximations at the level of content, which is what we'd need to look at when we use a piquet deck or deem that the good cards actually give a bad message, in which case we're scaling from red to black, from happiness to terror. Let's see what I mean. As I was writing this chapter, I was also paying attention to what happened in the Playing Cards Foundation Course online at Aradia Academy. A student asked a question that generated an important discussion and point. Upon seeing the cards of 7 Hearts, 9 Hearts, and 6 Hearts, the student asked: 'this lady asks if she is going to be fired from her job. Insofar as the string ends in red, I would say no. The situation will be solved happily and her wish to continue in that job will come true.'

Another student offered this insight: 'to me this looks like a yes, she will get fired, not simply because we are with the hearts. Things begin with some troubled heart(s) (7H), and if the heart is troubled in the work place or elsewhere, it often wishes or wants for a change (9H). So, she is let go, as in, sent off (6H), but it is done with good will; we're with the Hearts here, not Spades.' I pointed out the following: 'although we got all red cards here, and we may think that there's no cause to fear, it's likely that it ends with a new path (6H) as per the company's wish (9H). The focus must thus be on the company, not on what we presume about the woman's state of mind, or heart, or about what she wants, and how she'll resolve her wish. Therefore the more precise answer is to simply say that although the company feels bad about it (7H), they wish (9H) for the woman to find another path (6H).'

So here we are with the situation when the good cards deliver a bad message, and we scale the focus down from the woman as a subject implicated in the question to the company as a subject that has agency. While we can, indeed, infer that the reason why the woman asks if she will be fired is because she fears the outcome, the question was not about her but about her company's decision. In other words, we must read the cards with view to addressing the primary subject. We thus predict the moves of the company in this case, rather than speculate on causality pertaining to the querent that is irrelevant to the question. How one feels about a situation is irrelevant, when they are not the ones deciding. In this case we are not interested in this woman's heart.

I begin this final chapter here with this example because if we have to say something about how we can jump ship, as it were, and use a pack of 32 cards rather than the 52-standard, and apply the same reading principles throughout, then this is the place where we start. The 3-card draw is our template for reading like the Devil. If we can read it with some measure of accuracy, then we can read the 32-pack and the 52-pack by using the exact same approach to paying attention. The idea is to extract from the cards what is most obvious in relation to the context, the question, and our predicting approximations to what we can expect within the range of what is plausible and probable. In other words, we work with analysis and cultural statistics, probability and framing.

Now let's give two examples of a reading, first with the reduced deck, the piquet deck, and then have all the 52 cards on the table for a complete picture. We look at method from the perspective of formal properties, while keeping an eye on how we stretch our elastic where the delivery of content is concerned.

In my general practice of reading with the playing cards I mostly use the full deck, 52 cards. But as it happens, since I own an exquisitely rare hand-stenciled deck, featuring golden edges, a vivid red of passionate messages, and no indices — such is the privilege of owning an untaxed luxury pack — I find myself on occasion reading with the reduced number. Again, what characterizes the piquet deck is that it has only 32 cards in it, numbered from 7 to 10, with the Aces and the court cards similar to the standard 52-pack. No jokers.

Apart from seeing the cards as a fetish, when I appreciate their looks and the tactile experience they give me, I like reading with the piquet deck because it allows me to think differently. In French cartomancy reading with the piquet deck (reversed cards included) is seen as a normal practice, but in the Anglo-American context this raises some questions about preference. Why is reading with the piquet deck interesting when we might as well just read with the full pack? It's a fair question, especially if we like the numerical story that goes from 1 to 10. Personally I also find that reading with 52 cards saves me from the hassle of considering all those reversals that one finds in French cartomancy or its derivatives. We could say that the French read with 32 cards, but in reality it's more like the double, so we're with 64 very rigid meanings for upright and reversed cards that we must all learn diligently if we're to prove ourselves as serious diviners. But set meanings, reversals, and illogical conservatism is not my idea of fun.

What do I do instead? To begin with, I do the same as always: I follow the color and the number progression. Reds are good, blacks are bad. We go from hot to cold. 1 is a little. 10 is a lot. In between is a variation on the numbers 0 and 1, and to make it more fun, we can say that all the 7s are trouble, as they come right out of a new way of doing things (6s), preparing our entrance to the public sphere (8s) where we can present what we've been thinking of (9s) and realized (10s). There's no end to how many more variations we can offer when we talk about the numbers going from 1 to 10 as a linear story. Given this method, how then to read with 32 cards, the Aces and the court cards plus the 7 to 10 suits, if we want to use the basic idea as the above?

The reason why I want to maintain the above is simply because I prefer to read cards the logical way. As far as I'm concerned, I'm not interested in meanings that are generated by the illusion of some invented tradition. For me tradition is this: following a solid logic behind the mechanics of reading the cards. If I can follow the argument as to why, for instance, the Jack of Spades reversed should be associated with betrayal in love, when we have more immediately the Jack of Hearts reversed that might fulfill exactly that same function, then I can accept it as 'traditional' meaning. If I can't find any common sense to it, I deem it a waste of my time and send the so-called 'traditional meaning' to hell.

The same reasoning applies to considering how the 7 Spades in some Baltic cultures is associated with love, rather than a troublesome stab. While we can dismiss the idea of Spades having anything to do with love, as soon as we start thinking about the possible reason for this particular association, we can activate our cultural competence and offer this idea: back in the day, and I mean, back to the Akkadian records in Babylonia, and ever since then actually, love has been considered a pathology. When you're in love, you're ill. You don't have your wits about yourself. You're destroying yourself, digging your own grave. Love as a romance is a novel and modern idea. Back in the day people would marry strictly for political and financial reasons. The ones in love experiencing passion were deemed crazy. They were not looked upon with kindness, as everyone knew that great passion can lead to crime. Here comes your candidate for this very picture, the card of 7 Spades. As you can see then, in this case here, while I myself don't think of 7 Spades being about love, I can easily accept the tradition, and in the proper context see it as a representation of a pathology, when 'the heart is not up to speaking,' a line found in a number of cuneiform medical records.[1]

Before I move on here, let me make the observation that, in spite of my personal opinion of what a good method or tradition is, where arguments are concerned it's like in math. A theorem for which we have proof is only good so long as no one contests it. In other words, arguments are not infallible. In the context of reading cards this is what makes it most fascinating, namely, the fact that we can propose a simple method by following a certain system – logical or not – and then see how others use their brain-power to either add to it or to dismantle it.

Let's now have a look at a 9-card draw & surprise, and read the standard way: horizontally in trios from left to right, ditto vertically, and then we cross the tableau with an X. As you can see next, I got all the numbers from 7 to 10. Given that we lack the 2 to 6, here's what I think is an efficient way of keeping with the logic.

----

1 See a discussion of this in the first volume of the *Read Like the Devil* trilogy, dedicated to reading with the Marseille tarot (EyeCorner Press, 2021: 316). The quote is from the *Corpus of Mesopotamian Anti-Witchcraft Rituals* (2010).

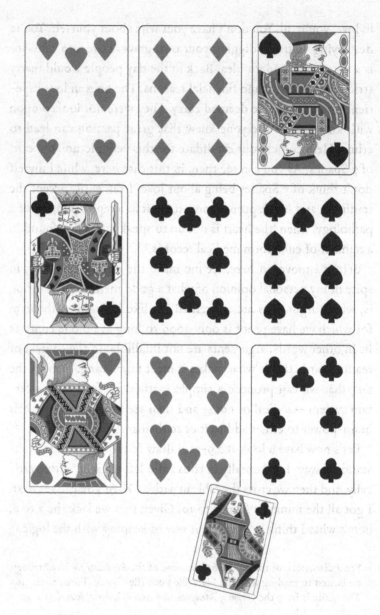

Before I tell you what the question is, look at the 7s. What do you see? Two rows of 3 symbols flanking one symbol in the top half. The most immediate response to this card is to think of 6+1, or the ways of the 1, the 6s being suggestive of pathways. But we can also see an empty 'house' — the lower half consisting of 4 symbols and nothing else in the middle — and 'the body' with two legs, two arms, and a head, our number 5 for the body, or number 2, separated from the 5 and indicating an exchange.

So, in the number 7 we have represented the number 3, 6, 4 and 5. How about the number 8? Two rows of 3 listening to the 2 in the middle. So here we have represented the ways of the 2 negotiating, in conflict, or in love. We can also say that increments double in the 3s raised at the power of 2. How about the card number 9? A nice and solid assembly — 4 on each side of the table — talking about the 1. And the 10? The assembly can also be ambivalent and divided. Or else, everyone rows to destination.

The point here is that if you're now confident with the story of 1 to 10, you can maintain it by looking at how the 1 to 10 numbers manifest in the 7 to 10, with the Aces and the Courts retaining their significations and functions. In addition, you still read the cards with a sense of elasticity: what contracts and what expands? How fast or slow is the escalation or declination? As to who is doing what to whom, we apply the same consideration of agency as before, with the court cards performing the functions of the specific suits.

Now that we have the dynamics in place, with the other missing numbers represented nicely in each of the 7 to 10 cards, let us attempt our reading revolving around the idea of preserving or conserving energy. I get this question often from people who feel

drained of energy and want to know what to do to protect themselves against it. The angst is about having your vital force stolen
away, with the consequence of feeling disconnected. So the concrete question from a woman was this: 'how can I protect myself
from energy drain at work?' Here's how I went about it, reading
with the piquet deck, without having picked a significator beforehand. But by glancing at my cards, it was plain that the King of
Clubs represented the boss, and the woman querent showed up as
the surprise, Queen of Clubs. I read the Jacks here as a representation of the dynamics among colleagues.

READING THE PIQUET CARRÉ

Rows: The ways of the heart cannot be mended by the mere ac-
quisition of cash. A skeptical young man is interfering with your
energy and affairs (7H, 9D, JS). Your boss instigates to work that
splits the camp, the result being that everyone feels the pressure
of antagonism and conflict (KC, 8C, 10S). There's satisfaction in
working with a young and well-intended colleague, but there's
still trouble in sight. (JH, 10H, 7C, the latter as modified by 10S).

Columns: It may be that the heartache is due to absent-mind-
edness, the young jovial man being non-responsive to the directives from the boss (7H, KC, JH). The young man doesn't seem
to be interested in being patrolled by the boss. He is looking in
the opposite direction. Yet, talks or meetings about the financial
strength of the company bring joy (9D, 8C, 10H). In spite of this,
however, there's opposition; a more disturbed youth seems to be
creating a major practical problem (JS, 10S, 7C) that makes you
feel responsible in the wings.

304

The X marks the spot: Double trouble (7H to 7C) and conflict between the ones in the business of learning something. Some resist (JS) some don't (JH). Interesting corners, by the way, with 2 sevens and two Jacks 'aiming' at each other.

Now, what does all this tell us about the energy of our querent? What we got here is a very simple and straightforward message that was delivered thus: 'conserving your energy is not easy, with people slanderously plotting against you, lording over the negotiating table with malicious intent, and influencing the immature ones. Make sure you bank on the youth who inspires.'

Here we might add that what gives away the theme of the reading is in fact remarking the manner in which we have an equal division between the cards that flank one or two other symbols. So what causes the drain of energy is divisive talk against the one idea. Our querent needs to be on guard with regard to whose opinion she runs with, and not let small problems (the 3 factions in the 7s) get the better of her.

The 10 Spades following the King's management of his workers is not good news, which make us think that the trouble is with the King, as he is in charge of the work environment. It's not good for him either if his young employees are either too relaxed (JH) or too recalcitrant (JS). Some are jovial and have good will, but can they work? Some are adversarial, but does being in opposition equal efficiency at work? Although it's not our querent's table to call the shots, knowing something about what her boss is up against may help her with her project of conserving energy. There's a reason why she appeared in the wings, in the surprise card, a position that tells her, 'by the way, you're not in the big picture. Not your monkey, not your circus.'

Evidently one can be affected by leadership that's not entirely thoughtful, efficient, or skillful, but it pays off to know your place precisely when experiencing stress, as not all positions carry the same amount of responsibility. I advised this woman to not make the strife between the boss and the young men her battlefield. She was well-advised to sit and watch and say nothing. There's nothing that can preserve energy quite like the position of silence and quietude. Here the piquet deck enforced this old wisdom.

Thus, whether reading with 52 cards, 32, or whatever other number, if you remember the simple rule of 1 to 10 in addition to the principle of expansion and contraction, you can divine until the hereafter. There's nothing mysterious in reading like the Devil. All you need to do is follow the suit, the color, and the number. The art is in putting two and two together in accordance with your position and what is made available to you in terms of context and a coherent formulation of the question.

READING THE GRAND TABLEAU

Reading a grand tableau with 52 cards on the table is like good detective work. Past, present, and future lines intersect and weave a fascinating story. There are characters at every corner, and surprises that astonish us. The grand tableau tells us the story of ourselves in relation in great detail. It can cover a wide time span from one day to a year. It can be used for mundane questions or the types that lend themselves to more reflective work. I cast a grand tableau all the time as I enjoy immensely seeing what stories and situations emerge from it. Once in a while I try to think of a metaphysical question and its relation to a concrete manifestation. I like seeing many playing cards on the table as they do not immediately conjure visual representations such as we may find them in cards that signify a particular concept on a more loaded symbolic level. For instance, we see the card of the Emperor in the tarot, we think: power. We see the Lily in the Lenormand Oracle and we think: beauty, sex, and family. When we divine with these other cards, we can also go with the extended meanings of their symbols and see the abstract power of the Emperor as a more concrete sign of tyranny or benevolence; the trio of significations in the Lily card can be an expression of your funeral: you seduce with your beauty, then have sex, get married, and get responsibility. You're a dead woman as far as freedom is concerned.

When reading with playing cards we may get such associations as the above, where we can say that the card of 4 Clubs signifies on a literal level a desk or a table (clubs connote the natural world, trees growing in the air out of which we build a house or make furniture), or we can say that 4 Clubs signifies on a symbolic level security at work (with clubs we also fight, and we can have competitive branches in a company). A whole range of metaphors and puns present themselves to us, as soon as we lay the ground for our basic principles for seeing the obvious.

Let us now formulate a question, and then proceed to saying something about the various steps we can go through in order to start the work of interpretation on a solid structure. There are several ways of reading the grand tableau, but my own preferred method is to lay the cards down in 5 rows of 9, with the remaining 7 cards placed in the last row at the bottom. As a general rule and as part of the process of scanning the tableau by making preliminary observations, I go through a number of quick steps.

In order to challenge myself, for this grand tableau I wanted to pose one question that would give me two answers. It is not always easy to pose such questions, but some contexts lend themselves easily to this. So I asked: 'what does my heart desire?' I may know what I want from the culturally sanctioned point of view, but often this knowledge lacks precision, simply because it's not the result of taking the time to think for myself about what I want, independently of endorsements or external validations. As a question such as this opens op the road for discovery, it's likely that the reading of the grand tableau for it discloses several layers of significations.

In principle, this question can also be answered by 3 cards, but in the context of the grand tableau, what you get is actually also an indication of the fact that what the heart desires may not necessarily be what you need or what is good for you. Sometimes I like to think of the great distinction between what we want and what we need. Ideally the two should match, but more often than not there's great discrepancy between need and desire. What the cards do is help us with narrowing down the divide between need and desire, by making us aware of where our wishes go wrong, if they do, and what we should focus on instead.

Let's look at the mechanics for answering this question first. To begin with, it's important to stress that unlike in the method of reading with the Lenormand cards, when we derive meaning from pairing the cards, reading in line, or linking the cards, in reading with the playing cards all the linking is done after reading the cards primarily in sets of three. For instance, for the reading of the

first row of nine cards, we could have 3 sentences based on reading the 3 sets of 3 cards each, and so on. We can then either link
these sentences to what else we observe in the course of developing a coherent narrative, or let them stand on their own. This is a
practice for the initial stage, as what we are always looking for is
to formulate a master sentence that encapsulates coherently what
we see. Our final verdict respects the law of clarity and brevity.

Why the insistence on reading cards in trios? Simply because by
noticing how color gives tension or release, we can get a sense of
direction and movement. Is the tableau tilting towards trouble or
resolve? Ultimately this is what we all want to know, regardless of
the nature of the question.

ELEVEN STEPS

[1] The significator. Before you cast the cards, it's best to choose
the relevant significators, both at person and topic level. For this I
chose as the significator for the heart's desire the card of 9 Hearts.
The person card is the Queen of Diamonds (woman with white
hair). So my reading will proceed from a consideration of both.
Left of the significator is the past. Right of the significator is the
future. The vertical line in which the significator card finds itself
in is the present. We read from top to bottom. The person significator card and the topic significator card must be read as the
middle card of the trio in which each of the two appears.

[2] The main lines. Read the vertical (present) and the horizontal
(future) lines in which the significator cards land. Here, my primary focus is the 9 Hearts. Note also that although this is not a
'person card,' I assign it agency nonetheless, due to the nature

of the question. So I look at what the hearts 'wants,' and I imagine what the heart can 'do.' In other contexts make sure not to assign agency to objects or abstract concepts, as they don't have any power to act. Assign agency only to the court cards.

If you have more than one significator, you can look at their intersecting points both on the vertical and horizontal axis. For a variation on your quick glance, you can use here the method of reading a line of 9 cards from the significator. Once you get to the 9th card from the significator, you read it as part of a trio that you create with the next 9th card, and the next again, beginning with the 9th card you land on in the first count.[2]

[3] The theme. Read the first 3 cards for the general impression of the tableau. These cards set the theme and the tone for the reading and tell you about what is being brought to the table. Where do you come from with your question? Here's the diagram for how you lay down the cards.

```
  1   2   3   4   5   6   7   8   9
 10  11  12  13  14  15  16  17  18
 19  20  21  22  23  24  25  26  27
 28  29  30  31  32  33  34  35  36
 37  38  39  40  41  42  43  44  45
     46  47  48  49  50  51  52
```

2 See Robert Chambers' classic: *The Book of Days: A Miscellany of Popular Antiquities*, 1869.

[4] The corners. Draw two diagonal lines down from position 1 to 41, and from position 9 to 41, position 41 being the intersecting point. Then similarly you draw two diagonal lines up from position 37 to 5, and 45 to 5, position 5 being the intersecting point. The cards in the intersecting points, cards in the positions 5 and 41 can be said to mirror one another. Now read the cards in trios in these positions: 1, 41, 9, and 37, 5, 45. These trios tell you something about what the question is up against, and how the overall answer can be framed by the X'ing of the tableau.

[5] The core. Look at the 9-card *carré* in the middle of the tableau. These are the cards in these positions: 13, 14, 15; 22, 23, 24; 31, 32, 33. You can glance at this core and perform a scanning of its significance, as you would a regular 9-card draw. Note that you will have another X'ing here that you can use to mirror the X'ing that the corner cards perform above. A lot hinges on it for the idea of how the macro level mirrors the micro relations.

[6] The knighting. Read the knighting positions, that is, draw a line from the significator in the shape of the letter L, like in chess. Just as the knight in chess can discover hidden things around the corner, so here we can get some information about what is not explicit in some relations. The significator card always begins the knighting trio. For instance, if the significator is in position 41, you can draw several L-shaped lines from it, upwards and downwards, so you read these trio relations from card 41: 42, 33, 24; 40, 31, 22; 32, 23, 22; 23, 23, 44. Read only the clusters that yield relevant information. Not every knighting move is urgent.

[7] The bridge. Read the final row of 7 cards. The card in the middle, card 49, is the bridge that links to the idea of 'as above, so below.' We mentioned already that card 49 mirrors card 5.

[8] The mirrors. Read for mirrors. If a significator card falls in one of the margins, say, position 28, it can be said to mirror the card in position 36. If the significator is in position 29, then it mirrors the card in position 35. The same applies to the vertical mirroring relations. By looking at these cards you can get a sense of what is collaborative or adversarial as fas as the significator is concerned.

Thematically, the same applies to the card 41 at the intersecting point between the diagonal lines drawn from the top corner cards. We can argue that by looking at the mirroring relation between the cards in the positions 41 and 5, we can learn something about the tension between the causal relations in the tableau, or that which you cannot escape, or begs to differ. The clench in the cross, that is, the cards in positions 32, 41, 49 and 40, 41, 42, also tells us about what the querent could have asked but didn't. So this internal cross at the bottom of the tableau mirrors the outer cross that starts with the corner cards.

[9] The bend. Read past and future lines, but make sure that you don't stop there. This reading can begin already at step 1. Think of bending the lines backwards or upwards. If your line of interest goes from 1 to 50, then you can go up again via the cards in positions 43, 35, and 27. Alternatively, take each end point of a line and look at the card that falls next to it. If the line goes from 1 to 50, then look at how the card in position 51 may modify the linearity of your narrative. This way we end up reading not only linearly but also in a circle and a spiral. I'll point to this in my sample reading below.

[10] The surprise. In classical cartomancy we also have a surprise card. Depending on what layout you use for the grand tableau, you can lay down the cards in such a way so that the last card falls

outside of the tableau. Especially those using the piquet deck like a surprise card. In my own tableau here, all the cards are in use. But if I want to have a surprise, I can devise beforehand what card is my surprise. In my practice I take the card in position 11 as the surprise and the card in position 22 as the card that can either trump the surprise, or foreshadow it. This is personal design, as I like to create elastics that give me a sense of intensity at work.

[11] *The law.* Always use your common sense. If you have a 'feeling' about the cards, don't let it hang there undeveloped. Look for evidence in the cards that supports your feeling. This is an honest way of validating not so much the truth of the emerging story, but more so the event of telling the story. What touches us is not the truth, but the event that creates the truth. My own mantra is: evidence, evidence, evidence. Think of yourselves as card lawyers.

THE HEART'S DESIRE

Let's have the question again: 'what does my heart desire?' First we locate the main significators, the card of 9 Hearts for the heart's desire and the person card, the Queen of Diamonds. We find both cards in the third column, thus sharing the space designated for the present, the now. Already here we can make this statement: since the heart's desire is in the proximity of the Queen of Diamonds, above her head and separated from the her only by one card, the 7 Clubs, we can infer that this Queen is already familiar with her own wishes of the heart, taking also the path of the heart. But how? Let's consider what is happening, also by going through the steps delineated above.

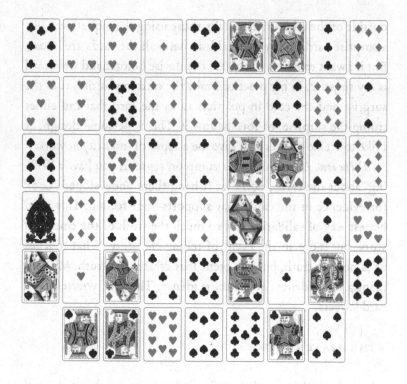

Step 1. The significators. After I picked the significators (person and topic), I cast the tableau. I located them individually (here, both are in the third column) and started preparing mentally to construe sentences based on reading three cards at a time.

Step 2. The main lines. I observed the following: the heart desires a stable work collaboration with the King of Diamonds (4C, 2C, KD). The Queen of Hearts disrupts the cash flow (QH, 4S, 9D) or the inspiration that the heart seeks. Presently the heart struggles with a learning community whose path the heart wants to improve (7H, 8C, 9H) (9H, 6C, QD). The Queen of Diamonds being an

314

intellectual, it is no surprise that she won't tolerate immature or shallow thinking, here as indicated by the presence of youth in her line. The third column where the 9 Hearts is located finishes with the Jack of Clubs who mirrors 7 Hearts. Within a community invested in working for pleasure (8 Clubs below 7 Hearts), we can think of the educational system. When children work, they're in school where they *play* with knowledge. Hence the idea that the Queen of Diamonds is a teacher. This holds quite so, as my line of business has been teaching in several schools and universities. In my private business I now also run Aradia Academy.

If we use the method of counting 9 cards from the significator, the 9 Hearts, and then 9 again until we don't have more 9 cards left to count, we get to this trio: the first 9th is the 6 Clubs, the second 9th from 6 Clubs is the Queen of Diamonds, and the third 9th from the Queen of Diamonds lands on 10 Hearts. We can now say that the heart's desire is to make the Queen of Diamonds go 'all the way' regarding her working with education.

Step 3. The theme. Judging by the first three cards in the tableau, 7 Clubs, 4 Hearts, and 7 Hearts, we can infer that emotional tension is maintained between troubles with planning and troubles with the heart of integrity that goes into it. Will the Queen of Diamonds pass on to her students the truth that may offend? (Ace of Diamonds, 7 Spades, Jack of Hearts). A curious thing to note here is the appearance of all the 7s in the first line. Four sevens and two Jacks. Are we here with the full range of 'troubled' students?

This observation may be a strong indication that whatever the heart desires, it is associated with challenges that this Queen will face in her encounter with her students. The other two Jacks are directly connected to the Queen of Diamonds, the Jack of Clubs being right below her and the Jack of Spades right next to the bridge, the 8 Clubs card where the intersecting points drawn from the top corner of the tableau meet. There's a meddler in the Queen's classroom, a young and immature person who resists her teaching.

If we want to get more information as to how the heart's desire relates to the challenges posed by the Jack of Spades, going ahead of the Queen of Diamonds, thus being in her future, we can cross the horizontal line in which the card of 9 Hearts is with the vertical line in which the card of the Jack of Spades is. We note that the two cards intersect in the King of Diamonds, another person of intellect. Usually what makes young men be in opposition is often provoked by intellectual ideas. A young man of war is not in the business of thinking, so we can expect a clash by default. But perhaps this is exactly what the Queen's heart is after, namely, to make a troubled student be more receptive. Receptive of what? We find the Ace of Clubs flanking the Jack of Spades to the right, followed also by the King of Hearts, a benevolent man. The card of 10 Spades next to the King of Hearts finishes the line, suggesting that this King's magnanimity is threatened.

As we can see here, just by looking at the theme that presents itself to us as it relates to both significators, we can quickly begin to form a narrative by simply drawing a few lines from the follow-up thought we develop as we move freely through the cards, while at the same time keeping an eye on the interconnections provided by the constraints of the method, that is to say, the idea that we red the cards in trios, and look at the intersecting points between the significators and the surrounding cards that lead us straight into the next observation.

Step 4. The corners. Troublesome plans cost money (7C, 8C, 7D). Perhaps the heart's desire is about conserving energy and cash – a classic, as we've seen earlier – especially since there's trouble 'down under' (QS, 5S, 10S). Not all are well-inclined towards the Queen of Diamonds. Here she's separated from the Queen of Spades only by the Ace of Hearts. This suggests that the enemy is closer than desired, basically in the Queen of Diamonds' own camp. As the Queen of Spades has the Ace of Spades on her head, literally, with the Ace immediately flanking the 8 Diamonds card, we're here with the notion of envy. What the Queen of Spades is after is the Queen of Diamonds' intellectual property & network.

Personally, as I've encountered this situation before, with other Queens leaning too closely into my ideas and work process, I'm not surprised to see persistence. Although they say that imitation is the sincerest form of flattery, when I look at the Spades on the table in this context, I don't feel reassured. Alas... But people are as they are, and not all make precise distinctions between what is their original thought and what is factually inspired. As to intended malice, let's just say that the Devil makes people do all sorts of things. Traditionally the suit of Spades has been associated with all the vices, from jealousy and greed to murder. As the King of Spades is also nearby, a corner card too right under the Ace of Hearts, we might even talk about joint forces whose aim here is to destabilize the Queen of Diamond's work with the students. Some policing is undermining the Jack of Clubs' full dedication to the work (JC, 10H, 8S). From this we can conclude that the corner cards announce challenges regarding dealing with close opposition. A sincere heart favors fairness. In its absence, what the heart desires is to waste less energy on remediations.

Step 5. The core. We now glance at the center of the tableau, the 9-card arrangement. The Diamonds are predominant. 6, 5, 4 Diamonds at the top of this 9-carré suggest taking the path towards crystallizing an idea. The King of Diamonds right below the 4 suggests an intellectual who works well with another professional, the Queen of Clubs right below him. The 2 Clubs card at the core displays collaboration. The Queen of Clubs likes what she hears (6H, 3D), as she sees that the structure of what is proposed is solid (6D, 4C). As these two court cards are linked to the Queen of Diamonds via the Jack of Spades, we're again with the theme of education on the table, perhaps even education that has a correctional dimension to it, given that the Jack of Spades in this picture is not exactly open-minded, such as the other three may be.

Step 6. The knighting. Let's look at how the heart's desire, 9 Hearts, represents the Queen of Diamonds' interests. I say 'interests' because if we follow the knight's jump, as it were, then we notice that two of the moves bring us to the 2 Diamonds and 4 Clubs respectively. This simply means that an exchange of ideas is on the table (the L shape from the Queen of Diamonds brings us to this trio: 2 Diamonds, 9 Hearts, 4 Clubs). The heart is invested in this: if you have a good idea, you share it. Others may steal it, but this possibility doesn't make the heart's desire any less inclined towards sharing the illumination. Here other knighting positions apply, but we'll highlight just this aspect as it's the most relevant.

Step 7. The bridge. The last row in the tableau gathers gravitational energy, with the card in the middle acting as focus point. 8 Spades mirrors 7 Spades in the middle of the first row of cards. Indeed, as above so below. The Spades rule here. Being of the earth, we get the impression that a secret is buried. What is this secret?

Old wisdom has it that the heart contains many secrets, the nature of the secrets being to be told, not revealed. What can we say here, then, without revealing too much? The trio that we can read first consists of 10 Hearts, 8 Spades, and 9 Clubs. Loving kindness doesn't work. This last row is led by the King of Spades and finishes with 5 Spades. Not healthy. Too much ill-inclined energy. Just in this row of 7 cards we have 3 court cards, the Kings of Spades and Clubs, and the Jack of Clubs. Melancholia.

There's misunderstanding here. The card of 8 Spades testifies to it. Although an attempt is made to change the negatively loaded situation, it all ends with the pain in the body. If we apply the hermetic principle of 'as above, so below' and 'as within, so without' to the heart's desire, then we must conclude that what the heart's desire is all about is to recognize that inspiring others through intellectual work can be draining, especially if one has to deal with a community of skeptics.

Step 8. The mirrors. On the horizontal axis the Queen of Diamonds mirrors the Ace of Clubs. Re-calibrate. 9 Hearts mirrors the Queen of Hearts. Lovely symmetry. The heart's desire is to 'reside' in the body of a Queen of Hearts. On the vertical axis the Queen of Diamonds mirrors 10 Clubs. 9 Hearts mirrors 6 Clubs. Too much work here. The heart desires less of it, from 10 to 6. If only this Queen would listen…

Step 9. The bend. If we follow the diagonal line from the card in position 1 to 50, we land on 9 Clubs. Upwards again to the right, we land on 9 Diamonds. From the card in position 9 to card 48, we land on 10 Hearts. Back up again, we land on 9 Spades. Luckily the tough card of disappointment is in the past, left of both significators. 9 Diamonds is a better bet for changing the mind.

A working routine can change with the changing of metaphors. That's where the bend is. 9 Spades for 9 Diamonds. An auspicious exchange.

Step 10. The surprise. I picked the card in position 11 to surprise me. Here my surprise is 3 Hearts. A celebration. What kind of celebration? Of work. The card in position 22 can be seen as the shadow of the surprise, or as a collaborative ally, yet with understated energy. Work seems to follow this Queen. What is she doing all day? How about writing? Doesn't the card of 4 Clubs look just like a writing desk? It does. What does the heart's desire have to say about this idea of celebrating work by sitting at a desk all day? The heart's desire, 9 Hearts, intersects with the surprise, 3 Hearts, in 2 Diamonds and 9 Clubs. Surprise, surprise. This Queen's dance with ideas is all about work. Resilience rules.

There's a lot of insistence in this tableau on sharing ideas with groups of people. Where do we find this? In a school, or other such educational places. Diamonds and Clubs shake hands here in all the important places determined by our choice of geometrical symmetries. Grievances are related to envy and recalcitrance, with the occasional joy almost always being squeezed between nasty looks. This Queen is exhausted. As her line finishes with 10 Spades, she is well-advised to heed attention to her heart's desire to work less. If work must be celebrated, then it should be in this form. As to the envious, 10 Spades of hell is also for them.

The Queen's future diagonal lines lead her first to the Jack of Diamonds, and finally to the 10 Hearts. She will have done well for her students and for herself to her heart's desire, with the full blast of 10 Hearts satisfaction. The dedicated ones get this queen's effort, and they testify to it by showing true appreciation.

320

Remember Peter Carroll's words quoted earlier? 'Enchant long and divine short?' When we read the grand tableau we do exactly this. When we probe for information by looking at lines, symmetry, mirrors, jumps, squares within squares, and treasures marked by the X on our map, we enchant ourselves with view to arriving at processed information in as coherent a manner as we possibly can. The cards provide visual clues. We have a path called 'spreads' or 'layouts' that determine fixity, yet a kind of fixity that's malleable and relative to the question. We can read the cards in their positional meanings, assigning a temporal sequence to rows and columns. We can make inferences that have causality in focus.

This process is called analyzing a visual text according to deductive methods. The fortuneteller is a detective. 'My husband is cheating on me,' is a classic predicament. The fortuneteller takes a snapshot of the situation with her cards. 'You have a powerful enemy,' the fortuneteller also delivers, then proceeds to probe the secret place and intentions of the other pestering the querent, who may turn out to be afflicted by greed, jealousy, envy, or anger. Also a classic.

As you've already noted, in my reading of the grand tableau, I've referenced these possibilities already, trying to probe for what ails the heart, so the path to fulfilling its desires is clear. I weaved the mundane with the lofty ideal, cliché with the extraordinary.

The art of interpretation is not an exact art. Where we can be exact is in knowing what we aim for and where to look. Divination is not about looking for a needle in a haystack. Divination is about assessing how much hay there is to begin with, where it is transparent or opaque, where it is rare or dense. We squint at the haystack in order to sense its resistance. What does it smell of? This alone can make us drunk with excitement to the point where we can even forget that it's the needle we want to find. What I'm trying to say here is that divination is all about process and performance. We get a question and off we go. The cards on the table open the roads. Some are crooked, and some are straight.

Divination with playing cards can produce some of the wildest stories; stories of love, magic, working relations, vitality or sickness, and the power of money. No question is too small. If the question, 'does he love me?' hits so hard, it's because everyone can hear the whisper of infinity: 'he loves you forever.' Isn't this beautiful? Even when relationships break, 'forever' still resonates. The clever fortuneteller has trained herself to hear all the tonalities in this song of forever, and she dispenses useful advice in accordance with her discernment.

A reading of a grand tableau with all 52 cards on the table can yield enough information to fill an entire novel. In my regular practice it's common that I write an analysis that goes over 20 solid pages. What you got here in my example is just a short 'method' enchantment for the divination that can be much longer. You can turn a tableau on all its facets, as the reading of the cards according to the set rules allows you a lot of sophisticated freedom.

In contrast, a reading of a 3-card layout yields information that invites us to practice the art of brevity. We keep it simple. We scale from a lot to just what is necessary. In practicing both types of readings with a few cards on the table or many, it's good to remember an important event in your life. Try reading with that in mind, and see how fast your sentences form. Scale from memory to magic, as that is exactly what you need in order to read like the Devil for another person you know nothing about. We are here with the art of recognition, the art of identifying human nature and what makes the heart move. We are not here with labels, 'I'm a traditional reader,' or kindergarten comparisons, 'my predictions are better than yours…' We are here with the heart and with what moves it. We're here for the sincere acknowledgment from our returning clients, who insist that what you do is change their lives, move their motivations, inspire and educate them, and finally enchant them.

The only condition for satisfaction is that you press for the end, the end point. This end point that is on point can be a sharp turn for the querent, who may signal already on your first line that there is comprehension followed by a desire to change. Can you sense how the point is on the tip of my tongue? I could have a run with puns on point on the very idea of the point. But this is precisely what does it in cartomancy, being on point, being an enchanting fortuneteller who is able to both inspire and educate beyond expectation. When a whip is necessary, then a whip is used. When encouragement is necessary, then encouragement is used. Each has its function, aim being to move the heart.

If divination doesn't move the heart, it has no point. What moves the heart is the obvious in all its glorious singularity. The obvious is not a tired cliché, but rather a pair of eyes that see in the dark. Now it's your turn, witches.

REFERENCES

ABUSCH, Tvzi and Schwemer, Daniel (2010). *Corpus of Mesopotamian Anti-witch-craft Rituals.* Brill

AMRON, Louise (1800). *La véritable cartomancie expliquée par la célèbre sibylle française: mise en tableaux par l'héretière de Mlle L. Norma.* Paris: Chez Delarue, libraire editeur.

BARTLETT, Robert C. and Collins, Susan D. (2011) *Aristotle's Nicomachean Ethics. A New Translation.* Chicago: The University of. Chicago Press.

CARROLL, Peter (1992). *Liber Kaos.* Red Wheel. Weiser.

DEPAULIS, Thierry (2005). 'Cartes et cartiers dans les anciens états de Savoie (1400-1860).' In *Journal of the International Playing-Card Society.* Nr. 4, April 2005.

CHAMBERS, Robert (1869). "The Folk-Lore of Playing Cards" in *The Book of Days: A Miscellany of Popular Antiquities.* London: W. & R. Chambers.

ELIAS, Camelia, (2021). *Read Like the Devil: The Essential Course in Reading the Marseille Tarot.* EyeCorner Press.

_____ (2020). *The Power of the Trumps and Pips. The omnibus edition.* EyeCorner Press.

_____ (2020). *The Heart Sutra and Tarot.* EyeCorner Press

_____ (2019). *Divination with Cards: A Short History.* EyeCorner Press.

_____ (2018). *21+1 Fortune-teller's Rules: Read like the Devil Manifestos.* Edited collection. EyeCorner Press.

_____ (2015). *The Oracle Travels Light: Principles of Magic with Cards.* EyeCorner Press.

ETTEILLA (pseudonym of Jean-Baptiste Alliette) (1785). *Manière de se récréer avec le jeu de cartes nomées Tarots. Paris: Lesclapart.*

FOLI, P.R.S. (1897). *Fortune-telling by Cards.* I. & M. Ottenheimer Publishers

GÉBELIN, Antoine Court de (1781). *Monde primitif, analysé et comparé avec le monde modern. Monographie imprimée chez l'auteur.*

GUÉNON, René (2004). *Symbols of Sacred Science.* Sophia Perennis.

HUSON, Paul (2004). *Mystical Origins of the Tarot: From Ancient Roots to Modern Usage.* Destiny Books.

JACKSON, Dawn R. (2006). *The Wise and Subtle Arte of Reading Cards as examined by a Witch who practices said Arte* [http://www.hedgewytchery.com/] Defunct website.

KAPLAN, Stuart (1978). *The Encyclopaedia of Tarot.* Vol 1–4. United States Games Systems.

KENT, Cicely (1921) *Telling Fortunes by Cards.* London: Herbert Jenkins.

MADAME Camille Le Normand (1872). Fortune-telling by Cards. New York: Robert M. De Witt, publisher.

MADAME Zezina (1979). *La Cartomancie.* Ed. S. Borneman. Paris.

NICOARA, Pavel (1961). *Despre preziceri, oracole si ghicit.* Editura Militara.

PAPUS (2008). *The Divinatory Tarot.* Aeon Books.

PLATT, Charles (1920) *Card Fortune Telling: A Lucid Treatise Dealing with All the Popular and More Abstruse Methods.* London: W. Foulsham & Co.

RAPOZA (1910). *How to Tell Fortunes by the Cards.* London: Weldons Ltd.

SEPHARIAL (1911). *A Manual of Occultism.* London: William Rider & Son.

TAYLOR, S. Rev. Ed. (1865). *The History of Playing cards: Conjuring, Fortune-telling and Card-Sharping.* London: John Camden Hotten.

ACKNOWLEDGMENTS & PERMISSIONS

I AM IN DEEP GRATITUDE to my students who have dedicated themselves to the study of the playing cards for fortunetelling and divination. Without their contribution I would not have been able to find so many fine examples of just what is challenging in the reading of these cards, and then point to how we can find better, stronger, and more precise ways of interpreting visual text.

I AM ALSO GRATEFUL to Roxanne Flornoy for her continued support of my work and kind permission to use Jean-Claude Flornoy's reconstruction of the Jean Noblet Marseille Tarot (1650). Here I use 4 cards from this deck (p. 69).

THROUGHOUT THIS BOOK I used the classic playing cards by Goodall & Son (1897), in public domain (vector rendition courtesy of Adrian Kennard).

THE MASTERPIECE, 'Christ Mocked' (p. 41) by Hieronymus Bosch from ca. 1480 is in public domain.

ALL OTHER IMAGES in this book are my own.

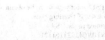

CPSIA information can be obtained
at www.ICGtesting.com
Printed in the USA
LVHW042238161121
703472LV00025B/1214

9 788792 633736